LIFE AND LETTERS

OF

WILLIAM BEWICK.

BIOGRAPHIES OF BRITISH ARTISTS

General Editor: Professor H. A. Miles

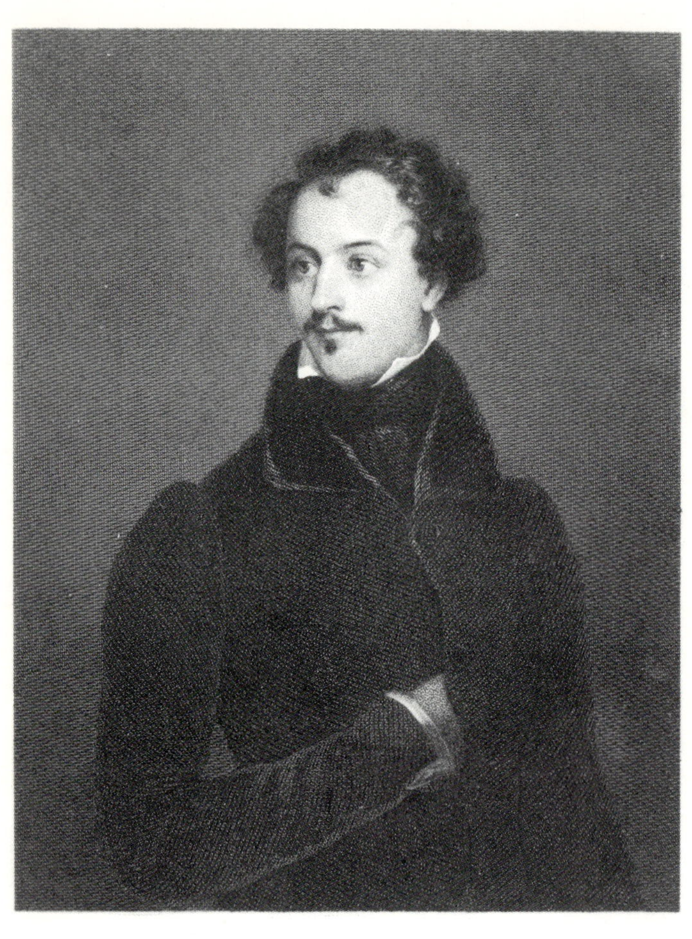

William Bewick.

LIFE AND LETTERS

OF

WILLIAM BEWICK

(ARTIST).

EDITED BY

THOMAS LANDSEER, A.R.A.

VOL. I.

EP Publishing Limited
1978

This book was originally published, in two volumes, by Hurst and Blackett, London, 1871. It is here reprinted in one volume, with new indexes of people and places.

Republished 1978 by
EP Publishing Limited
East Ardsley, Wakefield
West Yorkshire, England

ISBN 0 7158 1350 1

British Library Cataloguing in Publication Data
Bewick, William
    Life and letters of William Bewick (artist).
    – (Biographies of British artists).
    1. Bewick, William 2. Painters, Victorian –
Biography
    I. Title II. Landseer, Thomas III. Series
    759.2   ND497.B5
    ISBN 0-7158-1350-1

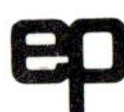

Please address all enquiries to EP Publishing Limited
(address as above)

Printed in Great Britain by
Redwood Burn Limited
Trowbridge & Esher

INTRODUCTION.

THESE records of the artistic life of William Bewick* consist, with very little exception, of autobiographic and literary sketches by himself, and of his correspondence with distinguished artists and intimate friends. He had the happiness to be on terms of friendly intimacy with many renowned artists and literary men during the first half of the present century; and his remains contain a rich store of anecdote

* William Bewick was born at Darlington, October 20, 1795—a fact which, so far as the date is concerned, he has forgotten to mention in the autobiographic sketches with which this work commences.

respecting a number of the most illustrious authors and painters of that brilliant period. Enjoying the friendship of Hazlitt, Haydon, Shelley, Keats, and others—entertained by Scott, Hogg, Jeffrey, Maturin, and many of the most distinguished novelists, poets, and essayists of his time—he had the best opportunities of collecting incidents in illustration of the career of men of whom we can never know too much. In his early life he was the pupil of Haydon, and was employed afterwards to execute some very important commissions by Sir Thomas Lawrence, President of the Royal Academy. He lived on intimate terms with Wilkie, the Landseers, and Gibson, the sculptor, whose friendship he enjoyed in Rome, and who, in testimony of his esteem, executed a very beautiful bust of him.

These records, though pretty full with respect to some periods of his life, still leave gaps which it would have been desirable, if possible, to fill up, but unfortunately the materials are not extant. We trust, however, that, imperfect as in some respects they doubtless are, these memorials will be found to contain a fair portrait of one who occupied a good position as an artist, and was highly esteemed as a man by his friends of all ranks and professions.

CONTENTS

OF

THE FIRST VOLUME.

CHAPTER I.

CHAPTER II.

CHAPTER III.

CHAPTER IV.

CHAPTER V.

CHAPTER VI.

CHAPTER VII.

CHAPTER VIII.

CHAPTER IX.

CHAPTER X.

CHAPTER XI.

LIFE AND LETTERS

OF

WILLIAM BEWICK.

CHAPTER I.

EARLY DAYS — DARLINGTON — SIXTY YEARS AGO — SCHOOL LIFE — THE BOY ARTIST — AUNT SARAH — BARNARD CASTLE — ITINERANT ARTISTS — GEORGE MARKS — THE 'EXAMINER' NEWSPAPER — HAYDON — THE ELGIN MARBLES — LEAVING HOME.

I WAS the third son of a family of seven boys and five girls. My father, William Bewick, married Jane Roantree, a native of Harworth-upon-Tees, and a descendant of linen manufacturers of that place. He was by trade an upholsterer, a plain, industrious man of business, strict and methodical in everything, and averse from all innovations to the routine of his household. My mother, half-Quakeress, and unsophisticated as she was beautiful, was more of an ambitious character, and not seldom found herself in something like a defensive argument with my father as to the capabilities and future prospects of her sons. Her ambitions were all virtuous, and her whole life, thoughts, and anticipations were wrapped up in the welfare of her numerous and innocent family. When a little girl, and very beautiful, she was a great favourite of the blunt and uncouth mathematician, Emerson, who used to amuse her by playing a curious kind of music upon an instrument of his own invention, described as something like a mandolin, formed of a small hollow wooden barrel, with a handle and three strings ; and he used to sit at the end of his long, passage-like study by the fire, his legs covered with leather leggings to prevent their being burnt.

In due time I was sent, in company with an elder brother, to a respectable school kept by a Quaker, in which girls and boys studied together. Here I learnt to read and write, and here I fagged through arithmetic as far as ' vulgar fractions,' which, with the rules of grammar, were my utter abomination. There

were two or three boys who had half days in
the week allowed for drawing, and, charmed
with this exceptional and delightful accomplishment, I cried to my mother to allow me to join
the favoured boys. She seemed pleased to consent ; I obtained a drawing-book and pencils,
and began the outline of a gabled barn of the
simplest construction and the fewest lines. My
shrewd schoolmaster smiled at my first attempt,
and in expressing his encouragement put my
modesty to the blush by saying that I should
become a famous artist. These drawing-days
greatly increased the pleasure of my school-
days, the love of pictures and prints became a
passion with me, and I never lost an opportunity of gaping in at the print-shop windows, or
wherever a drawing or engraving was to be
seen. The little work-a-day country-town in
the north of England, where my parents lived,
contained little or nothing of art ; nor was there
any taste for art among the inhabitants, it being
what may be termed a ' Quaker town ;' for here
a great many ' broad-brims ' had taken up their
abode. The love of making and accumulating
money was their ruling passion, and every

elegant accomplishment was suppressed with studied perseverance. The God Mammon flapped his drab-coloured wings over the little town, and the drama closed its scenic arena. Sock and buskin were contemptuously huddled beyond the precincts, and sent out of the place, as though it were criminal to represent on the stage the follies, the passions, the virtues, and the vices of mankind. The 'divine' Shakespeare's works were banished from the Public Library, and the 'novels of Sir Walter Scott,' subsequently shared the same fate. Dancing was to be decidedly discountenanced, as bringing young people together for no good. Poetry was described as a false jingle of words, wherein truth and sense were often perverted for the sake of the rhyme. Music was pronounced a great waste of valuable time, in which useful knowledge might be acquired instead; indulgence in the fine arts, time and talents spent with no profitable result. He only was said to be 'getting on in the world,' who was increasing his property; the term gain not being applied to knowledge, virtue, or happiness, but reserved solely to describe pecuniary acquisition, synonymous in short with gold, as if nothing but gold were gain. The man whose gains were known to be rapidly increasing, was not only spoken of by the multitude under their breath with veneration, but, as if he more nearly approached creative power than any other human being, he was said to be *making money*; and when that was said, eulogy was exhausted, and he was considered to be crowned with all praise. To live in my native town was to live in the very Temple of Mammon; and it was impossible to see the God worshipped daily, to stand in his presence, and behold the reverence he inspired, without catching the contagion of awe. The worship of the beautiful and good found no place there, for 'from the least of them even to the greatest nearly every one was given to covetousness.'

It may easily be imagined what an epoch in my childhood was a visit to a relative of my father's, known in the family as Aunt Sarah, who resided near Barnard Castle. Boy as I was, her delicate features, her slender figure, and pensive expression, struck my imagination.

When she held me close in her loving embrace, and kept my little hand in hers, which trembled with emotion, while her beautiful eyes were dim with tears, I felt that I was in the arms of one of strong sensibility and ardent affection; and as she arranged the dark curls that clustered round my face, and presented me to her numerous friends, I forgot everything in admiration of her sweet smile and lovely face. I remember thinking that her features and complexion were more like 'wax-work' than anything I had seen before. My remembrance of her is still vivid,—gentle, serene, pensive, and graceful in all her motions. With a romantic and chivalrous turn of mind, she had the appearance and bearing of a highly poetic character. And, certainly, she was unlike any one I have ever seen; for, with her enthusiasm for historical and traditional narrative, she combined a gentle, loving spirit; and her heroism, her admiration of deeds of daring in a virtuous or generous cause of honour, of loyal fidelity, did not interfere with the most tender domestic affections. As memory carries me back to those days of my youth, I see her plucking wild flowers for me in the romantic woods that surround this once famed and stately castle ; or, exploring with me the extensive ruins, pointing out tower, and keep, and pinnacle, or dungeon deep, subterraneous caverns, secret passages that were supposed to communicate for miles underground with Raby, Athelston, or Rokeby : thus affording means of escape, or conference with friendly allies in times of trouble or danger. She would point to Baliol's and Brackenbury's Towers, mysteriously hinting at the prisons and cruelty of former times, my lady's chamber, and the Duke of Gloucester's state apartments, with his arms carved in the bay window, still to be seen. What a picture of sorrow she seemed when dropping a tear upon the bloody arrow found in the *débris* of the ruins, or hanging with a sigh over the stone coffins dug out of the Castle Garth ! With what true archæological feeling she would endeavour to clear away the rust from some old coin, and to decipher names and dates ! Every little object and circumstance connected with '*the Castle*' became in her eyes sanctified. And the ruins of Barnard Castle, its woods, its water, its picturesque beauty from every point of view, its history, the romance of its many legends, and its connexion with great historic names, made it the homestead of her existence. She might be said, indeed, to live only in the barbaric ages of feudal despotism, her mind being so much engrossed with the past, that she hardly seemed cognizant of the present. As we roamed the woods, or followed the fisher's path by the 'rugged Tees,' or midst the ruinous walls of the Castle, my aunt would recount its fitful history, beguiling my young imagination with dreams of the past. She went as far back as 1300, when the Beauchamps, the Nevilles, and the Plantagenets held the place; then the Duke of Gloucester (Richard III.), who obtained undivided possession of the Castle and extended parks in 1477. She then descended to Elizabeth's time, when occurred the remarkable and noble defence of the place for eleven days by Sir George Bowes, of Streatham, against the rebellious earls of the north of 1569.

In 1590 the Castle appears to have been in tolerably good repair, until it came into the possession of Sir Henry Vane in 1626, who in 1630 unroofed and totally dismantled it for the sake of the lead, iron, wood, and stone contained in it.

'Oh! misery! can one thousand pounds worth of lead, iron, wood, and stone be more worth than a Castle which might receive a king and his whole train? Indeed, my dear nephew, it is miserable to think that the Vanes have done more to pull to pieces, and utterly destroy and ruin this noble monument of former greatness, than all the wars, sieges of barbarians, ay, or even the ruthless destroyer Time, during the many centuries before or since they have had possession of it. It is lamentable to reflect on the want of proper feeling for the history and great antiquity of such an object of interest as this once beautiful Castle, now, alas! a total ruin, mouldering fast to decay, and, I fear, soon to utter annihilation.'

Thus my aunt would lament the fall and spoliation of her beloved castle. And as I am desirous of rendering her character more complete to the reader's perception, I will endeavour to describe her dwelling, for often in domestic

arrangements we discover the tendency of menta
solicitude as well as particular housewifery. The
striking novelty to me in my aunt's home was
the profusion of works of art, of all classes and
descriptions ; for from the ceiling to the floor
the walls were covered with varied art represen-
tations — in painting, drawing, or engraving.
There were, I remember, prints of Angelica
Kaufmann's sentimental and allegorical designs,
—some of Boydell's prints from Shakespeare's
historical plays,—a large painting, size of life, of
Venus, nearly nude—with one of her own lap-
dog. There were landscapes of wild and romantic
character,—pictures of sentiment or poetry—of
beauty or heroism, — caricatures, too, of every
conceivable grade and allusion. One I noticed was
of a lay-brother carrying upon his back a huge
bundle of fire-wood, in which were seen peeping
out behind the shoes and ankles of a female,
underneath which was written 'SUPPLIES FOR
THE MONASTERY.' Besides pictures, there was
great store of curiosities and antiquities,—old
swords, old pipes, old coins and vessels of earthen-
ware, old cabinets, oak chairs, china, guns, bows
and arrows, Eastern slippers and embroidered

gloves, daggers and rusty spurs. The chair I sat upon was of oak, carved all over, and dated 1342 upon its back; it was of curious form, but lame and rickety; and there were others similar, but differing in form, age, &c. The tables, too, were odd, with spiral legs—and of various forms and workmanship. This sitting-room was lighted by a bay-window, filling which was an exuberant hydrangea in full bloom, with bunches of flowers the size of my head, and a magnificent geranium, the full height of the window. These so screened or shaded the light of the apartment, that with its pictures of half-revealed figures and heads, and other objects, together with the conglomeration of strange antiquated things about, seemed to strike at first the beholder with quaint mysterious impressions. On my first entrance I remained in silent wonder; while my aunt was as much amused at my abstraction as I was occupied in speculation on the novelties around me. She had the tact not to interrupt or disturb my youthful meditations, but smiled in self-satisfaction.

She led me upstairs to my bed-chamber, a large antiquated room panelled with oak, and old enough to be of the time of the Duke of Gloucester. It was dark and gloomy, where one candle only made 'darkness visible.' There were pictures here, which, however, I did not examine, but retired to bed, wearied and satiated with all I had seen during the day.

On waking in the morning, the light of day revealed to me this ancient chamber, and straight before me, over the mantel-piece, there hung a half-length portrait, the size of life, representing a beautiful lady, looking right down upon me, with an arch Cupid by her side, the little god and herself portrayed as divinities, as was the fashion of a certain period. And what attracted my young observation was that, as I moved to different parts of the chamber the eyes of the picture seemed to follow me. This strange illusion I could not account for at the time, but I climbed upon a table to ascertain if the eyes were part of the canvas, or not; and, sure enough, my astonishment was increased on finding the surface flat and perfect, and only painted over like the rest of the picture. On frequently resuming my examination of this work of art since the period above alluded to, I have always been charmed with the colouring of the flesh, the purity, and bloom, and richness of which seemed to me unsurpassed by Titian. The ruby freshness of the lips, and the transparency of the shade-tint, quite won my admiration, and I returned to it with ever new and increased appreciation of its rare merits; so much so, indeed, that I have no memory of the other pictures or objects in this room. The effect of this beautiful picture, its harmony and glow of colour, was to charm my young fancy, — my soul yearned towards the possibility of being able to realize such perfection, and PAINTING became from that time the lodestar of my ambition.

My Quaker schoolmaster, although familiar with almost every scholastic or scientific difficulty, possessed very little skill in the fine arts, and his pupils were left to improve themselves as best they could by 'copies' provided for them in the way of coloured engravings. When the time came for my being removed from school, and placed in my father's business, the passion for Art still clung to me; and as days and years passed on I was still true to my infatuation, taking every spare moment, early in the morning and late at night, to practise the delicious enjoyment of reproducing enchanting scenery, or exercising my hand upon the difficult human 'face divine.' My poor father became alarmed at last, lest this '*ignis fatuus*' should be leading me away altogether from what he deemed my best interests in life; and when my mother, delighted, exhibited my portfolio to some of her admiring friends, who praised and expatiated upon the wonders of 'genius,' my father would be groaning in spirit in an adjoining room. It was curious to observe the bewildered and divided expression that his face assumed on these occasions. If one side smiled with some degree of inward pride and satisfaction, the other assumed an aspect of rebuke, and he felt disposed to hurry to my mother's exhibition, shut up the folio from whence she brought out her son's wonderful works and exclaim, 'Nonsense, nonsense,—this will be the boy's ruin, I foresee!' But my father loved my mother, and no doubt suffered in his own breast rather than mortify his beautiful spouse, —for the praises of her child were a heaven of bliss to her. The boy's extreme modesty caused him to run away and hide himself on these occasions, while new sensations thrilled every nerve and agitated his whole frame, and he felt that he must live for other and nobler objects than those which occupied the men and women around him. When a fox-hunting squire saw the collection of my works, he would expatiate to my mother on the heavenly gifts of genius; how those gifted with it pushed themselves forward in the world, overcame all difficulties, cleared the fences, and reached their goal. 'Then, ma'am,' he would say, 'fame, riches, and honours come "thick as leaves that strew the Vale of Vallombrosa," as the great poet hath it; and he would leave my poor mother in an ecstasy from which it would have been sin in my father to have roused her. What glory it is to have praise in youth for any rare skill, physical or mental!

The part of the country where we lived at the period of which I write, had acquired fame for its peculiar breed of cattle, which it has ever since maintained. Exhibitions of the most extraordinary mountains of fat made the tour of the three kingdoms; paintings and engravings of these bovine wonders were fashionable; and it is not strange if a young artist should copy a series of these monsters. I accordingly had drawn, on large paper, bulls, oxen, and heifers, the most famous on record. With these I also executed sets of fox-hunting and greyhound-coursing, large views of the lakes, the scenery of Wales, the various picturesque rivers, and remarkable places or noble seats.

An unfortunate son of the brush arriving in the town and proposing to teach, I hastened by stealth, unknown to any of my friends, to his studio, and took my place for a set of six lessons, and accomplished under his tuition what to me was a fresh delight. It was a miniature of a beautiful girl, with a white veil spreading from the back of her head over her crimson satin dress, which showed in varied transparency the form beneath,—she might be a bride, most beautiful she appeared to my wondering eyes,—the graduated effect of the veil, in its soft transparency, seeming magical to me. This professor had been on intimate terms with Morland, and had advanced him from time to time sums of money until he had no more to advance. He said, whenever he went to Morland for the restitution of his accumulated debts he always left him with an addition to the sum due; but yet he loved him, he said, and was charmed with his genius and his society.

Another of these itinerant geniuses was detained in our town by sickness; he was a son of the 'sock and buskin,' but being accomplished in the arts, and no longer able to 'strut his hour upon the stage,' he wished to teach drawing; and to him I went for six lessons more in water-colours. Here I drew single figures, grotesque or humorous, taken mostly from such subjects as he painted. My portfolios being crammed with an extensive and miscellaneous collection, and my age approaching seventeen, I turned my thoughts to a higher pursuit, and became wholly absorbed in the study and practice of oil-painting, the smell of which was to me aliment and perfume inexpressible.. In these times of eight-horse waggons and stage-coaches there were no establishments to supply you with artists' colours from the shops in London, as there are now ; so I had recourse for my first supply of necessaries, colours, oils, varnishes, canvas, the loan of an easel and palette, and so forth, to one of those country artists who, uniting the fine arts to a department of trade, have, by a very celebrated bard, been denominated the 'Dick Tintos' of the provinces, and, like most English artists, adapt the supply of their genius to the demand. Thus he was at once house, sign, coach, and heraldry painter, while for all who might be pleased to patronise his graphic pencil, he ventured upon the higher departments of art, landscape or portraits, as well as those luminous displays yclept 'transparencies,' painted upon a system of glazing of the Venetian school. As this universal genius made up his own materials, and ground his own colours, there was no difficulty in obtaining from him whatever I needed.

And here let me endeavour to place before the reader's eye the picture of a '*brother chip,*' long lost to the provincial world of art and science,—I say science, for he was scientific as well as everything else, by turns, being in fact a universal genius ; and there was nothing

in the heavens above, the earth beneath, or
the waters that encompass it about, of which
he did not know something. His acquirements,
indeed, were extraordinary. Self-taught and un-
appreciated, he lived and died a recluse, known
but to few; his acquisitions of information were
scarcely known to himself; it was only when
subjects were brought under discussion that
he found himself prepared to enter on subtle
arguments and nice distinctions that would have
surprised and delighted learned professors.
Like many unfortunate geniuses, he was eccentric in person and manners. His figure was ungainly. By an accident in early life he was
lame in one leg, and crippled in one hand and
foot, and his head appeared (as well as his nose)
to have been knocked to one side, perhaps by
the same accident. He met your gaze with
one eye only, and if by some chance you caught
a glance of the other you would observe that
there was a decided obliquity of vision in
that organ, which he invariably kept closed
in company. He was decidedly a bookworm,
and when poring over some mouldy old tome
he wore a pair of wide - rimmed spectacles,

partly horn, partly metal, that conveyed to the observer such an open-eyed stare as not unfrequently caused him to be taken for one of those individuals called in Scotland 'uncannie,' so that he was suspected by several of his credulous neighbours of being able to unravel the mysteries of futurity, or of having communications with the Evil One; and many refused to enter the precincts of his sanctum, for he was a solitary man, and would be shut up in his wonderful chamber in silence and study until after midnight. He combined many pursuits; he was by trade bookbinder, bird-stuffer, botanist, herbalist, geologist, mineralogist, geographer, astronomer, surveyor, engraver; his closets and shelves were crammed with tools, instruments, books, portfolios full of old prints of all descriptions and sizes, stuffed birds and animals, an eccentric collection of branches, and clogs, and stumps of trees, with mosses and lichens, walls covered with pictures all painted by himself, besides his slabs and mullers, easels and colours, oils and varnishes. It was in this chamber I found him. As I entered his back was towards me, a lighted candle was in his hand, and as he turned his remarkable head towards me, his hair standing on end, his spectacles shoved up on his capacious forehead, his eyes looking different ways with the singular effect of light and shadow—I myself being at this time rather timid and imaginative, though bold in my errand—I confess to have been taken rather 'aback,' and I gazed at him with some trepidation; but he spoke encouragingly, bidding me 'come in.' So I threaded my way to where he was, and explained my wishes. To my infinite delight I found in him a kindred spirit, and he promised to furnish me with all I desired to have, canvas, colours, easel, &c.*

It was by him that I was initiated into the mysteries of 'oil;' it was by him I was told of the wonders of the palette, its mixtures and compound tints, those which were evanescent and those which stood the test of time, the 'rubbings in,' the first, second, and third paintings, all the secrets of glazing, and the constant habit and practice of the great masters,

* The name of this unknown genius was George Marks.

their experiments after the yet undecided 'vehicle,' that *ignis fatuus* of artists.

Need I tell of the sleepless nights, the raptures of anticipation of an artist's first beginning in oil? When I did sleep, my dreams were of pictures of ineffable harmony and brilliance, my visions of beautiful paradises and glowing sunsets, of Jacob's Dream and the ladder with the Angels ascending and descending,—of the tender aerial landscapes of Claude and the depth and richness of Titian, — all the wonders of the pencil, and of nature, arose before my ardent imagination. At last the materials came, and lighting my fire at five o'clock next morning, when all the household were fast asleep, I arranged my apparatus and set my first palette ; and after rubbing in and rubbing out, and dabbing away until breakfast, I had to my mind made little progress in getting over the first trouble of a new process, and found that the colours either *ran* or *crept* or did not cover the ground, and seemed so hard and harsh that the disappointment was great enough, when I had to scrape all off and begin again *de novo*. And so I went on morning after morning, month after

month, until at length I began to find the difficulties in the management of oil-colour give way
a little to perseverance. I often visited my singular friend to ask questions, to hear about
painting and about artists, and once a-week, when
the *Examiner* newspaper came to him, it was my
wont to repair at night to his sanctum to hear
the descriptions and critiques contained at that
time in this talented paper. It was thus that
I became familiar with the names of living
painters, with their works and the peculiarities
of their style, their merits and defects. In
these critiques Haydon was mentioned with
great praise, his 'Judgment of Solomon' ex-
tolled above any other historical work of the
English school (and with justice). It was by
this paper I was informed about the extraordinary wonders of the 'Elgin Marbles,' the
doings of artists in the great metropolis, and
all the interesting particulars of the art of this
period. Is it to be wondered at, then, if my too
sanguine imagination was fired, and my desire
painfully. excited to see the works of the men
of whom I was constantly reading ?

Most parents who have a family of sons find

it difficult when the time comes to decide what calling or profession their boys shall pursue during life. My parents were not exempt from this difficulty, and I was the one selected for my father's business. Obedient to their wishes I remained thus employed until twenty years had rolled over my head. Then, burning with desire to tread the illusory but flower-enamelled way that leads to fame, and urged by an impulse that grew irresistible, I started for London, a country youth in a modest suit of brown, with twenty pounds in my pocket, earned by my brush—all I could call my own; for my father told me that if I persisted in following the desire of my heart, I was to look for no assistance from him, saying at the same time, that he had no faith in such visionary pursuits. London appeared to me the heaven of youthful hopes and expectations, that Armida's garden of enchantment where all bright visions must be realised or disappointed. Viewed from a distance, it appeared decked in dazzling beauty to my youthful imagination, especially when a journey of three long days and nights by a stage-coach lay between me and my heaven of bliss. So it was some fifty years ago when the 'Highflyer' or 'Wellington' stopped at my father's door, and I quitted my indulgent home for ever. Silent and simple I travelled, with visions alternately sad and brilliant flitting before me. Everything was strange to my wondering eyes. As the coach entered the suburbs of the great City, in a heavy shower of rain, I was warned not to take my impressions of London from that day, which was dreary and gloomy enough, for with the dense smoke and wet it seemed as if we were entering into an inhabited cloud.

Alas! how was I situated!—I had no introductions, no friends, not even an acquaintance, in the whirlpool of life that I was entering.

I had come against the wishes of at least one parent, contrary to the advice of friends, who would come to my father to tell him of the risks and ruin of young men indulging in visionary pursuits, and urging him, as he loved his son, to induce him to return home, and to make him turn his talents to business.

CHAPTER II.

IN London, Bewick found himself involved
in all the difficulties to which the young and
unknown artist is exposed on his first arrival in
the metropolis. He appears, however, to have
made the acquaintance, at an early period of his
residence, of various persons who were able to
guide him in the cultivation of his art, and to
contribute in a great measure to his ultimate
success. He thus gained the advantage of seeing, in the beginning of his career, some of the
noblest works, both of ancient and modern
painters, and had opportunities of listening to
and profiting by the observations of competent

critics. Nor, while studying the works of others, does he appear to have neglected the practice of his art, as he employed his time both in retouching old paintings, and in producing new ones, some of which he was able to dispose of to the patrons of young and promising artists.

Among persons of more or less distinction with whom he became acquainted, perhaps none excited higher admiration, or exercised a more profound influence upon his mind, so far as regards his views of art, than Mr. B. R. Haydon, whom he calls the 'first painter we have.' Haydon gave him a letter of introduction to Fuseli, with the view of obtaining for him the privilege of drawing in the Academy, but at first he was unsuccessful. Haydon, indeed, appears to have acted towards Bewick with remarkable kindness, urging him to press forward to the higher walks of art, and amid the disappointments which might beset him to exercise industry, patience, and perseverance. In his intercourse with this renowned artist, he enjoyed the privilege of becoming acquainted with some of the most distinguished men of the day, poets, sculptors, and painters, not only of England, but also of foreign countries. From their conversation he derived the utmost benefit, his views of art, of literature, and of life being at once greatly enlarged, and at the same time rendered more precise. His position, too, as a pupil of Haydon's, in some degree exposed him to the animosity from which that artist was seldom free. In a caricature of Haydon and his pupils, which was published, Bewick was made the most conspicuous figure after Haydon himself. But of this period of his life the following letters, addressed from London to his brother, will give the reader an interesting outline.

DEAR BROTHER,—You will think, no doubt, that I am rather inert or forgetful, not to have written you ere this, but my desire was to have something satisfactory to tell you. I have no doubt you will want to know how I am situated here. Well, I am not doing anything, but am occupying my time in seeing the exhibitions, &c. &c., which will prove very useful, as I shall hereby improve my ideas. What a pity it is that I have not some little independence at the present moment, as I have got leave to study from the celebrated marble statues which Lord Elgin brought from Greece, — likewise from a plaster cast of Phidias, now exhibiting in the Mews Gallery. Such an opportunity would be likely to found me on the Grecian purity of design. I had the other morning a long conversation with Mr. Day (the proprietor of the King's Mews Gallery). I showed him my picture of Niobe, and he passed high encomiums on it. He is an artist, and has been in Italy, from whence he brought the celebrated cast from a statue of Phidias, twenty feet high, together with several valuable paintings by the old masters, Raphael, Carracci, Rubens, &c. ; all of which he is now exhibiting. I am to go with him to Lord Elgin's (Burlington House) to-morrow morning, to see his moulders at work. He brought them with him from Rome, having there borrowed them from Canova, the celebrated sculptor, who was over here six or seven months ago. Mr. Day is very polite, and asked me from what part of the country I came, and who were the principal noblemen in the neighbourhood. I told him that the Earl of Darlington was one, and that I expected a letter of introduction from Lady Chaytor to Lady Darlington.

I should like to stay here as long as possible, as I can employ my time either in a drawing-school, in portrait-painting, or anything else that would be to my advantage. However, I must take my chance. I have not had much good fortune thus far.

I remain your ever dutiful brother,

WM. BEWICK.

Mr. John Bewick,
    Newgate Street, Newcastle-on-Tyne.

London, July 14th, 1816.

DEAR BROTHER,—I have had a great many disappointments, and some flattering hopes. In my last I think I mentioned Lady Darlington, —that I had received a letter from Colonel Chaytor desiring me to wait upon her ladyship. I mentioned this to some of my friends here, asking their advice. They advised me to take a fine day, as it affects much the exhibition of any works of art. So, after waiting two or three weeks, during which period I retouched a picture, I repaired to Cleveland House on Monday morning, and was mortified and disappointed to learn that the family had quitted London the day before. Judge my feelings at this disappointment after I had anxiously waited so long. However, I must wait patiently, and employ my time as my means will permit. I am at present painting a companion to the 'Marriage.' It is the 'Presentation at the Temple.' I am to have ten guineas for it.

You would hear, if you received any of my letters to my parents, that I have been honoured with the acquaintance of Mr. B. R. Haydon, so much talked of in the papers. He is the first historical painter we have. I was drawing at Burlington House, a place where he studied. He invited me to go to his house to see his things. I got breakfast with him, and saw all his drawings from the Elgin Marbles, likewise the astonishing picture of 'Christ riding into Jerusalem,' which he is now painting. His 'Judgment of Solomon' you will have heard of. It was purchased for seven hundred guineas; he was engaged on it four years, and during that time he did not earn a shilling by his profession. He has been so kind as to give me a letter to H. Fuseli, professor of painting. I took the letter with a drawing, to obtain permission to draw in the Academy. The Council met on Friday, and I am not admitted. There were about fifty drawings not admitted. Mine was only the second finished drawing I ever made. I am not acquainted with any of the Royal Academy, and Mr. Haydon was expelled the Academy. But I understand I should have given the porter at the door a shilling to have given the letter to Mr. Fuseli himself. I was not aware of this, and one can't tell how the letter may have operated with the Royal Academicians. My means are limited: if I can manage until Lady Darlington returns, I will remain here, as I should like to be satisfied that I have tried everything. I send you a copy of Mr. Haydon's letter to Mr. Fuseli :—

'MY DEAR SIR,— The bearer of this is a Mr. Bewick, who is industrious and very eager to get on. He brings a drawing to show you, that he may be allowed to draw in the Academy, if you think it sufficiently well done. He seems to have a feeling for doing things in a large way, and I do think promises something.   Excuse my troubling you.

I am, dear Sir, yours respectfully,

B. R. HAYDON.

I thought of sending something to Mr. Bewick, the engraver ; I have nothing yet good enough.   There were two portraits of him in the Exhibition.   He is thought a clever man here.

As to my health, I am well, I have something else to think about.

I remain your affectionate Brother,

W. BEWICK.

London, Sept. 17th, 1816.

DEAR BROTHER,—You will have heard how I have been befriended by a celebrated historical painter, B. R. Haydon, Esq.   He has written to my father relative to my remaining here ; perhaps they will send you a copy of his letter, I cannot tell what he has said.*   My father has

---

* The letters written by Mr. Bewick and Mr. Haydon to his father were intrusted to a brother of Mr. B.'s, who has unfortunately mislaid them.

answered his letter, and in consequence I have received a note from Mr. Haydon inviting me to tea. I went, and had the kindest reception, evidencing friendship and an ardent desire for my getting on in the higher walks of art. He promises every assistance in his power; all he requires in return is, that I be industrious and have patience and perseverance (what less can I do ?). He says it entirely depends on myself whether I get on or not. I shall do all in my power to be industrious, &c., and a few years will show what I can do—how far my abilities (genius if I have any) may reach. He showed me a valuable collection of engravings. ' See what you like, do what you choose, and have anything I can conveniently spare,' these were his words at tea.

He is going in a fortnight to have a figure cast life-size, and he has given me leave to draw from it. This is a particular favour. I cannot give you an idea of my feelings. He will arrange for me to see all the exhibitions, &c. of pictures free. I must attend the dissections in a week or two, the weather is too warm at present. You will know that Mr. Stamper and I live together at Dr. Wilson's, two rooms first-floor.

Mr. Haydon has given me some precious advice, in fact more by half than I could have expected from a father. If I ever do anything the family will be indebted to him.

I am your dutiful Brother,

WM. BEWICK.

London, Jan. 12th, 1817.

DEAR BROTHER,—You will please to excuse my writing much at present, my time is so much engaged. Since I last wrote you, a circumstance has occurred concerning me at the Royal Academy. On Monday I took a drawing there, desiring to be admitted a student,—the man at the door asked me if I had a letter of recommendation, I said, No. 'You would have got in much better if you had had a letter from a Royal Academician or an Exhibitor.' I told him I had none, and that if my drawing was not sufficient to gain my admittance, I must be content. I went to tell the circumstance to Mr. Haydon; he advised me to go back and give the porter a shilling, but I despised this underhanded bribing work, and determined to take my chance.

I called a few days, after and heard to my surprise that my drawing was admitted. I naturally asked to have it, but I was told I could not. What they mean by this, I don't know, as it is not the usual method: it must have been that they think I am not able to do another as well. I hope I shall do better, and that the Academy will prove a useful place for study.

You will have heard that my mother received a letter from Mr. Haydon. I wish I could describe my feelings at receiving such friendship from this great man. He has even gone so far as to lend me money; and when I offered it him again he would not take it. I told him I really did not know how I should be ever able to recompense him for all he had done for me. His answer was, 'Only be industrious, and suceeed in your art, that is all I require.' Think, dear John, what must be my feelings to be thus honoured by such a man, while his acquaintance is courted by all the noble in the land. Write me the first opportunity, and say if you are determined to stay in Newcastle; I hope to see you in London.

I am, dear brother, yours affectionately,

WILLIAM BEWICK, jun.

Extract.

London, March 16th, 1817.

DEAR BROTHER,——   .   .   .   .

I last Monday set my name down as a student in the British Museum.   .   .   .

London, March 30th, 1817.

DEAR BROTHERS,—Your letter of the 24th inst. I received safe, enclosing 2*l.* for which I return you my sincere thanks and hope it may be soon in my power to refund it together with the 5*l.* you have already lent me.

You desire me to tell you how I am circumstanced. In answer: the last money I received from Darlington was 5*l.*, the remainder of the other payment for the last picture I did for Jas. Janson, Esq. (I have got 15*l.* for it.)

What I am to do now I really don't know. I was at Mr. Haydon's to tea on Monday last. We talked matters over, he thought like a father, and with as much concern as if I had really been his son, he confessed to me that he only had 5*l.* left. 'However,' says he, 'I'll let you have five shillings, that will help a little:' think of a man like this letting me have five shillings out of the only 5*l.* he had.

He likewise offered to pass his word for the payment of a quarter-year's living at an eating-house; but as I was so unsettled, and did not know whether I should change my lodgings, I thought it not advisable to accept his offer, and it seems much better to pay as I go on, as I should not like at the end of three months not to be able to pay.

A few weeks ago I paid a visit to Geo. Allan, Esq., M.P.* and had a glass of wine with him. I am to go with him to Mr. Haydon's to see his much-talked-of things.

My student's ticket for the Academy is sent to be engraved. There is one gentleman, about twenty-three years old, who has drawn in the Academy seven years; another, aged twenty-one, has drawn three years, and the Council have thought them not admissible for their ticket yet. They are very particular now, not as they used to

* For South Durham.

be. My drawings, unknown to me, were sent in to the Professor of Painting; he said he liked them very much: the man who was in the room at the time told me all he said, which I need not repeat here.

I told Haydon of it, and he said it looked like something when the Professor took notice of me. 'Tell the Professor,' says he, 'plumply, if he speaks to you, that you are a pupil of mine, I want it to be known.' What must I feel, John, when Mr. Haydon rejects so many young men who come to him with letters of recommendation, and who have offered him large sums of money — one young man came recommended from Edinburgh. Mr. Haydon (as he says) soon found out what he was, and recommended him to begin immediately with portraits.

I shall finish dissecting next week.

I am, dear brother, yours affectionately,

W. Bewick.

Extracts.

London, May 30th, 1817.

Dear John,—I intended to have written to you last night, but being out to tea, it was

late before I got home. Your letter and five-pound note I received safe, I cannot express how much obliged I am to you. When I look back at the many stops and turns, &c., which have occurred since I came here, I cannot but believe that there must be a Providence which directs and guides all our actions in a certain way to a certain point,—at least I think it is a fine consolation to believe so .   .   .
At Mr. Haydon's I am daily, and here I am introduced to all kinds of known characters, authors, poets, painters, sculptors, &c., not only of this, but of every other country of Europe   .   .   .   .   .

London, Feb. 11th, 1818.

To Mr. J. Bewick, Newcastle-on-Tyne.

DEAR BROTHER AND SISTER,—How do you do? I hope you are quite settled and happy; I hear you have taken a house. I have an opportunity of sending this by a friend, Mr. Harvey (pupil of Bewick the engraver); he is a very clever fellow, and I have no doubt but he will get on. I found him in an obscure part of the town. He has very few acquaintances, and wants bringing forward (his genius would bring him out). I have introduced him to the Landseers, &c. He has the right feeling, and as I said something to you about craniology, he has a good frontispiece. Will you give my best respects to Bewick, and son and daughters, and give them my address? I shall be happy to see any of them if they come to town.

I have been at two or three very intellectual dinners since I came. Amongst the company were Horatio Smith (author of *Rejected Addresses*), Keats the poet, Hazlitt the critic, Haydon, Hunt the publisher, &c., &c. I expect you will have got the numbers of *Annals of Art* from Bewick. I have taken rooms at No. 15 Nassau Street (Middlesex Hospital), unfurnished. It will be rather expensive for me just now, but it suits my purpose.

I have been drawing the skeleton of a lion, &c., for comparative anatomy, and a head in the British Museum.

Hazlitt is giving lectures on poetry; they are said to be the finest lectures that ever were delivered. He gave me a ticket of admission; I have attended.

He is the Shakespeare prose writer of our glorious country; he outdoes all in truth, style, and originality,—you must read his Shakespeare's characters.

I am, dear brother and sister,

Yours affectionately,

WILLIAM BEWICK.

Mr. J. Bewick, Newcastle-on Tyne.

London, March 20th, 1818.

MY DEAR BROTHER,—There will be published in the *Annals of Art* for the 1st of April a caricature representing Haydon and his pupils. Your brother is made most conspicuous, being placed in the centre, and figuring away in a most energetic style. I have had an impression given me. Haydon is flying in the shape of a bird, he has kicked his palette and colours behind him, and is blowing a trumpet as director of the public taste, with two large pens before him denoting his authorship. It will be the best thing for us that has happened, for it connects us altogether,—brings us into public notice, and if we produce anything it will make it tell so much the more. The fools! they cannot see that the more they talk

about us the better for us; they cannot anni-
hilate our works; they cannot criticise our
drawings, so they show their jealousy in this
way. You are free from all this glorious work,
this jealousy, this envy. Write to me as soon
as you can. Mrs. Harvey's brother is coming
to town, endeavour to send a letter by him if
he comes soon.

My love to Ann, and that you may both
live and die happy, with a religious sense of
duty towards your Creator, is the prayer and
hope of your brother,

WM. BEWICK.

Mr. J. Bewick, Newcastle-on-Tyne.

CHAPTER III.

IN the period which intervenes between the last letter and that which follows, Bewick appears to have visited his friends in the north; but during that time he seems to have been by no means forgetful of his vocation, enlarging his views of the domain of art by the practical study of it. The circle of his acquaintances was gradually enlarged; and among others, he obtained the friendship of Allan, the distinguished Scottish artist, and late President of the Royal Scottish Academy. A painting on which he had been working diligently for some time was got ready for exhibition in the British Gallery in January 1822;

and when Haydon exhibited his 'Judgment of Solomon,' and other pictures in Edinburgh, some of Bewick's first works were submitted to the public judgment along with them. Yet, though he was thus encouraged by the dawn of success, his position was still uncertain, and he was greatly harassed by the difficulties with which he had to contend. Embarrassed, however, as he was, he never lost his courage, but continued to labour in the assurance that he should yet overcome every difficulty, and reach the goal which was the object of his ambition. In the following letters to his brother, written in the years 1821-2, Bewick gives a very interesting account of the more prominent events in his career.

London, April 29th, 1821.

MY DEAR BROTHER, — Since I returned from the country I have been *fagging very hard* at my picture ;* it will, I hope, be out next spring,—God grant me health and means. I dine to-morrow (Sunday) with Allan, the painter, of whom you will read in *Peter's*

* 'Jacob and Rachel.'

Letters to his Kinsfolk,—Mr. Haydon and Mr. Geddes, all painters. Next Sunday I expect to meet the famous Belzoni, he that has been so indefatigable in his researches in Egypt, &c. He has published a very splendid and able account of his journey, discoveries, &c. He has brought to this country a collection of Egyptian antiquities, which he is now exhibiting to the public, so that he is very popular, and well deserves to be so. In his person he is a giant, and formerly exhibited himself in this country, performing feats of strength. I know he was at Newcastle. If you see the portrait at the beginning of his book, and then add his figure, you will have an idea what a grand fellow he is. Pray let me hear from you; my kind remembrance to Ann, and believe me,

Your affectionate brother,

W. BEWICK.

London, Nov. 16th, 1821.

MY DEAR BROTHER, — I am very much obliged for what you sent me by Mr. Harvey. My picture will be exhibited at the British

Gallery in January.* I have got very rapidly forward within the last two months, and I see now that I shall get through in time. Mr. Haydon is highly delighted with what I have done. I hope to God that it will be successful. I have just ordered a gold frame for it, and all is going on very well, except that I am harassed in my circumstances; but if I keep my health, I hope to get over it. I have an opportunity of sending this by a parcel to Mr. Harvey, and I avail myself of it merely to thank you for the kind remembrance of me. Mr. Haydon and Mr. Harvey have gone to Edinburgh to exhibit the 'Judgment of Solomon,' and other pictures, together with some of my first beginnings.

I hope you are all well. Excuse this short letter; I will write you a good long one by and by,—and believe me, dear John,

Your affectionate brother,

W. BEWICK.

Bewick now seems to have been infected with Haydon's passion for large pictures, a new

* 'Jacob and Rachel.'

one on which he was engaged, 'David bringing
the head of Goliah to Saul,' being on a very
large scale. From the correspondence which
follows, it is evident that he was gradually
conquering for himself a high place in the estimation of the public; and this no doubt encouraged him to undertake more important
works than he had previously ventured upon.
In the midst of his artistical aspirations, it
is very pleasing to find in these letters the
simple expression of his feelings as a man, his
domestic affections, his unshaken adherence to
principle, and that simple piety which formed
the basis of his character.

London, May 11th, 1822.

DEAR BROTHER, — Miss Harvey tells me
that you are offended at my not writing to
you before this; the truth is, that I have been
harassed to death in every way for the last
four months. But to tell you this, is hardly
enough; you sit by the fireside comfortably
every evening, you take your regular rest, nothing to disturb your thoughts, or drive them
from the regular routine of occupations from

day to day, from week to week, from month to month ; you can have no idea of the occupations or habits of study of a painter, or you would readily excuse me.

I am now as much engaged as ever with my new picture ; it is much larger than the last (14 feet by 10 feet), and the subject is of course more difficult ; it represents David bringing the head of Goliah to King Saul—who was jealous of him from that day forward,—while. the soul of Jonathan was knit with the soul of David,—and the women came out of all the cities of Israel, singing, and dancing, &c.

' Jacob and Rachel ' is now being exhibited at Leeds : it is not sold, which makes me very much pushed for money.

Mr. Harvey is going to send, and I take the opportunity of forwarding a hasty ' how do you do.' I hope Ann and your family are well.

Believe me ever yours affectionately,

W. BEWICK.

Mr. J. Bewick, Newcastle-on-Tyne.

Darlington, Oct. 6th, 1822.

MY DEAR JOHN,—We are all extremely sorry to hear of the loss you have sustained in parting with your dear little Mary Ann. This is your first paternal loss, and both you and Ann must feel it very much; but I hope you will both bear it with fortitude, as strong in the belief of the wisdom of Divine Providence. I am very busy from morning to night, and I begin to be afraid that I shall not be able to get over to Newcastle. If you get the *Tyne Mercury* (Tuesday last) you will see a very flattering account of my picture. Indeed they have made it the first subject of their remarks, which is more than could have been expected, considering that the established artists, Howard, R.A., and Martin, are exhibitors.

You must get a *Newcastle Magazine*, which contains more than the *Tyne Mercury*. My mother and all the family join in condolence with you both.

I am, dear Brother, yours affectionately,

W. BEWICK.

Though Bewick continued to labour with undiminished zeal, he was still unable to support himself by the proceeds of his art, and had to make, from time to time, applications for assistance to his friends. To add to his other difficulties, he was unfortunately involved in the troubles which continually beset the existence of his early friend and patron, Haydon. In order to assist one who had shown him so much friendship he incurred obligations which he was ultimately unable to meet. He alludes to these and other events in the following letters to his brother :—

London, May 8th, 1823.

DEAR JOHN,—The exhibition of Mr. Haydon's picture goes on remarkably well and profitably, but it is not sold yet, which makes him very short of money. Every person—enemies as well as friends—agrees that the ' Raising of Lazarus ' is the sublimest conception and best picture that has been painted in this country ; and that the figure, expression, and the sepulchral effects of Lazarus, are among the finest things ever conceived or executed. If you should think it any honour to have sat for the head of this fine figure, you may be interested to know that I served as model ; and it is not unlike me when I am worn out with fatigue,—in fact, it was painted from me just before I set off for the country last time, when I was so ill that I looked certainly more like a ghost than a living man. I am getting on rapidly with my picture, and working very hard. I know this must be an expensive time for you, but if you could send me a little more assistance, I should be greatly obliged, as the expenses are very great, and I have no means at present of raising any money, my time being wholly occupied with my picture. My kind remembrances to Ann and to little Emma.

Ever yours affectionately,

W. BEWICK.

Mr. J. Bewick, Newcastle-on-Tyne.

London, May 19th, 1823.

DEAR BROTHER,—I am all anxiety and misery. Mr. Haydon's affairs are in confusion, and I am uncertain as to how far I am involved, and how to proceed; send me what assistance you can. I have got on very rapidly with my picture, but this business stops me for the present. I have many good friends here who will advise me for the best; and whatever I may have to suffer in conjunction with other friends of his, I hope it will be a lesson to me for the future.

Believe me ever yours affectionately,

W. BEWICK.

Direct to me at Mr. Harvey's, 24 Norfolk Street, Middlesex Hospital.

CHAPTER IV.

BEWICK, who possessed the artist's talent for close and accurate observation, was in the habit, as we have seen in the preceding letters, of committing to paper his impressions of the various remarkable characters whom he met casually in society, or whose acquaintance he enjoyed. Some of the most celebrated literary and artistic men of that period have been very fully and accurately portrayed by him, and the reminiscences of his personal intercourse with such distinguished writers as Scott, Hogg, Wordsworth, &c., are full of interesting anecdote and acute criticism. No one had ampler opportunity of becoming perfectly acquainted with Haydon, and his portraiture of that great but erratic genius appears to find its place most conveniently in this chapter.

HAYDON.

'But I'll remember thee, Glencairn,
And all that *thou* hast done for me.'

Haydon is a subject that I hope to touch with circumspection, delicacy, and, if possible, justice. Many have written against his character, his talents, and his painting. Some have pursued him and his memory with never-tiring zeal, finding numberless points—God save the mark—at which to launch their shafts; and when it is no longer of any avail to attack his acknowledged genius, they turn to abuse the particular branch of art which he held to be the only one worth a life of deep study, and worth a man's ambition to excel in. This ambition even is a fault, and they say, 'It must be acknowledged there are too many examples to prove that painters will persevere in a peculiar style of art, notwithstanding every discouragement attending their labours. Our own Haydon is a case in point, a man of unquestionable genius, but entertaining views of art which the public either would not or could not understand, and persevering in his promulgation of them with a pertinacity that set at defiance general opinion till he " perished in his prime." '

What a piece of time-serving cant this is ! No doubt there may have been some Grub Street scribe at the time that Milton wrote his ' Paradise Lost ' who abused the selection of the subject, asserted the unsaleableness of it, and blamed the pertinacity of the unfortunate author in continuing to exercise his genius upon a work of such great labour, for which he would only receive 5*l.* reward. No doubt it was an imprudence in a pecuniary point of view, but we look upon that noble poem with very different conclusions at the present time, and no one attempts or desires to rob the author of his high fame. So it will be with Haydon when his ' Judgment of Solomon ' will stand out to justify his pretensions in the higher walks of painting, and show him worthy of public patronage and of the reward assigned too often to mediocrity and to the time-serving drudges in the middle and lower ranks of art, who, if they can only make money, would be lauded by such encouragers of art as the writer of the above.   Take, for instance, Thorn-hill, Barry, West, Reynolds, Northcote, not to speak of the most famous living artists. Compare West's 'Death on the Pale Horse,' Barry's Societies of Arts pictures, Reynolds' 'Ugolino' or 'Death of Cardinal Wolsey,' Northcote's 'Princes in the Tower,' all or any of them with Haydon's 'Judgment of Solomon;' consider the composition, the power of telling the story, then the breadth, mastery of light and shadow, appro-priate tone of colour and harmony,—above all, take the expression, action, costume, then sub-mit it to a scrutiny of parts—take a toe, a finger, an eye, a nostril, a hand, a foot, a head—and see if you can match Haydon's drawing, masterly handling, the colour, or the solidity of the flesh. There is no picture of the English school to be compared with it, and this will be admitted by all capable of judging before many years elapse. Why speak of the *pertinacity* of his character? Surely it is a virtue pertinaciously to follow out what we conceive to be meritorious, and Haydon was pertinacious in following the bent of his genius which was for *great works*, not for little ones.

He tried portraits and exhibited the results

of his experiments at the Royal Academy, but the public would not encourage that style of handing them down to posterity, requiring something more bland, more flattering. He tried smaller pictures, but it cannot be said that he was successful, although he painted many re-petitions of ' Napoleon looking on the Sea ' for as low a price as would satisfy his most humble-minded counsellor. What then was he to turn to ? ' Gentle critic, tell me what ? ' But why overlook the truth of the position of this artist and scholar ? After painting his ' Solomon,' he never was the healthy, vigorous man he was before. His health and the affliction of his eyes prevented him from applying himself to his next work with perseverance and assiduity, and he was six years before he brought out his ' Christ's Triumphal Entry.' He had thus six years of em-barrassment upon him, and this incumbrance he never got free from : it weighed upon him, broke down his spirits, interrupted his labours, disturbed his tranquillity, weakened his powers of mind, and prevented that concentration of genius which is required for the achievement of difficult intellectual productions. Many great

men have succumbed to pecuniary embarrassments. Harassed by bailiffs and tax-gatherers,
what can the intellect of a man achieve ? What
mastery of mechanical manipulation can he ac-
quire ? Nor does the public look at his works
with favour, but in his struggle, he fights, as it
were, with the sun in his eyes, helpless and bewildered, until insanity or death comes to end his
mortal turmoil, and his character is left at the
mercy of his enemies. But if he have done anything worthy of envy his works live after him, and
honour and glory will crown the name of him to
whom mere bread could not be granted in his lifetime. If to Mr. Haydon such a pension had been
conceded as was enjoyed by Mr. West so many
years (1000*l.* per annum), how differently, in my
belief, he would have repaid his country ! what
works of grandeur and historical interest would
he have executed ! Honour and reward foster
genius and cause it to expand ; neglect, em-
barrassment, disappointment, wither and blast it.

When I first knew Haydon, he was very
joyous, and even frolicsome ; he delighted in fun,
he would roll on the carpet at the facetious
drollery of Charles Lamb, whose quaint humour

was to him irresistible; but he never could do more than laugh heartily at Horace Smith. Smith, he used to say, was too respectable-looking to suggest any tomfoolery, or boyish excitation of excess, or exuberant merriment. His hilarity and high spirits never flagged even in times of difficulty and anxious pecuniary straits; he seemed buoyed up by some inward conviction that he should overcome all his troubles, and so he struggled on—hope strong in his nature, and his high purpose giving vigour to all his projects and to all his labours. A good day's work at his picture was more to him than any other stake in the game of life.

One fine day after I had been sitting to Haydon, he took me to Kensington to see Wilkie's picture of 'Reading the News of the Battle of Waterloo,' which he was then painting for the Duke of Wellington. The picture was far advanced, and I was exceedingly struck with it, and admired many parts of it. The painter was pleased and in very good humour, and Haydon and he seemed to enjoy each other's company vastly, they had great confidence in and estimation of each other's judgment; and Wilkie asked Haydon advice about parts of the picture which he had some doubts about, or which were not exactly to his satisfaction. The conversation was extremely interesting and instructive; and I was astonished at the perspicuity and nice discrimination that Wilkie evinced in his explanation of the how, the why, and wherefore of his doubts. He then showed his sketches, and they deliberated and decided. It was beautiful to observe the brotherly friendship and sincerity that seemed to exist between the two great painters, both at this time at the height of their celebrity; and I came away impressed with the conviction that no one knew more than Wilkie of that intricate and difficult part of the art, composition of lines, of masses and breadth of effect; and surely his execution is inimitable when confined to subjects of the size of this picture.

Haydon praised what had been done since last he saw the picture, and Wilkie was delighted. Indeed I never saw him so light-hearted and playful. Haydon took hold of his hands and said, ' Look here, Bewick, these are what I painted my Christ's hands from. Wilkie's hands are the only part of his person that are like his pictures, they are made for fine execution,—my hands are very good, but they are not so tremulously nervous,—so delicate or refined. These will never paint *large* works with power, nor will mine ever paint small pictures with sufficient delicacy or refinement. You would never suppose that these hands would have such a miserable mess upon the palette as you see there (looking down at Wilkie's dirty palette). Wilkie's hands were copied for the *real mother* in my picture of Solomon, and it has been said that they are the most tender and expressive part of the whole picture.'

Wilkie was mentioning to me something about the material or vehicle he painted some parts of this picture with, and Haydon, laughing, stopped him, saying, 'No! now, Wilkie, don't pester Bewick with that,' and added to me, 'Every man, I suppose, must have his hobby, and Wilkie's hobby is, and always has been, *vehicle*. He has been running after this mystery, this *ignis fatuus*, ever since he began to paint; and like Sir Joshua, who did the same thing, he will always and for ever get further and further from the objects of his search, and there will be a pretty look-out fifty or a hundred years after this, when his pictures fade, or crack, or turn black, or do something to astonish and disappoint posterity.' Wilkie laughed and said, ' Well, well, it is after all an important matter.' ' Yes,' replied Haydon, ' it is important to be contented with what has already been found to stand the test of time.'

An appointment was made to go to the National Gallery to examine the Piombo picture of the ' Raising of Lazarus,' Wilkie having said he had been thinking that Haydon wanted some ' bits of bright colour, perhaps *yellow*, in his picture.' Wilkie went deliberately over every part of this work ; and it was after this visit that Haydon introduced those bright effects in the back of his picture.

Haydon and myself returned home through Kensington Gardens. It was a delicious day, and I enjoyed the freshness of the country, the air, and the walk, the more so from my constant confinement at my studies. We approached a seat and sat down under the grateful shade of some of the magnificent trees. The air was fragrant with the perfume of the linden, and the bees were busy profiting by the profusion of expanded flowers, and with the birds were making a humming music very conducive to meditation and silence. The sun danced upon the waters of the Serpentine, and a slight breeze played in the branches above us.

Haydon was pensive, and began to tell me the following incident of his pathetic story by saying, ' This reminds me of bygone days: it was here I sat on my return from my friend Wilkie, at the time I was painting my " Solomon." The picture of "Macbeth " had been returned by Sir George Beaumont because I had increased its size, and I was in the midst of my next even larger picture of "Solomon," when in consequence of not receiving the price agreed upon for "Macbeth," I was without funds, literally without a shilling to get my dinner. I thought what was to be done, and as I had already served Wilkie in another way, and we were on the most intimate terms of friendship and con- fidence, I determined to ask him for the loan of five pounds for my immediate necessities, in fact existence, as my father had withdrawn his former allowance to me. I therefore walked to Kensington, the pride of my youth was on this occasion very much subdued. Well, my friend as usual was delighted to see me, and after a good deal of hesitation I plumped out the object of my visit. I was struck with his blank expression of face; if I had given him a blow he could not have been more staggered. I knew he had received some hundreds for his last work, and I *ought* to have done the same. Wilkie put his hand to his mouth and pressed his under-lip between his finger and thumb, like one of the figures in his " Rent Day," and drawled out in cold Scotch, that he " raaly couldn't " let me have it. I said, " You can't, eh ? " he replied, " No, *indeed* he could not." I was silent, numbed; my young heart, warm then in the feelings and sentiment of friendship, had received a shock. I felt my cheek hot with the blush of wounded pride and disappointment, and could only say, " I am sorry for it," and wishing him a good morning, left him to himself and his hundreds.

' I had returned as far as this seat. Beginning to feel extremely hungry, I sat down to consider what was next best to be done to obtain my dinner. Hunger, they say, sharpens one's wits—but it did not mine; and I pursued my walk towards home. When I came near the old haunt for dinner, appetite pushed me on, and I determined to try on trust for once. I had always dined and paid at the same place for some years, and the waiter knew me. So into the eating-house I dashed, and, putting a good face upon the dilemma, asked for my usual chop, and dinner was never more gratefully consumed. When I had to pay, my hand went into my empty pocket in make-believe, and I said, "Oh, I've forgot my money to-day, I will pay you to-morrow." The reply was "Very well, Sir;" and I stepped to the door with as much momentary satisfaction as if I had had in the bank the amount Sir George owed me, or Wilkie's hundreds. Just as I put my foot upon the step of the outer door, a gentle tap on my shoulder stayed my progress, and I was very civilly invited by the keeper of the eating-house to walk into his room, as he wished to speak with me. I returned with him. He then shut the door, and, after apologizing for the liberty he was taking, said he had read in the newspapers how badly I had been used with regard to my picture, and that if dining there, or living entirely at his house, would be any convenience to me, he should be quite delighted, and I might pay him when I was able. I agreed to dine there for the future, with many thanks for this noble, disinterested kindness.

'And there I continued to dine until my "Solomon" was completed. It was exhibited at Spring Gardens, had a good light and was well seen, made great success,—sensation, I might say—and was sold for 800 guineas. I paid all my kind creditors and my noble eating-house keeper, who, afterwards having retired from his successful business to his villa in the country a rich man, often drove in his carriage to pay his respects to me. I still continued my friendship for Wilkie, and did not let trifles of this kind come between us to mar our mutual satisfaction in the pursuit of our loved art. He seemed to enjoy my success as much as anybody; and I was now puffed up in all quarters as the first painter England had ever produced; and it must be my boast that I am a true *Englishman,* for my art and my country are

the only enthusiasm that possess my whole
soul. I have invitations to reside in other
countries, but I refuse all—it is *here* my *fate* is
fixed.'

At the time Sir R. Peel bought the famous
' Chapeau de Paille' of Rubens, it was exhibited in Bond Street, and I accompanied Haydon and Martin to see it.   Haydon went off to
a proper distance under the light of the window
and exclaimed, ' By G—d, Martin, that's wonderful ! charming !—how pure and brilliant ! What
lustrous, beaming eyes ! what a creature of
brightness, of silvery splendour !' ' Oh,' Martin added, ' it *is* fine !' We were permitted
to go within the enclosure to examine closely
this extraordinary specimen of a very wonderful painter, take him all in all.   Both
our great English artists viewed it closely,
admiring its solidity, its transparency, its fra-
gile brightness, its softness, its purity of tint,
and its elastic touch, without uttering one word ;
they did not seem to breathe.

After they had apparently satiated themselves, Haydon said to me, ' There, Bewick,
take your fill of that ; it is a perfect lesson to

any painter.' We then left the place, and the only remark I heard Haydon make as he got into the street was, that 'it at first struck him as being what is called "fishy" in the complexion;' to which Martin assented, but he confessed he did not know much of the practice of flesh-painting, nor was he aware by his own study of the great variety of delicate tints and half-tints required to make up the one colour or effect of flesh; he apprehended that flesh was one of the most difficult of an artist's tasks in the search after expression. On which Haydon remarked how few modern painters had attained to anything like what we had just seen, and that perhaps might not rank with some of the flesh of Titian, or of Murillo, or even, I am tempted to say, with some very few specimens of his pupil Vandyck. Sir Joshua had a fine conception of the general effect of flesh, but he seems to have wanted delicacy and tenderness of half-tint, and the fine drawing, and execution, and purity you find in Vandyck. Titian is mellowed, but there is not the purity which charms us in Vandyck, and even Guido.

'I should like,' said he, 'to have been able to

put what we have just seen by the side of a Titian. I apprehend Rubens in the head might seem cold, if not vapid. Those Venetians sacrificed all to their flesh, and produced tremendous effects of golden brilliancy and power of colour. Rubens is brilliant too, but there is not that *depth*—that power of *rich tone*. His pictures, though wonderful, have all the appearance of haste, of slightness, and want of solidity, whereas the Italians, the Venetians in particular, are finished with great care, with masses of solid colour,—with power, fine drawing, rich glazings ; nothing can stand against them. Some of the Spanish painters have all this solid *impasto*, and transparent toning too, with the power and drawing, and we have an appreciation and sympathy with both schools. The Dutch school, as it is called, is perfection of execution in small, but where carried to a large expansive scale, it does not transfer its power, but appears attenuated or vapid.'

Martin had a peculiar habit of sneezing twice, or rather snorting with his nose, when conversing, and this would increase in loudness and frequency as he warmed to his argument. Haydon also had the same curious propensity, but not quite so loud as Martin.

In the dead silence of the room where the picture was exhibited these curious sounds were remarkably distinct, and seemed like the faint expressions of the thought of a dumb person or the sneezing of dumb animals, or like a sound and its echo. When old Kean played Sylvester Daggerwood (for his own benefit), he imposed upon himself this same odd habit, and when presented on the stage it was laughable enough.

Martin was of about middle size—fair, extremely good-looking, and pleasing in his expression; there was nothing remarkable or eccentric in his appearance; he was smart and trim, well dressed and gentlemanly, and when seen out of doors he seemed to delight in a light primrose-coloured vest with bright metal buttons, a blue coat set off with the same, his hair carefully curled, and shining with macassar oil. He was prepossessing, with a great flow of conversation and argument. He was also imaginative, and kept to his points with a tenacity not easily subdued.

Wilkie was tall, ungainly, and awkward in his manner, and, though not quite deserving the description of Mrs. Flynn, the beautiful housekeeper of Castle Howard, who spoke of him as 'the ugliest man she had ever seen,' he was by no means the 'golden-haired' Adonis his fellow-countryman, Allan Cunningham, would have liked to make him. He had rather a drawling, hesitating speech, and when in close argument would forget himself, and the 'twang' of his Northern tongue would be very strong. Indeed, he never was quite free from it, although he could not be persuaded that it was possible for anyone to discover by his speech that he was a Northern, and he sometimes got out of humour when told of it. Haydon would laugh at his provoked expression when he twitted him with his Scotch accent, and Wilkie would insist upon his pronunciation being 'pure English.' Haydon would cry out, 'Ha, ha, ha! what a delusion!' and as Wilkie became warm and vexed, his native Scotch was evident enough. Haydon would then repeat and imitate the broad intonation of a particular expression that Wilkie had in his heat allowed to slip out. When he found that he could not edge off, or get out of it in any way, Wilkie would laugh too, and return the quiz upon the Devonshire peculiarities by saying, 'Well, and *yew tew* are Devon*sheere*, and fancy, like Northcote, that you speak pure English.' And so they would laugh and joke each other in a playful moment of relaxation like two school-boys. At other times they would consult and argue upon difficult matters connected with their art, and Haydon would be fluent, decided in his propositions, would cite precedents and authorities, and be even audacious in his language, whilst Wilkie with great patience listened, returned again and again to the encounter, and *hammered* in separate words, that seemed difficult of enunciation, and hard to get hold of; but his difficulty and hesitation did not in the least prevent him from following out his side of the argument, which he would put in various forms and lights to persuade or convince his friend, often repeating with a smile the persuasive expression of 'you see,' which, as he had a slight lisp, he would pronounce 'you sthee.'

CHAPTER V.

THE next of these autobiographic sketches contains the painter's reminiscences of Wordsworth and Ugo Foscolo, in which national temperament, as exhibited respectively by the English poet and his Italian *confrère*, is very accurately and forcibly discriminated. On the occasion when Bewick met Foscolo, the latter appears to have suggested the first hint of that important task on which Bewick was afterwards employed, namely, that of executing copies from the celebrated frescoes of Michael Angelo in the Sistine Chapel at Rome. The word-picture of the two poets, which the artist draws from life, is very effective, and we have no reason to doubt in every respect faithful.

FOSCOLO AND WORDSWORTH.

On one occasion I met the Italian poet and lecturer Ugo Foscolo with Wordsworth and some ladies, at tea at Haydon's in the evening. The contrast between the two poets was remarkable. Our own sat still and collected, philosophic and considerate. His soul seemed full of the religion of poetry. He had dwelt apart, and arrived at convictions through experience and inspiration. His tranquillity was noble and majestic, like the repose of the lion. Conscious strength, with mild reserve, beamed placidly over the features that spoke of content springing from the conviction of Universal Good. His Italian brother poet, volatile and passionate, ever and anon started from his chair, and vapoured about—whirling round the room,—twirling his quizzing glass rapidly in excitement, as if he were suffering under some galvanic influence, expressing by violent action and gestures, as well as in every feature of his remarkable face, whatever sentiment or proposition he wished to enforce.

One of the ladies present (Miss Wordsworth, I think) began by praising the Italian language, ' for its grace, its force, its suitableness to poetry and to song, its mellifluous sweetness to the ear, merely in sound,' &c. Wordsworth joined in, commending likewise the Italian pronunciation of the Latin language, ' which seemed to him always natural and proper, being emphatic as well as soft,' and, he said, ' he should fancy Milton would have adopted the Italian mode of conversing in Latin, as suiting his own ideas of fulness, rotundity, and power, combined with sweetness ;' adding, ' What a treat it would have been to listen to John Milton, the immortal, repeating the poetry of Virgil or of Horace !'

One of the ladies here asked Signor Foscolo to be kind enough to favour the company by repeating a few lines in the pure Italian tongue. The poet very obligingly complied with the request, and rising to his feet, commenced in the manner of the *improvvisatori* of his country, and recited with deep feeling, passion, fire, and pathos, not forgetting the appropriate gesture of the actor, his own lines, descriptive of himself. They were as follows :—

> ' Solcata ho fronte ; occhi incavati intenti ;
>   Crin fulvo, emunte guance, ardito aspetto,
> Labbri tumidi, arguti, al riso lenti ;
>   Capo chino, bel collo, irsuto petto :
> Membri esatti ; vestir semplice, eletto ;
> Ratti i passi, i pensier, gli atti, gli accenti ;
>   Sobrio, ostinato, umano, ispido, schietto ;
> Avverso al mondo, avversi a me gli eventi ;
>   Mesto i più giorni, e solo ; ognor pensoso :
> Alle speranze incredulo e al timore ;
>   Il pudor me fa vile, e prode l' ira.
> Parlami astuta la ragion ; ma il core,
>   Ricco di vízi e di virtù, delira——
> Fors'io da morte avrò fama e riposo.' *

---

* TRANSLATION.

Intent and deep-sunk eyes, a furrowed brow,
    Fair hair, thin cheeks are mine, and look possessed ;
Lips full and eloquent, to laughter slow ;
    Head bent, and well-formed neck, with shaggy breast ;
Limbs neatly made, simple yet choice in clothes ;
    I do the world (fortune doth me oppose) ;
Rapid in movement, action, thought, and word ;
    Temperate, yet firm, humane, and fond of truth ;
Most often sad and lonely from my youth ;
    Thoughtful ; by hope or terror seldom stirred ;
Shame makes me coward——anger makes me brave ;
    Reason speaks sweetly to me, but my heart,
In virtue rich, and vice, doth madly start ;
    Perhaps from death I fame and rest shall have.

No description can convey an adequate idea of the oratorical peculiarities of this original and eccentric foreigner, as he gave this portrait of himself, abounding in contrast of tones, of manner, of action, changing from the mild, placid, or mournful to the spirited, sarcastic, denunciatory, or severe.

No one unused to Italian recitation can form a just conception of it. Haydon's small parlour seemed too confined for the voice, or for the violent gesticulation, of Signor Foscolo. Wordsworth appeared astounded as the Italian proceeded with the description of himself, and seemed to be wondering to what excess this unexpected phrenetic display would lead ; and when the poet came to the last four lines, in which the letter r is rather frequent, our English poet seemed moved to fear, and opened his mouth and eyes, gasping for breath, so startling was the effect of the shrill trumpet-like voice of the speaker, as it vibrated, sonorous or deep, with the rough sound of the letter r rumbling in his throat or rattling on his tongue. The ladies fluttered in tremulous agitation, looking at each other, not without alarm, as this strange original was acting his wild part before them, throwing himself into all the contortions of which his pliant body was capable, while his voice and expression were equally variable and intense; his 'intent and deep-sunk eyes' darting like lightning, burning in anger, or melting in pensive softness, as occasion required. All this in so small a sitting-room, and so close to the audience, seemed excess even from an Italian point of view; and when it is thought that it was all about himself, it approached to madness, and the strangers naturally felt alarm lest it should end in some dire fit of insanity. The lady who had innocently induced this display had half repented, but she might afterwards be pleased to have witnessed so singular an exhibition.

Mr. Haydon, being acquainted with the Italian language, and always entering into the enjoyment of an original character like Foscolo's, was in his element, and he cordially thanked the Signor for exerting himself to so much effect. Wordsworth was silent and absorbed. The exhibition, altogether, seemed too much for him; whether it was the difficulty he might feel with the Italian language, or that he was puzzled and thrown out of his usual ideas of a quiet chanting mode of recitation, or that he could not make out to his satisfaction what conclusions to draw from this his first interview with the Italian poet.

But the last act of this eventful evening was still to come. After the various little episodes of a social party like this, where free conversation was passing round, and Haydon's small talk to the ladies, with his joyous laugh, was amusing them and making Wordsworth smile, some one having spoken in reply, and by way of badinage, of the beauty of disinterestedness, and the generosity of the nature of man in his undegenerate state, Mr. Foscolo started into life—for this was a subject that seemed to be his hobby—and directing his conversation to his brother poet, aimed some serious blows against the good qualities and virtuous intentions of human nature, insisting that man's actions arose entirely from self-interest, that his motives and springs of action were naturally and unavoidably selfish, traceable to those sources that tended to his benefit or advantage. Upon these premises he grounded his argument, which appeared as nothing compared with the energy and violence with which he delivered it. Indeed, he seemed unable to speak or converse at all unless he was upon his feet, giving loose to all the parts of his body at once; and, as his thoughts prompted the utterances of his tongue, his whole frame followed in the wake of that marvellous organ; and the louder he spoke, the more violent was the action of his various members. Indeed, his argumentation, or his conversation, was a species of acting, which, upon the stage and at a proper distance, would have been energetic and spirited; though, upon the English stage, it would have been thought overdone. Wordsworth allowed Signor Foscolo to proceed to the end of his reasoning without any interruption, when, finding a pause, he quietly said,—

' Suppose a person had fallen into the water, and there seemed every probability of his being drowned, and another person, entirely a stranger, and by mere chance coming that way, should, without premeditation, or even thought of consequences, jump in to save the drowning man, and happily, or not, succeed, what interest or benefit could the humane person expect to derive from his saving, or trying to save, the life of a fellow-creature ?'

F.—'There is not an instance of a person voluntarily risking his own life to save another, unless in the expectation of reward or benefit in some shape or other.'

W.—'I think there are instances in my own knowledge, and I hope many that I may not be aware of, nor have ever heard of.'

F.—'Ah! no.   Impossible!'

W.—'I assure you, Sir, that, in my own knowledge, a case occurred where there could be no expectation of reward or benefit whatever, for the parties were totally unknown to each other; and the disinterested individual who saved the other from a watery grave was not only unknown, but was never seen again in the neighbourhood after the interesting circumstance,—interesting, I may say : for the life so saved was a precious life : it was the son of a poor widow, whose labour was the only support of herself and a numerous small family. I often tried to find out the name of the heroic preserver of this young man's life, but in vain; nobody had ever seen him before the circumstance happened, nor up to this present moment has he ever been known to appear in the neighbourhood. I could mention other instances of disinterestedness, similar to this one, if necessary, to prove the humanity and instinct of noble self-sacrifice and generosity planted by Providence in the breast of man.'

F.—'Sir, there must be some mistake; it may have been done to satisfy some vain-glory of personal exhibition,—the art of swimming,— or the strength of the swimmer, to receive adulation for the courage, the success.'

W.—'As far as appeared the humane impulse came momentarily, without premeditation, and the feat done, he quitted hastily the scene of his heroism, and no one knew who he was, nor where he came from. Besides, there are many similar acts of noble and disinterested beneficence in the history of man. It would be ungenerous and unchristian to condemn the human race to such narrow bounds, when it is admitted by philosophy and reason that Christian benevolence is natural, that our Maker has bestowed upon us impulses of generous sympathy,— of heartfelt tenderness towards our kind.'

All this was uttered in the quiet solemnity peculiar to Wordsworth, as if dictated by profound conviction of its truth. His brother poet listened with attention, for Wordsworth's manner was impressive. But no sooner had he concluded his observations, with the seeming satisfaction of having performed a duty, than his opponent (for the conversation now took the semblance of disputation) sprang upon his feet, eyed the philosophic poet at the opposite side of the room, for a moment only,—

> ' Collecting all his might, dilated stood,
> Like Teneriffe or Atlas unremoved;'

then walking up directly in front of his antagonist, deliberately doubled his fist, and held it in Wordsworth's face, close to his nose, staring at him with his curious Chinese eyes, and crying, or bawling rather, in rude emphasis,—

' Bah! It is all to satisfy self, Sir, to please self, to gratify self-love or pride, to have the satisfaction of performing something that will in his expectation be substantially rewarded, or secure the gratification of the passion of self-esteem ; and in this way the effect revolves and turns round—what you call ?—to meet the pleasure of self,—the doer of it,—derived, in the first instance, from the impulse of anticipation or expectancy of recompense ; and in the second place, of self-gratification, vanity, pride, ambition, or the innumerable small selfish passions in the breast of man.'

Having uttered these *liberal* sentiments with the vehemence natural to the Italian, holding his clenched fist all the time in our poet's face, he started off suddenly with a triumphant wave of his extended hand, and spinning quickly round the circle of the company, he nodded as he passed each his self-satisfaction, as if he had quite confounded his adversary, tossing and twirling his quizzing-glass the whole time in agitation and excitement. The self-complacency and apparent conceit could only be equalled by a Malvolio ; and as he repeated his circuitous turns round and round, the ladies drew in their feet and costume, not a little apprehensive, for they were shocked at the liberty taken with a gentleman of such moderation and mildness as Mr. Wordsworth, however amused they might be at the novel antics of the foreign poet.

Mr. Haydon put on an expression of alarm when Foscolo stepped up to Wordsworth with so little ceremony; and although an excellent conversationalist, seemed inclined to allow the argument to be fought out between the literary gentlemen, enjoying the high treat of the contrast of character in these two gifted men.

Whilst Signor Foscolo was executing his rapid gyrations within the circle of the company, Wordsworth remained unmoved, and I observed he shut both eyes, as if looking inwards to collect and digest arguments so contradictory to his own convictions, and so unfavourable to his view of humanity, and I perceived he breathed a faint sigh within himself. There was now a pause, and silence pervaded the company. I ventured to observe that I could have wished for the presence of

Mr. Coleridge, as the subject of conversation put me in mind of what he said to Mr. Hazlitt in *The Valley of Rocks*, where the fisherman gave an account of a boy who had been drowned the day before, and whom they had tried to save at the risk of their own lives. He said 'he did not know how it was that they ventured, but, Sir, we have a *nature* towards one another.' This expression, Coleridge remarked to Hazlitt, was a fine illustration of that theory of disinterestedness which he (in common with Butler) had adopted.

Signor Foscolo bent his eye upon me, but did not deign to make further remark, and Wordsworth opened his eyes and smiled to me, saying, in low and subdued tones, 'Well, I must and do believe that there are such things existing as sincere disinterestedness, philanthropy, and even patriotism.' He then came and took a seat beside me, and told me how pleased he had been with my drawings from Raphael's Cartoons and the Elgin Marbles that he had seen exhibited, and what desire he had to see similar comprehensive copies from the celebrated frescoes of Michael Angelo, such as the

Prophets and Sibyls, and the compositions from the Sistine Chapel at Rome. 'Angelo,' he said, 'is the great epic painter, the poet executing his high imaginings with the pencil; no one touches the hem of his garment in that lofty comprehensiveness that soars beyond the regions of commonplace, adding ideality and greatness to ordinary forms, giving sublimity and distinctive character to what in other hands might only be dramatic. Although I appreciate, and I hope can admire sufficiently, the beauties of Raphael's transcendent genius—and let us observe that in him there are no inanities—yet we must brace the sinews, so to speak, of our comprehension to grapple with the grandeur and sublimity of thought and imagination, the epic greatness, of Michael Angelo, who has the merit of eclipsing in these respects, as well as in the difficulties and technicalities of his art, every other artist that had preceded him;—I mean of that epoch. And we must not forget that it was the splendour, the brilliance, the superlative lustre of this sun of Art, that shone, and enlightened with new and ennobling impressions and enlarged conceptions the re-

fined, pure intelligence and the beautiful soul
—if I am permitted to say so,—of Raphael.
The brighter luminary glanced, as it were, a
ray of its peculiar force to the already divinely-
endowed genius, and added a new lustre to
that already there. It was an additional ray
of sunlight into the prism of genius, which
there blended with other bright hues, strength-
ening the glittering beauties that sparkled in
their primitive modesty, delicate and sensitive.
Raphael was strengthened, both morally and
physically, by Michael Angelo, for by him his
mind expanded, his hand was emboldened, and
he depicted his conceptions with greater power
and distinctive character; and what, perhaps, is
extraordinary, without diminishing in the least
his wonted delicacy, or grace, or refinement.'

Mr. Wordsworth seemed greatly relieved
from a metaphysical dispute so disagreeably
conducted, and smiled with pleasure in dwelling upon the beauties of art and the poetry of
painting. It seemed balm to him to return to
social converse and pleasant themes. 'Let me
take this opportunity,' he said to me, 'to express
my admiration of those beautiful works by your

namesake, the engravings on wood, transcripts of nature, that I look at with ever-recurring pleasure, and wonder at the variety and texture the artist has contrived to produce upon such difficult material. I hope, when you have an opportunity, you will not forget to make my compliments and respects to Mr. Bewick.'

Perhaps it may be interesting, and not out of place, if I quote here a description of the person of our English poet, by one who knew him well. 'Mr. Wordsworth, in his person, is above the middle size, with marked features, and an air somewhat stately and quixotic. He reminds one of some of Holbein's heads, grave, saturnine, with a slight indication of sly humour, kept under by the manners of the age or by the pretensions of the person. He has a peculiar sweetness in his smile, and great depth and manliness and a rugged harmony in the tones of his voice. His manner of reading his own poetry is particularly imposing ; and in his favourite passages his eye beams with preternatural lustre, and the meaning labours slowly up from his swelling breast. No one who has seen him at these moments could go away with an impression that he was a "man of no mark or likelihood." Perhaps the comment of his face and voice is necessary to convey a full idea of his poetry. His language may not be intelligible, but his manner is not to be mistaken. It is clear that he is either mad or inspired. In company, even in a *tête-à-tête*, Mr. Wordsworth is often silent, indolent, and reserved. If he is become verbose and oracular of late years, he was not so in his better days. He threw out a bold or an indifferent remark without either effort or pretension, and relapsed into musing again. He shone most (because he seemed most roused and animated) in reciting his own poetry, or in talking about it. He sometimes gave striking views of his feelings and trains of association in composing certain passages. If one did not always understand his distinctions, still there was no want of interest — there was a latent meaning worth inquiring into, like a vein of ore that one cannot exactly hit upon at the moment, but of which there are sure indications.

'In art, he greatly esteems Bewick's woodcuts and Waterloo's etchings. But he some-

times takes a higher tone, and gives his mind
fair play. We have known him enlarge with a
noble intelligence and enthusiasm on Nicolas
Poussin's fine landscape compositions, pointing
out the unity of design that pervades them,
the superintending mind, the imaginative principle that brings all to bear on the same end;
and declaring he would not give a rush for any
landscape that did not express the time of day,
the climate, the period of the world it was meant
to illustrate, or had not this character of *whole-
ness* in it. His eye also does justice to Rembrandt's fine and masterly effects. In the way
in which that artist works something out of
nothing, and transforms the stump of a tree, a
common figure, into an ideal object, by the gorgeous light and shade thrown upon it, he per-
ceives an analogy to his own mode of investing
the minute details of nature with an atmosphere
of sentiment; and in pronouncing Rembrandt
to be a man of genius, feels that he strengthens
his own claim to the title. Those persons who
look upon Mr. Wordsworth as a merely puerile
writer, must be rather at a loss to account for

his strong predilection for such geniuses as Dante and Michael Angelo.'*

Like Mr. Wordsworth, Signor Foscolo in his person was above the middle height, but in every other respect he differed greatly. He was, to be sure, rather bony, but then he was wiry, alert, energetic, wild, and betimes uncontrollable. If, as Mr. Hazlitt says, Wordsworth seemed 'either mad or inspired,' the Italian poet was ever in a *ravissante* posture, ready for attack, always in extremes and excess. *His* madness never seemed the inspiration, but rather the vexed passion, of the Muse, — the boiling, lashing surge of a stormy sea, tossed by unknown or unapparent causes, which might be lying at the bottom of his own fiery temperament.

He never appeared, like Wordsworth, to 'relapse into musing,' but was ever on the watch, like some untamed animal of the Abbruzzi, who waits the moment of attack, and spring supon his game with ferocity and rage,

'By anger brave,'

---

* Hazlitt's *Spirit of the Age.*

—as he says of himself. After mauling his adversary with loud and fiery dashes of his withering tongue, he thinks he has destroyed him, or his argument, and whirls about the circle of the company in triumphant bombast, as much as to say, ' See the extraordinary power of superior genius over this quiescent and spiritless antagonist.' But he mistook his man when he assailed Wordsworth, for he was a real John Bull; he came again 'to the argument,' and by quiet unimpassioned facts confuted his sounding words and flighty brawling, his solemn tranquillity even seeming to enrage him the more.

It cannot be said that Ugo Foscolo possessed ' marked features ' in the sense Mr. Hazlitt means of Wordsworth, yet he had something distinctive in his features, although his face was not an uncommon one. His face was long with ' thin cheeks,' as he describes, and down the middle of these straggled a narrow strip of grizzly, sandy-red whiskers, coming in a point to the corners of his mouth. His eyes were like those represented in Chinese figures, the outer corners running upwards, as

Haydon said 'like those of a fox,'—deep-sunk and piercing, unsympathising, electrical eyes that you did not encounter with inclination or pleasure. His smile was odd, it was that vacant, unmeaning, and painful smile seen in insanity; you could not return it, but might wonder what it meant. As to his wardrobe being 'choice,' I did not perceive anything remarkably elegant or select in his apparel; his coat hung upon him as if it had been made for another person (perhaps *home-made*), the tails came together, pushing each other outwards, forming the letter V.

Signor Foscolo told how he had economised in furnishing his house in London, by purchasing wood, and having his chairs and tables, drawers and bedsteads, made in the house by 'day work.' The same was the case with the carpets and curtains, having women to sew them, &c. He told us what he had saved by this plan, and, looking very sinister, recommended it to others about to furnish. Haydon praised the thrift, but laughed afterwards at the idea of his filling his house with workpeople, shavings, and sawdust, and occupying his time in running round the town, cheapening materials at the wood-merchants' and the drapers' shops. 'Better far,' he said, 'had he gone to a furniture-broker's and bought second-hand furniture, with all the live-stock into the bargain.'

What different impressions the personal appearance of men make upon different individuals! I am reminded of this by the following circumstances, and by a certain similarity between Foscolo and Wilkie. They were both tall, both had sandy-coloured reddish hair, both were of manners unusual in society; but how opposite! what a contrast!—One was fiery, impetuous, restless;—the other gaunt, awkward, nervous,—slow to speak or to move,—painfully cautious and reserved, seldom caught approaching to enthusiasm, even about his art, in which he was so eminent. His finely proportioned and beautifully formed hands, a lady told me, were the only part about him to praise. From Foscolo's portrait of himself in his sonnet, you would think that he was an Apollo. Again, if we read the description of Wilkie's person by his countryman, Mr. Allan Cunningham, he appears an Adonis, with golden locks, curling and clustering round his beautiful face. While the housekeeper at Castle Howard, Mrs. Flynn, thus describes his visit to the Castle :—

' Mr. Wilkie came down here to the Castle to see the pictures, and the only words he spoke to me were—"When does Lord Carlisle dine?" His Lordship being told of the strange question Mr. Wilkie, a stranger, had asked, flew into a passion, and was highly offended, observing, "What does the fellow mean?—does he want to dine with *me*? I think my steward or housekeeper may content him." Now people of genius—clever people—are generally treated with great attention and proper consideration both by my Lord and Lady, but in consequence of this unusual question Mr. Wilkie was never invited to remain. But, bless me! did you ever see such an ugly creature? Forgive me, but Mr. Wilkie is the ugliest man I ever saw in my life — red hair, eyes like boiled gooseberries, staring at one as if he had never seen a woman before !—with not one word of civility to anybody. Now my dear friend, Mr. Jackson, was not, to be sure, to be called good-looking ; nay, he was ordinary; but then he made himself agreeable to everybody. Poor fellow! he used to take his morning walk there upon the lawn, before beginning to paint, always wishing me good morning, with some pleasant observations, and everybody here would have been glad to do anything for him. The family were all kind to him, and my Lord took an interest in all he did. This house, indeed, was like a home for him. Mr. Jackson was not very particular in his dress, although he was a tailor's son; and when he painted my dear little Lady Mary (called in the Exhibition, and in the engravings, "The Rose of Castle Howard"), he placed her upon a table, and the spirited little thing, not liking to stand cooped up so long, got out of humour with the painter, plumped upon Mr. Jackson's waistcoat, abused him for wearing such an ugly colour,—a vulgar pattern, which "she could not bear the sight of," and begged him to go and change it. The patient artist laughed at the dear little creature's discrimination, affected petulance, and promised he would change it if she would only stand a little longer in the right position, and so he managed to humour and coax her, till he produced that beautiful picture of her that is the admiration of every one. Yes, Mr. Jackson was only the son of a Malton tailor, and he is a Royal Academician, as they call them. I thought at first that Mr. Wilkie was perhaps the son of some of those poverty-stricken Scotch *lairds*, with more shabby pride in their heads than money in their pockets; but I understand he is the son of a Scotch clergyman, and it is a pity but his father had taught him a little more of Christian humility and good manners, so as not to come from Scotland here to a great house like this, and expect to dine with my Lord, *even without an invitation*. Now, there is my dear young Lord, he is not handsome, but what can exceed his goodness, his amiability, his condescension, and his gentlemanly courtesy? My young Lord is beloved by all classes, wherever he goes. Such is the difference of breeding, of birth, of a natural sense of propriety, that is given to gentle natures, not to speak of nobility.'

The good and sensible Mrs. Flynn, taking offence as his Lordship himself did at the strange question as to 'my Lord's time of dining ;' saw Wilkie under a different aspect, and under different influences, from his countryman, Mr. Allan Cunningham, though it is more likely Sir David (then Mr. Wilkie) asked the question with a view to avoid my Lord's dinner-hour, rather than that he was guilty of such an impropriety, so unlike his modesty and his independent spirit, as to desire to intrude into a family circle without invitation.

Having arranged to sit to Haydon for his picture the next day, I went to him accordingly, and after that rather tedious business was over he asked me to accompany him to Mr. Hazlitt's, to give him a description of the extraordinary exhibition we had witnessed the night before between Foscolo and Wordsworth. Mr. Haydon told exactly what had occurred, and how timid and alarmed the ladies appeared at the gesticulations and violent manner of Foscolo. Hazlitt laughed his curious laugh, a sort of hysteric shout—a quick 'Ah! ah!' stopping suddenly. He was much amused, and laughed at Wordsworth's *sang-froid*, saying, 'He was right to hold to the last, when he was in the right.' I asked if he did not suppose that

Hobbes or Helvetius was present at Mr. Haydon's? He replied, 'Well, either of those gentlemen would probably have taken the same side of the question; but I hope that for the sake of good manners, to say nothing of philosophy, they would have listened with more fairness and reasonable calmness to what such a person as my friend Wordsworth would have to say upon any subject that he thought it worth while to trouble himself to speak about.'

CHAPTER VI.

BEWICK'S LITERARY STYLE — REFLECTIONS SUGGESTED BY THE MEMORY OF HAZLITT — INTELLECTUAL AND SOCIAL CHARACTER OF THE ESSAYIST — VEHEMENCE OF HIS PASSION — POLITICAL TENDENCIES — HAZLITT'S HOUSE — BENTHAM — MILTON — HAZLITT AS A CONVERSATIONALIST — RAPHAEL — MICHAEL ANGELO, DANTE, MILTON, AND HOMER — TITIAN — ABSENCE OF MIND.

IT is by no means improbable that his familiarity with Hazlitt's characteristic sketches of poets, essayists, and painters, may have had considerable influence in suggesting to Bewick the idea of these literary portraits of his contemporaries, the presentment of which is in all respects so vivid. If so, the following chapter on Hazlitt himself, whom he knew not only by his writings, but by intimate personal intercourse, must be regarded as so much the more interesting. Perhaps in some respects the ambition to imitate the great English essayist, or some similar type of literary excellence, has tended to lead him away from that simplicity and directness of style which would have rendered his portraits so much the more truthful, and from which it is probable he would not have departed if he had trusted to his own instead of to foreign inspiration. The influence of Hazlitt is nowhere more apparent than in Bewick's sketch of that eloquent writer.

WILLIAM HAZLITT.

Man is said to be

' The paragon of animals,'

because of his intelligence, but if in 'action' he may be compared to a Deity, his frailties and unaccountable inequalities reduce him to the level of imperfect beings. Well has it been said, ' What a want of harmony there is between man and the other works of God ; how imperfect and unfinished, as it were, is man ; how the mind longs, struggles to penetrate the mysteries of its being ; how imperfect and without aim does life sometimes seem ! Everything besides man seems to reach its utmost perfection. Man alone appears a thing incomplete and faulty.

Other things and beings are finished and complete—man alone is left, as it were, half made up. A tree grows and bears fruit, and the end of its creation is answered. A complete circle is run. It is the same with the animals. No one expects more from a lion or a horse than is found in both. But with man it is not so. In no period of history, and among no people, has it been satisfactorily determined what man is, or what are the limits of his capacity and being. He is full of contradictions, and incomprehensible in his organisation. For while every other affection finds rest in its appropriate object, which fully satisfies and fills it, the desire of unlimited improvement and of long life —the strongest of all the desires — alone is answered by no corresponding object. And man would seem a monster in creation — compared with other things an abortion—and in himself, and compared with himself, an enigma, a riddle which no human wit has ever solved, or can ever hope to solve. And when we think of the great and good of other times, and of what the mind of man has in them accomplished, we feel that he has been made not altogether unworthy of a longer life and a happier lot than earth frequently affords.'

Such are the reflections that apply, aptly enough, to the memory of one of the brightest 'spirits of the age' — for in his intellectual strength, his frailties, and his inequalities, William Hazlitt was indeed 'an enigma and a riddle.'

If he was a scholar, philosopher, and subtle metaphysician, a severe critic and sarcastic politician, he was also a lover of truth for its own sake, and his mind was free and independent, and breathed the spirit of liberty in every form of language. He could discriminate and appreciate the beauties of nature—feel the charms and amenities of refined taste in poetry and art. To simplicity and genuineness of character were added the eccentricities of a wayward and impressive temperament, original genius, boundless stores of knowledge and of thought. A brilliant imagination and discriminating refinement gave him a power of language that surprised, if it did not charm, the world of literature and of criticism.

With all this varied intelligence and intellectual ability, the reader will see by what follows, how strange and unaccountable often were his actions ; in what relation he stood to the great family of mankind. For though odd and quaint, he was not a misanthrope ; he loved the companionship of man and the exchange of intellectual thought, was gentle and tender to the feelings of others, and guarded against giving offence to those he associated with. He was besides the most patient listener, and would consider and weigh the observations of the youngest and most inexperienced ; indeed, he seemed ever anxious to draw forth the opinions of the modest and retiring genius. Although the scope of his mind and turn of thought were original, and his manner simple, he carried about him the air and bearing of a scholar, and if he was unquestionably impulsive, he still possessed a mental reservation, so that he was, as I have said, 'full of contradictions.'

It so happened that I saw a good deal of this remarkable man, at the best period, perhaps, of his life and fame, and I will endeavour to remember and note down such incidents as are likely to illustrate his character, or are interesting as throwing light on the history of one of the distinguished literary men of the time.

William Hazlitt was one of the most unaffected men I have ever met with, undisciplined and unrestrained by the rules and usages of society. One may have observed the vagaries of pretenders, or, still more, the excesses of imbecility ; but these are explicable and contemptible enough. What was remarkable in Hazlitt was the simplicity and spontaneity of all his strangeness, and if he gave way to vehemence of passion or irritation, or was melted into moods of softer and even amatory emotions, he never attempted to conceal in the least his feelings, or repress the expression of them, just as if he believed all the world sympathised with his indignation, his jealousy, his romantic attachments, or his wrongs. It excited sorrow and pain to see a man of such intelligence, with features so capable of expressing the varied emotions of his too sensitive nature, lash himself into terrible bursts of uncontrollable rage, the effect of his excitable nervous temperament, where the slightest discord vibrated to his inmost soul, while it found no echo in the breasts of others, who could only gaze with wonder as at a frenzied being, amazed by the violence of the physical action which followed the phases of his mental excitement, at the expression of his features, and at his burning language.

Surely human face could not be more exquisitely formed for expression of the passions, equally capable of exhibiting the softer, tender emotions of the soul, with the sudden flashes and fury of turbulent anger.

In all the freaks of his wayward character, his wonderfully endowed organisation was ruled by the omnipotence of mind, and his excitable temperament, played upon like some stringed instrument, was moved to tenderness or intensity by the very slightest touch or variation of Nature, so that it might be said that this over-sensitive being was led on the uneven tenor of his way by the uncertain 'music of the spheres.' Yet, in his soul, dwelt supreme the love of freedom and intellectual independence ; and if he toiled for the liberty and happiness of the human race, though he might receive small thanks for his endeavours, his courage never wavered. His nature seemed to revel in attacking and upsetting what he conceived to be the despotism of mankind; and thus was engendered a hatred to the assumed *Divine Right of Kings*, for he deemed that assumption little less than blasphemy. In all his propositions, his criticism, and his political bias, he was sincere in his convictions, and expressed himself accordingly in vivid and eloquent language peculiarly his own.

I have no distinct recollection of my first interview with Hazlitt. It was probably at Haydon's; but I remember well being taken, for the first time, by Haydon to Hazlitt's residence in Westminster; that house so remarkable and interesting as having been the abode of Milton.

The house was curious. The entrance was a sort of porch opening to a small anteroom, with very red brick floor and upright posts, that one rubbed one's shoulders against, and the staircase was narrow and dark. The room where Hazlitt received us was, as he informed us, in the same condition that it had been in Milton's time; the same dull-white painted wainscot, the same windows looking into a garden-like piece of ground, tricked out into grass-plots, shrubberies, and winding walks, with two noble trees crossing the windows. From these windows might occasionally be seen the celebrated lawgiver Bentham, shuffling along in loose *déshabille*, his shirt-neck thrown open, the strings of his knee-breeches hanging about his shrunk legs, his loose habit of a coat seeming too large for his short puffy body. He staggered along with faltering steps, as if he would be tripped up by the least pebble or interruption in his way. We could hear distinctly his chirpy, garrulous voice, in broken treble tones or shrill uncertain sounds, answering to questions put to him by his companion, a spruce and well-adjusted divine, as they sauntered together in the open walks or leafy bowers, conversing, it is not improbable, upon the laws of the universe or ecclesiastical polity.

The contrast between the two individuals was remarkable enough, and seemed to indicate the past and the present age. The one scrambled along decrepit and negligent; the other trimmed and *débonnair*, in scuttle-hat, silk stockings, and silver buckles, paced elegantly with measured steps, as if walking to music. My fancy suggested that this clerical person might be a Paley, a Barrington, or a Bowles.

Seated, as I was, in that ancient chamber, once the honoured abode of the epic poet, and where I imagined he probably hymned and sung of Paradise,

> 'I beheld the poet blind, yet bold,
> In slender book his vast design unfold :
> Messiah crown'd, God's reconcil'd decree,
> Rebelling angels, the forbidden tree,
> Heav'n, hell, earth, chaos, all.' *

Overcome by emotions so profound and absorbing, I could picture to myself the imaginary groups that once dwelt or assembled here. I saw them, as they might have appeared in the quaint costumes and manners of the time, surrounding the venerable poet and his graceful daughters, with his Quaker friend Elwood. The air of the place seemed harmonised to sounds of heavenly music, as of the organ, in tones large, round, and full, expressive of the poet's verse.

It was an effort to recall my attention from the indulgence of imaginary conceptions to the

* Andrew Marvel.

reality, and to the conversation of the two living friends before me.   I remember well how silent I was, how engrossed my mind and faculties were during this, to me, memorable first interview at Hazlitt's residence.

The critic and essayist, like the painter, was a fluent conversationalist, and their candour and tone of intercourse were respectful and cordial; and however spirited their language, there was always that gentlemanly deference that characterised the minds of both. They spoke of books, of Waverley, comparing the author with Richardson, Addison, Madame d'Arblay, &c., with the French and Spanish novelists. But to this I need not further allude, as Mr. Hazlitt has himself given his sentiments on these subjects in another place.

Hazlitt was ever urging the painter into questions and debate about art, and when it did not seem agreeable (as it seldom was) for Haydon to acquiesce in this, he would start off upon his own views and opinions, and Haydon listened with great attention to his fresh and vigorous observations on the practice of the art, and his just and discriminating conclusions on the Italian schools of painting. The author was now artist, now politician or metaphysician, and with his vast and varied stores of knowledge illustrated in perspicuous language the sentiments and opinions he wished to convey. Happily for me, I could appreciate the part of his charming conversation which related to art. It excited my enthusiasm and inflamed my ambition, when with passion and emotion he 'confessed that his bias, his great love, was ART. He turned to *it* as the sunflower turns to the sun. And if he had to express his greatest ambition, it would be that his son should become a great painter, as he himself had unfortunately not become. Indeed, his own great thirst of fame was to be great in art. To be a great painter, he thought, above all other divine inspirations!'

He dilated upon Raphael, calling him 'the heaven-born!' 'the divinely-inspired!' 'celestial creature!' He questioned if the 'gentleness of Shakespeare' could be compared to 'the sweetness of Raphael's nature,' and with somewhat of bitterness said,—

'It is curious that Michael Angelo, Milton, Dante, and perhaps Homer, the great epic minds, should have been alike so persecuted during their lives. The first was harassed and unhappy by the jealousies and cabals of artists and their conflicting interests (for he had his nose broken by one of them in envy of his great powers), and by the intrigues of priestcraft, often interrupting his great works. Indeed he had to fly for his life, and place himself under the protection of another state. Milton, too, had his domestic ills, his political broils, was in daily fear of assassination, was compelled to hide himself, and had a mock burial to save him from the scaffold. So of Dante. Of Homer we know less. But is it not hard to think of these things, that men of genius, so elevated by nature, by endowment, above the capacity of other creatures, their inferiors in mental qualities, should be left at the sport of untoward circumstances, or be played upon at the mercy of grovelling incapacity, through the jealousy of a lower grade of mankind ? May we not be permitted to look for aid and protection from the Creator of such rare and mighty minds—of beings, by comparison almost superhuman ? If posterity mourn the sad hours of suffering, of bitter, because unmerited, persecution, we have at least the works, the sublime imaginings, of these inspired beings, left to us that we may judge of their merits and deserts, and venerate the memory of the exalted in retribution of their ignoble and despised persecutors.'

He would then branch off, with evident delight to himself as well as his hearers, into a discursive flight among the great painters of different epochs and countries, observing,—

' After all, I would rather be Titian than even Raphael, or Michael Angelo, or Correggio ; and why ? Because Titian has gone beyond all the painters of his own or any other time or country. He dipped his pencil in the gorgeous tints and tones of soul-subduing harmony, rich and full and fresh, and ripe as autumn fruit. His was a mastery of the scale of colour, and that, too, laid on, pencilled, in such perfection of execution, such wonderful manipulation, as to be a mystery and a lesson to all painters of future times. It is to Titian we attribute the perfection of the painter's art, and it is in that my soul is wrapt—enchained—in wondering admiration.' I have to express too, in all humility, my competitive incapacity, having tried with all the ardour and devotion I was capable of, to come near the rich brilliance and depth of this great painter's works, by copying them in the Louvre.

'Others have imagined finer compositions, more sublime conceptions, as some of the "Prophets" and "Sibyls" of Michael Angelo. Perhaps nothing has equalled, in epic grandeur and exalted thought, his "Jeremiah mourning the Destruction of Jerusalem," his whole body weighed and drooping like

"An aged tree surcharged with showers."

His "Prophet Joel," and the "Cumean Sibyl," are fine. All these grand conceptions are marked by distinctive character, intensity of expression, and are the work of a great master-mind. It was to this great man alone the privilege of the epic in art was given. None have touched his greatness.

'The "Paul Preaching" and the "Transfiguration" of Raphael, with some others, are noble compositions, and full of dramatic interest and fine expression, but are they so perfect in the painter's art? The fresco of Michael Angelo, and the cartoons of Raphael, are not, perhaps, fair comparisons, but the "Transfiguration" of Raphael is an oil-picture, and although there is refined and inimitable expression—the figure of the Saviour finely balanced, suspended, or ascending in the air, with the floating lightness of a bird, and the figure of St. John, all propriety, and beautifully graceful—yet all these fine things, to my mind, are inferior in execution and colour to the Titian, to that perfection of the painter's art that I have alluded to.'

Haydon assented, with some reservation as to the distinction of class, style, and purpose for which the works were executed, and perhaps Mr. Hazlitt had not appreciated this distinction. However, I wished to endeavour to remember his peculiar opinions as to Titian, and to record them.

When Hazlitt perceived Bentham enter the garden, he paused in his conversation, looking earnestly out of the window, and pointing him out, said, 'Ah! that is the great lawgiver, Bentham; a remarkable man: he would make laws for the whole universe, but, as the sailors say, "he doesn't allow for the wind."'

Upon hearing a noise at the door, and perceiving his only child creeping in upon all fours, he jumped up from his seat, ran to him, and clasping his boy in his arms, hugged, and kissed, and caressed him, like some ardent loving mother with her first-born.

The room we were in, I may remark, was in keeping with the general negligence and peculiarity of Hazlitt's habits. There was little furniture, no appearance of books, no pictures or prints of any kind whatever!—a confusion and apparent want of comfort and domestic order reigned in the apartment. Over the mantel-shelf, upon the wainscot, instead of picture or looking-glass, there was written, in good bold hand (Hazlitt's own writing) as high up as he could reach and covering the whole space, all manner of odd conceits (as they appeared to be), of abbreviations,—words,—names,—enigmatical exclamations, — strange and queer sentences, quotations,—snatches of rhyme,—bits of arithmetical calculations,—scraps of Latin,—French expressions, — words or signs by which the author might spin a chapter, or weave an elaborate essay. The chimneypiece seemed to

be his tablet of mnemonics,—his sacred hiero-
glyphics,—all jotted down without line, or
form of any kind, some horizontal, some running
up to the right, some down to the left, and
some obliquely. They seemed thoughts and
indications of things to be remembered, put
down on the instant, and I concluded that this
room might not be his study, but his living-
room.

When we took our leave my companion
observed to me :—

' What a remarkable man !— how profound
and abstruse he can be !—he touches the most
difficult subjects with a master-mind,—how he
must have studied, and refined upon those
subtle questions he delights to argue, — with
what fine, and expressive language he clothes
his thoughts, and one is as much astonished as
delighted that a being so wayward and uncertain can pursue with constancy abstract specu-
lations and investigations that seem to give
zest or energy to his curious mind. He delights
in metaphysics, as he does in art. His odd
manner, and absence of mind, are peculiarities
grown with his nature. What a curious organ-

isation !—what a strange mixture of genius and eccentricity,—of mental power and uncertainty of purpose, — of 'imagination all compact,' and the negation of realities about him. Keats says that a poet has nothing poetical about him; here is romance and poetry both in a living prose-writer! I do enjoy the conversation and sincerity of Hazlitt, perhaps more than any one else ; he is natural,—unaffected,—expresses himself with a frankness, impetuosity, and passion, that arrest one's attention and secure one's confidence, he sympathises with one's Art-notions too, and is on the whole the best conversationalist (except one) that I know.

'I will tell you of one of the many instances that I know of his absence of mind. When that little boy of his was to be christened, and the day appointed for the ceremony, all preparations made, and a pheasant provided by him, as an extra-course for dinner, the friends and sponsors all arrived and waiting for the officiating minister, the time passing agreeably and rapidly away, some one, who began to apprehend the chances of a dilemma, suggested the question, whether the clergyman had been informed of the necessity of his attendance? When our author, first in some confusion, then blank dismay, confessed that there might be some probability of his having forgotten to give that piece of information, so necessary to the consummation of their intended business. He then fell to accusations of himself, of his incomprehensible stupidity, that he never had the least thought of what was proper, &c. &c., adding with more good nature, " Well, never mind; it is too late, I suppose, now, to correct my folly in this affair: let us at all events enjoy the christening-dinner, even without the ministerial ceremony." '

CHAPTER VII.

I OFTEN met Hazlitt at Haydon's, and had good opportunity of observing his character, of witnessing the wonderful power and varied resources of his mind. He was apt to brood over metaphysical difficulties, and in his abstract deductions was never certain, he said, that he made himself understood. His company was always acceptable to Haydon, and he came occasionally on Sundays, bringing some of his lucubrations, which he would, at a fitting opportunity, and with modest awkwardness, draw from his coat-pocket. Then explaining the subject of his paper, he would read it with feeling and freshness, as though it engrossed all his mind. Glancing occasionally to observe what effect his language had upon his hearers, he would sometimes rise from his seat, and in the interest of the subject pour forth in impassioned tones, excited expression, and animated action, the violence of his emotion. It was in this way he read his Letter to Gifford,—The Description of a Prize Fight,—On the Death of Kavannah, &c. &c. If the paper so read seemed to have the desired effect, he would send it to the press.

Haydon could seldom be induced to converse about art, and Hazlitt seemed glad, on the occasion of meeting Wilkie, to draw both painters into argument upon this subject. The question he introduced was unimportant, if not foolish, as stated by Hazlitt, 'Whether a particular set of colours arranged on a painter's palette did not influence his style of art?—so much so, indeed, as to be a question whether any artist would not have painted in the same style, scale of colour, and peculiarities, with any given palette,—say, for instance, of Titian, Rubens, or Rembrandt,—and that a painter, with the palette so set of any one of these three, would have painted in the precise style of Titian, Rubens, or Rembrandt?'

Wilkie was first appealed to, and 'thought certainly that any one, with the particular set of colours and varied tints peculiar to Titian, or those of Rubens or Rembrandt, would be so influenced as to paint in the same style and colouring as these great artists. That is, suppose a palette with the *peculiar* and *particular* primitive colours, so arranged, with gradations of tints and variations, that palette would so influence his taste, his mind, his ideas, and his "feeling" for contrast and harmony, that he would indeed be induced to paint in the style and manner of the painter to whom that particular palette of colours had belonged.'

Haydon smiled, and shook his head, as disagreeing with Wilkie. Hazlitt pushed and provoked the argument by all the eloquence and energy of which he was capable, in favour of Wilkie's seeming views; and however preposterous and absurd the proposition, the controversy was carried on for some time.

It is probable that Hazlitt commenced the argument only to hear what the two great painters would offer in support or rejection of the question. Or, he might be curious to witness a combat of words between two persons so eminent for expressing their ideas by the pencil. Be this as it may, he seemed quite serious in the whole affair, and enjoyed the fray ; putting in a few words of encouragement or provocation on the one side or the other, fidgeting and smiling with delight when any difficulty seemed apparent in the argument. He seemed, too, highly amused at the dissimilitude of the two characters before him. Haydon was energetic, explanatory, voluble, and eager to convince; whilst Wilkie, on the contrary, was slow, dry, caustic, cautious, keeping much on the defensive, and when pushed hard would return to his argument in strong Scotch intonation. Although the great painter of 'Reading the Will' and 'The Pensioners' seemed to do his best in debating this extraordinary proposition, yet it appeared possible that he had taken that side of the fray to humour Hazlitt, whom he seldom met, and might wish to propitiate. When, however, the heat of debate had partly subsided, and there was a pause, Hazlitt turned to me, who had been a silent listener during the whole time, and asked, 'Well, Sir, what do you say to this interesting question?'

'If you will permit me,' I replied, 'to repeat an anecdote of what is recorded to have occurred to the two celebrated painters, Vandyck and Frank Hals, perhaps it may illustrate your present question. When Vandyck visited Frank Hals at Haerlem, he introduced himself as a gentleman on his travels who wished to have his portrait painted, and had only two hours to spare. Hals, who was hurried away from the tavern, took the first canvas that lay in his reach, and sat down to work in a very expeditious manner. He shortly desired the sitter to look at what he had done. Vandyck seemed pleased with what he saw, and told Hals that such work appeared so very easy he thought he could do it himself. He took the palette and pencils, made Hals sit down, and in a short time he painted his portrait, but the moment Hals cast his eyes on it he cried out in astonishment, that no hand except that of Vandyck could work so wonderfully. Thus, the palette and colours of Hals did not tend to produce his, or any style, but that of Vandyck himself.'

Haydon smiled at me in satisfaction, and Wilkie opened his mouth and eyes, and looked at me in silence, though pleasantly. Hazlitt said in soft and subdued tones, and with kindness, ' Ah ! *that is* indeed to the point, Sir; but as I never heard of it before, I hope it is true ?'

' It is quite true,' replied Haydon.

Wilkie still seemed inclined to hammer out in his hesitating way some proposition, and began discriminating his subtle niceties in his northern accent, for he was rather fond of puzzles in debate; and as he was circumspect, cold, cautious, and not easily convinced, so he was slow, and the last person to laugh at a joke, or appear to apprehend points of wit or fun.

Hazlitt and Haydon laughed to see Wilkie beginning to perplex himself anew about a question upon which probably none of the three entertained any serious views.

As Hazlitt and Wilkie seldom met, and were of such opposite characters, they did not get on very well together. Wilkie lacked the cordiality and frankness of nature and of manner that characterised Haydon, and which seemed to satisfy the author and set him at his ease; and Hazlitt enjoyed the society and appreciated the heartiness of Haydon's ingenuous nature. He would often say, 'Haydon is a fine, frank, as well as clever man, and albeit the *best painter* England has produced, I find him well read up in the literature of the day; never at a loss for subjects of conversation, whether of books, politics, or men and things. The only subject he seems to desire to eschew, with me at least, is the fine arts. I observe he keeps his great picture covered up, lest, I suppose, it should lead to or suggest that line of conversation; and this puts me in mind of what Goldsmith says of Sir Joshua,—

" When they talked of their Raphaels, Correggios, and stuff,
He shifted his trumpet and only took snuff."

Perhaps there is not much good resulting from painters gossiping about their art, for, after exhausting themselves during the day in the practice of it, they wish for the relaxation of some other subject, and Haydon has always plenty of good conversation without that, which he says satisfies no one. He talks well, too, upon most subjects that interest one, indeed better than any painter I have met. Northcote is talkative and original, but then he is narrow in his views, and confined in his subjects. Haydon is more a scholar, and has a wide range and versatility of information. One enjoys his hearty, joyous laugh; it sets one upon one's legs, as it were, better than a glass of champagne, for one is delighted to meet such a cheering spirit in the saddening depression that broods over the heartless despotism and hypocrisy of the world. His laugh rings in my ears like merry bells. When I do ask him to show me his picture, he does so without reserve, and with an open candour, courting my remarks. How finely he does some things! He has great power of expression, fine drawing, good, solid, and rich colour,— no difficulty in composition, and tells the story comprehensively. What refinement and pathos in some of his female characters! far beyond anything that has been done in modern times. His " Judgment of Solomon " is, to my mind, the very finest work of that high class to be found since the time of Titian. And to the excellence of that great painter some parts of the picture may be compared; which is the highest compliment I can pay, since Titian is my seal of perfection. Posterity will do Haydon the justice moderns may deny him.'

Thus Hazlitt would talk, as we sauntered homewards together in the evening from Haydon's house, parting with an invitation to me to call upon him—which I did very soon after, and was gratified by his showing me some of his productions with the pencil.

' Now,' he said, ' you have heard me preach and argue a good deal about painting and the arts, I wish to let you see that I have done something practically on canvas, and original. Here is the painting of an old head done from life; every touch, every line is strictly copied from the poor old creature who sat for it : she wearied and fell asleep, by which lucky accident I got near enough to elaborate all those wrinkles ; her mouth was pursed up into all those intricate lines you see there. I worked at it from day to day, and could have gone on for a month to reach the truth of Nature, or approach the force of Rembrandt. Indeed, I confess to you that I had the vanity to feel, or mistakingly judge, that my insignificant endeavour put me in mind of some of Rembrandt's heads. And I would ask to live a hundred years, and be permitted to paint every day of the year, could I come near the merit of that painter. You will observe in those flesh tints, and shadow colour, how difficult it is to produce the transparency, with the depth, force, and richness of that master's secret,—mellow without muddiness— bright without crudity. How the devil he produced the combinations, I am at a loss to comprehend. I am told it was *feeling*. Well, I suppose I *feel* what I wish to do, I *feel* what it ought to be, but I cannot *feel* how it is produced. My *feeling* does not teach me the colours to use, how they are to be manipulated ; whether with thick impasto and pure, or thin with vehicle and pellucid. Perhaps Rembrandt's secret is a combination of all these, only known to himself; his mind and hand execute as his genius guides and suggests : in fine, it is inspiration. We believe that the poet and the painter are born. But the latter has not only to possess the same faculties of conception—arrangement, and effect of his production,—he must do more ; he must be cunning and expert at handwork, the master of lines and touches, and sleight-of-hand glazings. His hand must combine the subtleness and delicacy of the skilled player on a stringed instrument. He must be subtle, and full of expedients for realising all the appearances of the surface of objects. He must produce the reality of life, of nature, in all the brilliance of light and colour,—all the solemnity of shade and contrast. He must combine a thousand mimic difficulties that the barren spectator never dreams of, and which he who has never tried his hand with the brush will never find out.

'How much, then, must we wonder at and admire those works of such infinite difficulty, that have the combined skill and perfection of a Titian or a Rembrandt, whose works seem to me to be inapproachable in certain difficulties of the painter's art.

'It is a difficult art. One is at a loss to select the precise colours to make up a tint, for instance, that lies between the light and shade of a coloured object, as of flesh, and that seems to be made up of a neutral variation of neither the one nor the other, yet allied to both. How differently the various great masters treated these half-tints to unite light and shadow!

'Rubens and Vandyck, the latter in particular, were eminently successful in these beautiful gradations, and so true to nature, blending all with such imperceptible softness and roundings, that you are as much lost in mystery as to how they produced the particular tint for these effects as you are with nature, so subtle and undefinable is the perfection of both. The intricate combinations of flesh-colour defeat the skill of the metaphysician, and I would give the world to ascertain how the purity, the mellowness, and the *rich glow* of Titian's flesh is produced! How he laid his grounds, by what gradations, whether he jumped at once at one solid painting, at the substance or body of his flesh-colour, and by what process of toning or glazings he afterwards modified, enriched, and perfected with such transparent glow, his unapproachable flesh! How he so operated as to rival Nature! By what conjurations, and what mighty magic, he won the palm, the crown of glorious colour, charming and enchanting the beholder with wonder and delight, with never-ceasing pleasure in the contemplation of gorgeous harmony! contrasts so blended, positive brilliance so set in tone and skilful artifice as to cheat the sense of its gaudiness, depth, or candity.

'Let us cast our eyes to the French school, or to German art, and then estimate truly what Titian's secret of perfection of colour and scale of harmony amounts to. We cannot but be struck with the wide difference between these schools and the Italian, Dutch, or Spanish. If we have no sympathy with their colouring it is because it does not represent the delicacy, the beauty, or truth of Nature. Their colour is crude, and it is false. Their action, too, in most cases, is the action of the stage, and that of the French stage too, where affectation and extremes of attitudinising seem to obtain. Artificial bombast is not emotion or passion. If we admit certain dexterity, arrangement, and extended composition, yet with unbounded national encouragement, every opportunity of free and noble institutions, and advantages for acquiring the practice of the art to anyone daring enough to touch the grand or historical department, still we are disappointed that the success in the painter's art is not commensurate, perfection is in no instance approached. In France the artist is lifted up into a position of honour, of estimation; he takes his rank with the first men of the state, has rewards and honours showered upon him. Here in England, how different! Genius must work its arduous and solitary way, uncountenanced by any national recognition or the help of Government employment, and unless he can unite with the higher style of art some other subordinate branch to satisfy his pecuniary wants, he must starve, or give up his high views of fame and honour to his country.

'Had I possessed the executive part of the art sufficiently, and could I have drawn correctly, with facility, or to my satisfaction, the subject I feel I should have desired to realise would have been "Jacob's Dream." I have the arrangement, the composition, and, if I may be allowed to say so, the poetry of the picture in my mind.'

He was in such good-humour on this occasion that he invited me to accompany him the next day to the Tennis-court, to see him play. This surprised me, as I had no idea of his skill in a game requiring so much physical exertion and activity. Besides, he would often lament his want of accomplishments of every kind. 'Egad,' he said, 'he could do nothing like most men. There is Mrs. —— plays exquisitely upon the flute; there is Mr. —— sings his own songs, and accompanies himself upon the piano, will dash off a leader for a morning paper, or write an important note to the Secretary of State, whilst discoursing in a room full of company; and I could name many who thus possess genius and varied capacity, whilst I can literally do *nothing*, nor ever could,' &c. &c.

The next day we went to the place, and as we sauntered along he informed me there would be no first-rate play on that day, but there would be some tolerable second-rate players; he himself was only second-rate. Had Kavanagh been there first-rate play would have been seen, for no one could stand against so extraordinary a racket as his. When arrived at the court, he ushered me into a sort of gallery at one end, supported by strong wooden posts, so that it was open below for spectators of the sport. The game of tennis was soon commenced in good earnest, the players becoming excited and eager for success. My friend, having stripped to his shirt, looked all alive, and being anxious to do his best, soon displayed himself not only an adept, but an original in his style of play. It was peculiar and characteristic of the man, and his sighs, groans, and lamentations left no doubt that he was becoming warm in the spirit of the game, and sad trouble he had to hitch up his trousers, it being his custom to be free of braces. He was the only one despoiled of his upper garments, so that I had no difficulty in following his rapid movements, and as his excitement warmed in the course of the game, so his exclamations became more vehement, and with his difficulties his ardour increased, until he lashed himself up to desperation, and looked more like a savage animal than anything human. The spectators below me appeared to be well aware of the ability and eccentricity of this hero of the game, as they peered forward to witness

any extraordinary feat of play. When a difficult ball was driven to such a distance from him,
and so skilfully dropped close to the wall, that
it seemed an impossibility to come near it in
time, or catch it with the racket if he did, he
would run with desperate speed, make a last
spring, and bending down his head to meet the
concussion with the wall, crushing his hat flat
over his eyes, dexterously tip the ball, sending
it to its intended mark with unerring truth
amid murmurs of applause. Then jerking himself upright again, his eye following the ball in
its lightning speed, he would pursue it, however
difficult the course. Thus he would repeat his
feats of agility and success, excited all the while
to a desperation and madness beyond belief.
It is impossible to give an idea of his expressions. His ejaculations were interlarded with
unintentional and unmeaning oaths that cannot
be repeated, but may be imagined. In this
way he would stamp and rave :—'Nothing but
my incapacity,—sheer want of skill, of power, of
physical ability,—of the Devil knows what!
There again! Ever see such play? Egad! I'd
better not take hold of the racket again if I do

not do better. Ah! well, that is better, but still bad enough—sheer incapacity, egad!' And so he ran on all the time he played, so that the energies of mind and body were fretted and embittered. The frenzy of his irritability, although curious as characteristic, yet became, if not alarming, at least not pleasant to witness. And as he came occasionally to set his back against the post under me, and rub himself to and fro with the force of irascible impatience, repeating the exclamations to himself, I could not but wish that all might end well, and that the game might close in favour of my friend's party. Fortunately it was soon over, and, as I wished, William Hazlitt had won his game at tennis. I could perceive him in all the joyous triumph of boyish pleasure, stooping low, his racket in both hands, and, bounding from the ground, throw it high up to the roof, exclaiming to himself, 'Hurrah! hurrah!' and as he waved his right arm over his head, catch with dexterity his falling racket, retiring with the satisfied beam of triumph in his face, to put on his coat and waistcoat.

Hazlitt came smiling with delight, and said,

'Well, we had a hard run for it, but we beat after all.' When we came to the street, he pointed to his cravat, and said to me with a somewhat mock solemnity,—'You see I am without my shirt; it was so wet with perspiration that I left it behind to get dried. You must not be seen walking with a person who has no shirt on his back, therefore we part here: you go that way, I this.'

He left me abruptly, and I could not but reflect what a strange being he was. Looking after him I could perceive him threading his way in the crowd, with the alertness and rapidity of one not at all exhausted by the exertions of the game he had played. What a serious strain upon a constitution not by any means strong, such an irregular life must have been!

Mr. Hazlitt having met Sir Anthony Carlisle, the Professor of Anatomy at the Royal Academy, at a conversazione at Mr. Basil Montague's, in Bedford Square, and having heard him, in his grandiloquent manner, utter some startling expressions about '*the uselessness of poetry,*' he was desirous to see more of a person who could propound with such importance so novel a proposition, and wished to satisfy his curiosity as to his ability and character. He therefore requested me to take him to hear one of his anatomical lectures, delivered to the students of the Academy. I consequently accompanied him one appointed evening to Somerset House. This celebrated surgeon generally treated the artists, his hearers, with some exhibition of novelty or interest, and his lectures were consequently always crowded. Once he had six or eight naked Life-guardsmen going through their sword exercise, exhibiting the varied muscular action of the human body. On another occasion he had some Indian or Chinese jugglers, performing their feats of agility, showing the flexibility of their joints, and what suppleness training may produce in the frame of man. On the evening I speak of, the lecturer, when speaking of the emotions and passions of the mind, handed round upon a dinner-plate the brain of a man, and on another a human heart. As these severally came to Hazlitt for observation, and to be passed round, he shrank back in sensitive horror, closed his eyes, turned away his pale, shuddering countenance, and appeared to those near him to be in a swooning state. I was glad, however, after a little while to observe him rally, when he whispered in nervous accents, ' Of what use can all this be to artists ? Surely the bones and muscles might be sufficient.'

He was highly amused to see the lecturer in full court dress, with bagwig, curled and powdered, his cocked hat, and lace ruffles to his wrists, and laughing, said,—

' I should not have known my unpoetic acquaintance in that disguise ; he seems like the owl peeping and winking in an ivy-bush upon some ancient turret, and I cannot conceive of such an arrant puppy finding anything good, or of *use*, or beauty in poetry. I now know *the man.*'

As we retired down the great staircase at Somerset House, some one passed us quickly, throwing his capacious mantle over his shoulders with an air of affected consequence. Hazlitt observed,—

' That will be some one of the mighty R.A.'s, but, depend upon it, he will never paint below the fifth button-hole.'

And so it has been.

It was after this that Hazlitt himself was called upon to appear before the public as a lecturer at the Surrey Institution. I remember well the nervous trepidation, blank dismay, and hopelessness of success, he manifested on his first attempt at oratory.

The friends who knew the sensitive and wayward character of Hazlitt were prepared for disappointment from his failure in self-possession and confidence. They therefore placed themselves in readiness,—but what did take place ?

The time arriving, and the audience expressing unequivocal signs of impatience, our lecturer, pallid as death, and hesitating, like some unhappy being about to meet his doom, approached the table, lecture in hand, and tried to clear his choking voice, but all his efforts failed to overcome his nervousness. The auditory, perceiving his timidity, clapped and applauded, crying, ' Bravo, Hazlitt ! ' This seemed to encourage him, and he began in faint and tremulous accents ; but as the noise subsided, and he became conscious of the sound of his own voice, lifting his too-observant eyes to the 'sea of heads' before him, all watching and gazing at him, his small modicum of voice and confidence oozed out, and fidgeting confusedly at his waistcoat pockets, he came to a full stop, closed his manuscript, and bolted off in quick retreat. In the room he passed into, however, he found friends ready to prevent his disappearance. They came round him, encouraged and persuaded him; he heard too the hubbub of applause, the shouting of his name, with many expressions of encouragement, and he slowly returned to the lecture-table, amidst vociferous clamours of 'Bravo, Hazlitt!' &c. He commenced once more his difficult task, and warming to his subject while he was stimulated by the frequent acknowldgements of his striking thoughts or brilliant language, before he had finished his first lecture he became quite at home with the indulgent friends before him.

By his request I often called upon him and accompanied him to the Surrey Institution. He was generally sitting alone in front of a looking-glass, putting the last touches to the lecture of the evening.   After which he would chat away in great good-humour, making pertinent remarks upon the requirements of popular lecturing, observing that '*He* at all events must always endeavour to express his own thoughts upon what he undertook to do, and not be led away by the mistake of pleasing the million, or speaking for the present hour.'

Hazlitt was afterwards engaged to deliver another series of lectures at the same place, and I called as before to accompany him.   At these times he would sip his cup of strong tea, and laugh and joke at the difficulty he had to surmount at his first course of lectures, adding,—

'But there are sometimes odd people connected with institutions of this sort: committeemen, directors, and what not, consequential individuals, who, although civil or courteous to you in success, may take offence.   It is best to be guarded against change, and not permit any one to become too familiar.   For one like myself who have seen the fickleness and experienced the frowns of mankind, it is best to treat those one does not know well, as if they *might* become enemies.'

When I observed that his last lecture was eminently successful, he replied,—

'Ah, well, yes, it appeared so to me. The subject of it was likely to be popular, and surely there was applause sufficient to satisfy any moderate expectations. But there seems to be generally something to check, if not mar, the little satisfaction or success that may happen to be awarded to *me*. What do you think of that handsome Mrs. Montague throwing herself into my way as I came out, and telling me, in plain, unmistakable terms, that she did not like my lecture that evening *at all!* But as I had just before received such unequivocal testimony of approbation from the audience, I made her no reply; and, as if I had not heard her cutting remark, said in the same jeering tone of depreciation, " Mrs. Montague, madam, allow me to compliment you upon the excellent *tea* you made in Bedford Square!" Then leaving her in the crowd, that she might have no further opportunity of saying anything ungracious, I slipped away to my own appointment. But is it not great pretension, if not vain conceit (I beg the lady's pardon), to make such unpleasant remarks to one whose ears were tingling with the general and unmitigated applause of so respectable and select an audience? She deemed it right, I suppose, as a *friend*, to prevent me becoming vain of that brawling popularity, blown so straight in my teeth, in this gentle way to put me down a peg. Indeed, I begin to think her not so handsome, and I laugh at her singularity, for, after all, what can she really know of so difficult a matter?'

Hazlitt became a favourite at the Surrey Institution, and stood up in his place at the lecture-table with all confidence, in the consciousness of having friends and admirers about him. In his flights of sarcasm, or bursts of censure upon the favourite authors of some of his hearers—Lord Byron, for instance—he would occasionally meet with disapprobation; and, as he calmly looked towards the place whence the hissing came, turning back the leaf of his copy, and deliberately repeating the sentiments with greater energy and a voice more determined than before, he exclaimed with slow emphasis, 'If my Lord Byron will do these things, he must take the consequences; the acts of Napoleon Bonaparte are subjects of *history*, not for the disparagement of the Muse.' Then tossing over the leaf with an air of independence and iron firmness, as if he was not to be influenced by opinions differing from his own on these subjects, he exhibited a striking contrast to the timidity and nervousness of his first appearance at the Surrey Institution.

CHAPTER VIII.

BEWICK'S DIFFICULTIES — FRIENDLY ADVICE — GOES TO SCOTLAND — EDINBURGH — SCHEME OF A GALLERY OF PORTRAITS — ENCOUNTERS HAZLITT — SHERIDAN KNOWLES — POETICAL REMINISCENCES ON FISHING — HAZLITT'S PERSONAL APPEARANCE — STARED AT IN MELROSE — CHALK DRAWING OF HAZLITT — EVENING WALK.

HAYDON'S pupils, Lance, Chatfield, Taham, and the Landseers, were soon afterwards dispersed. This event caused a coolness between the friends, and, as Haydon put it, Bewick mounted the enemy's colours at once. The following account given by Haydon himself of the manner in which Bewick was involved in difficulties through him, may be interesting to the reader. 'During "Jerusalem" — a picture on which he was engaged—'Lord de Talby gave me a commission. I begged him to transfer it to Bewick, as he was a young man of promise. He did so; and he was paid sixty guineas for his first picture. His second, Sir William Chayter bought, and during his third his landlord refused to let him proceed unless I became security for his rent. I did so. In the meantime, I was becoming rapidly involved, and having helped Bewick in his difficulties, I thoughtlessly asked him to help me by the usual iniquities of a struggling man, namely, accommodation bills; Bewick and Harvey both did so. Those were not accommodation bills to raise money on, but accommodation bills to get time extended for money already owing. When in the hands of a lawyer, if I wanted time, 'Get another name,' was the reply. As I wished for secresy, I asked these young men, into whose hands I had put the means of getting a living without charging a farthing. As the father of a family, I now see the indelicacy and weakness of this conduct. But at that time I was young, a bachelor, at the head of a forlorn hope, and I relied on the honour and enthusiasm of my pupils. I had reduced Bewick's liabilities from 236l to 136l., and Harvey's from 284l. to 184l., and whilst in the act of extricating them, I got through the "Lazarus" and was ruined. There is no excuse for my inducing my pupils to lend their names as security for bills, but I was in such a state of desperation that I wonder at nothing.'

As will be seen in a subsequent page of these memoirs, the accuracy of this account was afterwards called in question by Bewick.

Mr. Bewick found it impossible to deliver himself from the difficulties which beset him in consequence of the desperate state of Haydon's affairs, a position which he shared with most, if not all, of Haydon's other friends. By his own friends he was advised to retire for a time to the country, where, at a distance from the embarrassments by which he was surrounded in London, he might devote himself more unreservedly to his art, and in time hew for himself a way out of the difficulties in which he was involved. The manner in which he regarded his circumstances and prospects at that moment may be gathered from the following letter to his brother :—

London, June 12th, 1823.

DEAR JOHN,—I wonder that you have not written to me before this time, as I think you would receive a letter from me by Mr. Harvey, wherein I told you my misfortune in being involved in Mr. Haydon's distress, by having accepted bills for him. Mr. Harvey here is in the same situation, and we are both miserable. Of the two, I am in the worse situation, not having the immediate means of getting any pecuniary relief; although I have small commissions to the amount of 50*l.*, which I hope to execute in a short time. I have a portrait to paint for an institution at Glasgow,* for which I shall be paid 25*l.*; this will assist me very much. I have not told my father about my situation; it will be better not to do so until everything is settled.

Some of my friends here advise me to go into the country, to endeavour to paint portraits and to be out of the way until Haydon's business is settled, but I think I shall not do this on account of the inconvenience of being at a distance.

The sale of Haydon's property is to-day and to-morrow. You will think it strange that Harvey and I can be losers by him, but so it is,

* The Mechanics' Institution.

as well as all his best friends. His most staunch friends, those who have stuck by him through thick and thin, through good report and evil report, are the greatest sufferers.

Harvey's case is settled, but mine is not, which makes me anxious and uncomfortable. Kind remembrance to Ann and Emma,

I am, yours affectionately,

W. BEWICK.

Though unwilling at first to follow the advice of his friends, he was ultimately satisfied of the propriety of it, and made up his mind to leave London for a time. Early in the autumn of 1823 he went to Scotland, where he had relations who were sure to give him a hearty welcome. In Edinburgh, too, where he first took up his abode, he found at that time some remnants of that brilliant literary society which had rendered the northern metropolis so desirable as a place of residence at the commencement of this century. Many, it is true, who had combined to render it illustrious were already gone, either dead or dispersed in other lands; but there were still many distinguished men, poets, artists, and critics, who with an enthusiastic appreciation of literature combined a refined taste in matters of art, and with these Bewick soon found himself at home. In the following letter to his brother he gives expression to the impression produced on him by the city of Edinburgh, the grandeur of its site, and the beauty of its public buildings. He had already also, by means of the letters of introduction which he carried with him, obtained admission to that society which numbered so many members distinguished by their reputation in art and letters, and whose friendship he highly valued.

Edinburgh, August 28th, 1823.

DEAR JOHN,—I arrived here after a fine day's voyage in a Leith smack on Tuesday last, and was met by our cousin George, at an inn to which I came from Leith. My uncle and aunt with two more cousins, Tom and Joseph, live in a very romantic and beautiful place (Laughton Mills) where they have their spinning-mills and dwelling-house, and where for the present I am living very comfortably.

The letters and introductions that I have brought with me give me an opportunity for observing the varieties of Scotch character and manners, and may lead to something of more consequence to me than I thought when I got them; for I find I am associating with some of the first people here for talent and reputation.

I am going to Glasgow, but I need not be there before September or October, as everybody is bathing just now. It is the same here, but then there are more men of great talent whose acquaintance and society are of consequence to me, and who may eventually assist me to work out an idea I have of painting a series of portraits of eminent men.

I must now speak of the city of Edinburgh, and I must say that, though I have heard such eulogies of its beauty and site, I had formed no idea of the grandeur of the whole, any more than of the parts which form the whole. No description whatever could possibly give you the slightest idea of the immensity which nature has massed in piles upon piles of rock, backed by mountains that tower upwards either by gradual ascent or precipitous erections, making deep dells and dales vocal with brooks running between sedgy banks.

Any attempt at detail would be useless; but I send you a bit which I recollect.

Perhaps you cannot understand this sketch. When I come to Newcastle I will tell you more.

With my remembrance to Ann,

Believe me ever yours affectionately,

W. BEWICK.

Mr. Bewick's principal object in visiting Scotland was to recruit his funds, that he might be able to pursue works of greater importance than he had yet attempted. He had also formed a scheme for preparing a gallery of portraits of eminent men, and in this he was remarkably successful. They were the size of life, and numbered among them portraits of Sir David Brewster; Lord Jeffrey; Dr. Greville; Professor Wilson, author of the 'Isle of Palms;' George Thomson, the friend and correspondent of Burns; Mrs. Grant, of Laggan; Allison; Jamieson; Mackenzie; Combe, the phrenologist; McCulloch, the political economist; Liston, the surgeon; Nasmyth; Wilson and Allan, besides many more who enjoyed a fame in their lifetime which has scarcely survived them.

At Edinburgh Mr. Bewick formed an anatomical class, in which Liston, the surgeon, studied, probably his most distinguished pupil.

While in Scotland in 1824, he again met Hazlitt in the circumstances which he thus amusingly describes:—

'It was some time subsequent, in 1824, I received an invitation from Mr. Hazlitt, who was staying at Melrose, on a marriage tour, to meet Mr. Sheridan Knowles. Knowles, who had arrived before me, had gone out on a fishing expedition; and Hazlitt, after presenting me to his bride, proposed that we should take a walk by the river to find Knowles. We strolled out by the side of the romantic and picturesque stream, looking for the dramatic author, who, Hazlitt told me, was fishing from a rock in the middle of the stream.

'Let us steal slowly along unperceived,' said he, 'and I will promise you a higher treat than you have ever seen at Carlisle's lectures at Somerset House. It was down here I found him, and lest I should disturb his pleasure I sat down behind this bush and watched for half-an-hour his motions, as he threw the line from him among the rocks with such certainty and dexterity that I could not but enjoy his rare skill, the easy sway and graceful gesture of his whole figure as he threw his long rod and line with silent sweep, so that they seemed part of his frame, all moved by one spontaneous impulse. I never could have imagined that such beautiful grace and action could belong to old Walton's passion of angling. I was charmed by the variety as well as the elegant positions of our dramatic fisherman. Should you be the first to perceive him, pray do not speak or do anything to discover us, or disturb him, in some of those Apollo-like attitudes we chance to find him in. Could a sculptor have struck him out in marble, standing on the rock, in one of his fine positions, the statue would have made his fame, as the Gladiator did for the Greek sculptor.'

We did not, however, find the fishing Antinous in his place; but we met him returning from his labour of love, with his basket of fish at his back, rod in hand, in all the ruddy freshness and joyous spirits of one of his free Swiss mountaineers in *William Tell.* His bright blue eyes and sunny smile, buoyant with health and exuberant spirits, his neat costume, muscular and fine proportions, marked the·man of sudden and impetuous actions, of bright and brilliant thought, while Hazlitt presented a strange contrast with his attenuated frame, pale and contemplative face, loose and negligent habiliments, his delicate and tremulous hand nestling in his waistcoat breast, his head inclined on one side, and his searching and expressive eyes bent in silent meditation. His long black hair clustering in massy locks about a forehead and features the very image of intellectual refinement, of deep or critical investigation. There was, too, a pensive seriousness that at times gave an interest of a romantic character to the scenery with which he was here associated. Knowles stopped to open his basket and show us the success of his sport. Hazlitt, drawing his breath, peeped timidly in, and was as nervous as if he were looking into a cradle containing dead infants. As Knowles

took one of the fish in his hand, expatiating upon
its merits when cooked, and on the table, &c.,
Hazlitt, sighing, exclaimed,—

'How silvery! what rainbow hues and tints
glisten and flit across its shining surface! How
beautiful! Do you remember Waller?

> " Beneath a shoal of *silver fishes* glides,
> And plays about the gilded barge's sides;
> The ladies, angling in the crystal lake,
> Feast on the waters with the prey they take:
> At once victorious with their lines and eyes,
> They make the fishes and the men their prize."

'And somebody has written—

> " When thirsty grief in wine we steep,
> When healths and draughts go free
> Fishes that tipple in the deep
> Know no such libertie."

'I remember also reading when I was a boy, but
do not call to mind who is the author :—

> " Blest silent groves, oh, may you be,
> For ever, Mirth's best nursery!
> May pure contents
> For ever pitch their tents
>
> Upon these downs, these meads, these rocks, these
> mountains,
> And peace still slumber by these purling fountains;
> Which we may every year
> Meet, when we come afishing here!"

'Ah!' cried Knowles, 'do you remember these lines in an old song?—

" Of recreation there is none
So free as fishing is alone;
All other pastimes do no less
Than mind and body both possess;
My hand alone my work can do,
So I can fish and study too."

'But as we walk home by this stream I will repeat a fine merry old song.   (*He sings.*)

" Oh, the gallant fisher's life
Is the best of any!
'Tis full of pleasure, void of strife,
And 'tis beloved by many :
Other joys
Are but toys;
Only this
Lawful is ;
For our skill
Breeds no ill,
But content and pleasure.

" In a morning up we rise,
Ere Aurora's peeping ;
Drink a cup to wash our eyes;
Leave the sluggard sleeping ;
Then we go
To and fro

With our knacks
At our backs,
To such streams
As the Thames,
If we have the leisure.

" When we please to walk abroad
For our recreation,
In the fields is our abode,
Full of delectation :
Where in a brook,
With a hook,
Or a lake,
Fish we take ;
There we sit
For a bit,
Till we fish entangle."

We had by this time reached the inn at Melrose in a merry mood and hungry for dinner, without my having been fortunate enough to see the fine action and attitudes of the author of *Virginius.*

The reader knows that Mr. Hazlitt was in personal appearance something remarkable, unlike in looks and manner, as he was in temperament and intellectual peculiarity, to any other of the varied family of man. In the streets of Edinburgh he might have passed for a poring antiquary or bookworm, or some plodding editor of a Jacobinical review. But in a quiet provincial town or village such characters are rare, and therefore it may not create surprise that the author of *The Spirit of the Age* excited the curiosity of the good people of Melrose; who, when he walked leisurely through the town for the first time, and alone, turned out in a body to watch his return, that they might have a sufficient opportunity of scrutinising his person and belongings. He found them in ranks or groups in front of their dwellings, gaping and staring at him, as he told me, 'like so many idiots.' Instead, however, of taking no notice of this provincial attention as complimentary to his popularity, he was highly offended at the liberty taken with him as a stranger, and he made a full stand, fronting round to the principal position of the enemy, and with a countenance full of scorn and indignation, he addressed them in loud and thundering voice thus :—

'What the devil do you see in me? You staring hawbucks! Cannot a stranger walk quietly through your town without exciting this vacant and impertinent curiosity. What is there for you to see? You gaping Scotch ninnies!'

Strange and sensitive being ! I presume that any other person would have passed along the streets of Melrose without troubling himself about the over-curiosity of the people. This notice made the good folks stare still more, hardly, we may suppose, understanding one word the 'southern' said to them. They knew from report that he was a great writer, like Sir Walter, and their curiosity was natural. Perhaps they deemed a turn-out would be complimentary to the individual so honoured, as well as a gratification to themselves. But Hazlitt understood the gathering as an expression of rude curiosity, and he resented it on the spot.

'A stare,' he observed, 'is a rude liberty, and a piece of vulgar and improper behaviour; but a Scotch stare is a wide, open, cold, hard, fixed gaze, of both unmeaning eyes, not to be endured —a gaze without any redeeming expression or intention, but that of sheer impudence.'

His sensitiveness was more delicate than that belonging even to feminine nerves. He was pointing out the beautiful variation of colour and tint on the stones and moss of an old wall opposite the window of the inn, when he suddenly caught sight of a man being borne into the house who had received some serious injury. The dread spectacle of a dead man terrified him, and he rushed from the window to the opposite side of the room, while, covering his eyes with his hands, he begged me not to mention it. Thinking that something had happened to himself, I approached him, but he put his hand out, saying, 'Don't let me hear anything of it; the man is dead, I dare say, but I cannot look at anything of the kind, death or the appearance of it, and pray do not speak of it.'

When Knowles had left us, I made the chalk drawing of Hazlitt, size of life, still in my possession, and which called forth the following sonnet from his friend :—

' Thus Hazlitt looked !   There's life in every line !
   Soul — language — fire that colour could not give.
See ! on that brow how pale-robed thought divine,
   In an embodied radiance seems to live !
Ah ! in the gaze of that entranced eye,
   Humid, yet burning, there beams Passion's flame,
   Lightening the cheek, and quivering through the
      frame;

> While round the lips the odour of a sigh
> Yet hovers fondly, and its shadow sits
> Beneath the channel of the glowing thought
> And fire-clothed eloquence, which comes in fits
> Like Pythiac inspiration ! Bewick, taught
> By thee, in vain doth slander's venomed dart
> Do its foul work 'gainst *him*. This head must own a
> heart.'

The drawing is engraved in the *Literary Remains of William Hazlitt*, by his son,—a highly interesting work. Mr. Hazlitt, whilst at Melrose, was writing a criticism upon Lady Morgan's *Life and Times of Salvator Rosa*, for the *Edinburgh Review*, which he laid aside in good-humoured willingness to sit to me. He seemed highly amused and pleased to have the sketch made, and wrote a paper upon 'the pleasure of sitting for one's picture.' During dinner he was gracious and smiling, and asked me to put up the portrait for him to look at. I stuck it up with a fork at each corner into the wainscot over the mantelpiece opposite to him. He frequently laid down his knife and fork to contemplate the likeness, gazing earnestly and long, asking if really his own hair was anything like that of the drawing. Mrs. Hazlitt exclaimed.

'Oh! it is exactly your own hair, my dear.' With which he seemed quite satisfied, and in great admiration of what I had done, said, 'Well, surely that puts me in mind of some of Raphael's heads in the cartoons. Ah! it is, however, something to live for, to have such a head as *that.*' He contemplated the representation of himself for some time in silence, with evident expressions of satisfaction, not unmixed with some natural emotion of vanity, which in him was neutralised by the genuine simplicity of his character.

When the drawing was finished we walked out in the evening. It was twilight; a delicious freshness and serenity reigned over the face of nature. The silence, the stillness, and the solitude of our path seemed to affect both of us. We came to an old gate. There was a low mound upon which stood a small stone building in ruins, and by its side an animal quietly grazing upon the sward. These objects were in deep shade against a star-lit sky. My meditative companion paused, pointed to the group and whispered, 'There is a picture! No painter can produce the sentiment that pervades it, the wonderful breadth and harmony and depth of effect that "hangs upon the beatings of the heart !" and thus affects one like magic, for there is nothing here in the subject itself. I have been thus affected by some of Claude's land-scapes, but by no other painter's works. Poussin and Salvator have produced grandeur, rugged and romantic nature, and Titian the finest landscape of all, but none the poetical senti-ment that arrests your sympathy as occa-sionally in Nature and in Claude, to whom there seem, ' the soul's most intimate affections known.'

<blockquote>
' We all acknowledge both thy power and love
To be exact, transcendent, and divine ;
Who does so strongly and so sweetly move.'
</blockquote>

Thus he murmured as to himself, lingering by this tranquil picture, as if bound by some spell or enchantment, and he seemed to tear himself away with reluctance, and often looked back to the spot.

CHAPTER IX.

HAZLITT, by his own avowal, was subject to fits of absence of mind, during which he occasionally performed droll or foolish acts ; but such proceedings sometimes led to fortunate results, as was the case on the present occasion, for through the critic's forgetfulness our artist had the happiness of making the acquaintance of Sir Walter Scott, without whose portrait his gallery would have been incomplete : the 'Great Unknown,' as he was then termed, for the secret of the authorship of the Waverley novels had not then been revealed. Bewick had the good fortune to see him in the privacy of his domestic and home life, and the picture which he draws of

Abbotsford, of the guests assembled there, and of Sir Walter's friendly hospitality, is remarkably pleasing and attractive. The great story-teller at his own tea-table reciting old Border minstrelsy to his guests is as vividly presented to the mind of the reader by the artist's pen as his personal form and feature could have been depicted by the most skilful exercise of the limner's art.

VISIT TO ABBOTSFORD.

Hazlitt mentioned to me how absent he occasionally was as to things immediately before him, or connected with the present business of life, and 'Egad,' he said, 'it is curious how I came to Melrose at all, for I had no intention of being here. I will tell you how it happened. After I had handed Mrs. Hazlitt into the post-chaise, and seated myself by her side, the man held the door open with his hand to his hat. I put something into his hand, but he still remained, and thinking we were a long time at a stand-still, I looked at him again, and he said, " Where to, Sir?" The question took me by surprise, for, like a goose, as I am, the thought had not occurred to me. Looking out before me, I observed two pointed hills, and asked where are those hills? "Melrose, Sir." "Then drive there;" and to Melrose we came.'

Fortunate and happy mischance for me! for had he not been the absent 'goose' he called himself, and ordered in his confusion to be driven thither, I should not probably have seen either Melrose or Abbotsford. As it was, I saw both. While Mr. Hazlitt was engaged in writing, I walked out alone to Abbotsford to see the place, its scenery, and its mysterious belongings. I had before met Sir Walter Scott in Edinburgh, and conversed with him. On the the road there I met a carriage full of company, with the Great Unknown in the midst. He recognised me as they passed rapidly on, and I walked to the house and saw through the building. I was struck with a painting of the head of 'Mary Queen of Scots,' and mentioned it to Mr. Hazlitt on my return, who advised me to write and ask Sir Walter's permission to make a drawing of it, which I did, Hazlitt approving of my note. The permission was graciously given at once; and as Hazlitt read the reply, he seemed delighted with its gentlemanly tone and kindness, saying,—-

'Ah! he is indeed a fine piece of Nature's handiwork! I was convinced of that when I went to see him at the Court of Session, where he seemed to be working out some of his own pleasant thoughts with a good-humoured smile, as if it were all boy's play to him. I daresay it was so, for he is a true master of the craft, and one feels that there is no one else *could* write *Waverley* but himself. The mystery that exists about these works serves a purpose, the secret is well kept, and all is worked to admiration. Extensive demand follows the interest excited, but at the same time the ware is generally equal to the interest. Scott's large heart rises above his party prejudices; and he is a fine hale, hearty creature, full of genius and romance,—tells a story, a legend, a ballad, a plot inimitably. As a man, I am told, he is frank, free, and open-hearted, simple and natural in his manners, and ready to grant every one his meed of praise and justice. This is a fine character, and when added to great genius is, I am afraid, rare in these selfish and oppressive times.'

During my pleasant walk to Abbotsford, I had time to reflect that I was treading on classic ground, that I was approaching to a nearer interview and acquaintance with the home and person of the remarkable being who was as great a mystery, and was creating as great an interest throughout Europe as 'the man with the Iron Mask,' the 'Wandering Jew,' or any other hero of books or story. That he was the author of the novels and tales devoured so greedily by every class of readers, some believed, and many doubted; whilst other men, and even *women*, had occasionally been set up as the producers of these wondrously rapid productions of the pen; but the question was up to this period still unsolved.

I stepped under the portico at Abbotsford with some feeling of nervous trepidation, not unaccompanied with awe at the thought of entering the mystic circle of the Enchanter. Accordingly my pull at the bell was so tremulous that no servant made his appearance; but, instead, I heard the approaching sound of unequal footsteps (steps which anyone who had ever heard them before would recognise as those of the author of *Waverley*), and soon appeared the well-known face and smile of Sir Walter Scott. No doubt he had expected me, perhaps seen me arrive; and as the kitchens were distant, concluded the bell had not been heard. He, therefore, without ceremony, opened the door himself, saying something in excuse about the servants not hearing the bell, and with a hearty good welcome seized my hand, and after paying the courtesies of the morning, which he did with kindness and simplicity, he led me at once into the house to be introduced to his family and friends. I found a large number of guests congregated in the breakfast-room, and I was thus graciously introduced by the head of the house into an elegant and select company, that smiled their kindness and attention to me, as if they had long known me. It appeared that my coming had formed part of the conversation of the morning, for allusion to the object of my visit was soon made. There were present Lady Scott, Charles and Miss Scott,—a German, Baron D'Este, the

Rev. Dr. Hughes, of St. Paul's, London, and his lady, &c.

The name of *Thomas Bewick* had already gained for me the favourable attentions of Mrs. Hughes, who told me in a kind and friendly manner that my namesake had quite won her heart by the beautiful engravings in his publications. 'Indeed,' she said, 'I am so much indebted to him, that I could wish to have the opportunity of expressing my obligations, for you must know that, whenever my children were cross or ill, I had recourse to Bewick's tailpieces, or his birds and animals, to pacify and amuse them ; and they never failed to restore them to good humour and dry up their tears. And I am delighted to have the opportunity of telling my gratitude to one, even of the name of Bewick, and I hope you may be able to convey my acknowledgments to himself.'

This charming lady's cordiality set me quite at ease, and as the party separated to get ready for a drive, Sir Walter kindly inquired what I should require for making the drawing, and ordered a servant-man to attend upon me and get whatever I wished during his absence. Then apologizing for having to attend upon the ladies to show them something of interest in the neighbourhood, he left me to my engagement with the death-like features of Queen Mary, of Scotland, whose living charms, and grace and eloquence, have been so vividly portrayed in his 'Abbot.' Alas! the interesting memento that I copied is the lifeless head of features once lovely, struck off from the body of the Princess. The original painting is in oil colours, by Annius Cawood, dated Fotheringay the 9th of February, 1587. The head appears to be represented on a silver salver, or dish, covered with black crape; and Sir Walter observed that the room where the body lay after execution was locked up for three days, and it was supposed the painting was done during that time.

As some of my friends were afterwards interested to know all about the painting from which my drawing was done, I wrote to Sir Walter Scott, and received the following reply :—

'SIR,—I have pleasure in affording you all the information I possess concerning the picture, but it is not much. Mr. Bullock, the naturalist, brought me a message from a gentleman then going abroad and disposing of a collection of pictures, expressing a wish that I should be possessed of this one either by gift or purchase, naming a moderate price (10*l.* I think, but am not certain), if I preferred the latter arrangement.   He stated that the gentleman who had so kindly thought upon me, had received the picture in a present from a friend in Prussia, and therefore did not wish to expose it to public sale.   This is all I know of it.   I have forgotten even the name of the former proprietor, but I have it written down somewhere.

I am happy to have had an opportunity of gratifying your curiosity, which will not however be altogether gratis.   I am afraid the ladies will hold you but a perjured person unless you favour them with a copy of the sketch of Abbotsford which you had the goodness to promise them, and which will find us here if sent by any of the coaches.   I will be happy to see you if you will call as you pass through Edinburgh, being, Sir,

Your most obedient servant,

WALTER SCOTT.

39 Castle Street, 18 May, 1824.

I afterwards received the following letter from Colonel Shipperdson, of Durham :—

DEAR SIR,—I received from the hands of Mr. Balmer (the painter) your elegant drawing of Queen Mary's head. It will be interesting to you to read the following extract of a letter from Miss Scott, of Abbotsford, in reference to the painting from which your first drawing was made. The letter is addressed to Mrs. Surtees, of Mainsforth, who was so good as to write to Miss Scott, to inquire the history of the painting.

You ask about Mary Queen of Scots' picture. It was copied by Mr. Bewick, and is thought an original. It was bought in Germany ; not by papa, but by a very strange old man, who wished to give it to papa, thinking it of great value. This papa refused. He then offered to sell it, and named forty or fifty guineas, as he always said no one else should have it but him. All the artists admire the picture very much. This is all I remember about it. Letter written in Sir W. Scott's room, darkened on account of his illness, and during attendance upon him.

Your faithful, humble servant,

EDWARD SHIPPERDSON.

To W. Bewick, Esq.

After I had partaken of luncheon I finished my drawing and was preparing to take leave, but Sir Walter told me that as dinner would soon be on the table he should be glad if I would remain and dine, and 'Lady Scott desires me to keep you,' he added. 'I am not to allow you to leave the house before dinner, so, you see, your engagement is fixed by the fair, and is beyond the will of both you and myself, for you cannot say no to a lady's wish;' and laughing in his good-humoured way he sat down by me. Although I was very desirous to show Mr. Hazlitt the drawing of the head I had described to him, and about which I had interested him so much, yet there was no denying the wish of Sir Walter and Lady Scott, nor had I any inclination to decline the honour of sharing their hospitality. My first dinner at Abbotsford was elegant, and, as my friend Thackeray would have said, *recherché*. The conversation was light and agreeable, and went merrily round, for the party was not large enough to induce isolated gossip. The young Baron was entertaining and gentlemanly, and indulged Miss Scott with romance, music, and gallantry. The reverend Doctor was unfortunately deaf, but Mrs. Hughes made amends for all her good-natured husband's failings by her tact and gracious volubility. She sat near me, and spoke much about her son's taste for drawing, and his beautiful sketch-book, which she showed me afterwards. Lady Scott and she conversed about their families, and Sir Walter seemed to take the opportunity of expressing his mind about his son Charles, who he said was wasting his precious time from morning to night every day, either fishing or shooting, while he had not the pleasure or satisfaction of seeing his face for days together, for he was off by sunrise, and as far as he knew did not return till bedtime. 'It is all very well to make an amusement of sport occasionally, but that boy works hard at fishing every day, as if for his livelihood. But I suppose it will have an end at a given time, like every other hobby of youth, and I leave it to his own good sense, you know, Mrs. Scott.' Then turning to me, he said, 'I observe that Sir Joshua Reynolds was very fond of children, and the children reciprocated his feelings. He used to play with them, and he delighted to amuse them,—would roll himself on the carpet, and become himself a boy, with all the fun and joy and laughter of childhood. How delightful it is, and what an idea it gives us of his amiability and goodness! For myself, I have often tried to ingratiate myself with the innocent, dear little things. I admire their beauty, and enjoy their pretty prattle, but somehow or other I never seem to make a favourable impression. I do not succeed with them, they do not approach me with the familiarity or favour that they show to other men. I am sure I have often tried to take pains enough to gain their good opinion, and I would do anything to obtain their confidence and love.'

When the ladies retired I took the opportunity of intimating to my kind host that I had a long walk to Melrose before me. He gently laid hold of my arm, and in most persuasive accents said, ' Oh, dear, no, sir, the ladies are waiting for us in the drawing-room, and they expect you there to take your tea, and very likely they will favour us with a little music;' adding, as he rubbed his hands together, with his pleasant, open-hearted smile, 'They will not like your slipping away in this fashion, I assure you. Come, come away, let us to the divinities of the tea-table;' and thus in his own friendly way he ushered me into the drawing-room, where the reverend gentleman of St. Paul's and the Baron had already taken their places.

The brilliant gaslight, the elegance and taste displayed throughout this beautiful apartment, the costumes of the ladies, with the sparkle and glitter of the tea-table, its steaming urn and comfortable beverage, all tended to impress one with a sense of the luxury of a home and fireside in the high scale of society in which the owner of Abbotsford moved.

To see 'the great story-teller' seated upon a low ottoman by the fire, the lowliest of this gay party, sipping his bohea, conversing in his humorous way with the simplicity peculiar to him, appeared to me delightful. His stores of anecdote, historic ballads, legends, and exciting stories, seemed to be inexhaustible; and as he told them with suitable expression of mystery, awe, wonder, or surprise, he would chuckle and enjoy the effects he produced upon his hearers. Amused, too, he seemed as he observed Mrs. Hughes ever and anon busy with a small note-book, in which she jotted down words and memoranda, that we may suppose would be written out at length after she retired. When a quaint old Scotch ballad was repeated she had some difficulty in following the recital, and asked Sir Walter to indulge her again. He said, ' Never mind that now, Mrs. Hughes, I will take care to write it out for you in the morning ;' and at breakfast the promised transcript was handed over, with the observation, ' There, Mrs. Hughes, is what you wished, I have not forgotten you.'

Something was mentioned about Spence, and Sir Walter observed, ' There is another old Scotch ballad, *Sir Patrick Spence*, which I will endeavour to remember,' and pausing for a short time, with closed eyes, swaying his body to and fro, he commenced in a low, mournful kind of recitative, peculiar I presume to poets or minstrels, as I have never heard the harmonious chant from any other persons. As it must be interesting to all to read what Sir Walter took such pleasure in reciting, it is scarcely necessary to make any apology for the insertion here of the quaint old ballad.

SIR PATRICK SPENCE.

The king sits in Dumferline town,
    Drinking the blude-red wine:
Oh, where will I get a guid sailòr,
    To sail this ship of mine?

Up and spak an eldern knight,
    Sat at the king's right knee;
Sir Patrick Spence is the best sailòr,
    That sails upon the sea.

The king has written a braid letter,
    And signed it wi' his hand;
And sent it to Sir Patrick Spence,
    Was walking on the sand.

The first line that Sir Patrick read,
    A loud laugh laughèd he:
The next line that Sir Patrick read,
    The tear blinded his ee.

And who is this has done the deed,
    This ill deed done to me;
To send me out this time o' the year,
    To sail upon the sea?

'Mak haste, mak haste, my merry men all,
    Our good ship sails the morn.'
' Oh, say not so, my master dear,
    For I fear a deadlie storm.

' Late, late yestreen I saw the new moon
    Wi' the old moon in her arms;
  And I fear, I fear, my dear master,
    That we will come to harm.'

  Oh, our Scots nobles were right loth
    To wet their cork-heel'd shoone;
  But lang ere all the play were played,
    Their hats they swam aboone.

  Oh, lang, lang, may their ladies sit
    With their fans into their hand,
  Or ere they see Sir Patrick Spence
    Cum sailing to the land.

  Oh, lang, lang, may the ladies stand
    Wi' their gold combs in their hair,
  Waiting for their ain dear lords,
    For they 'll see them na mair.

  Have owre, have owre to Aberdour,
    It's fifty fathom deep:
  And there lies guid Sir Patrick Spence,
    Wi' the Scots lords at his feet.

No one reading the above lament, who is not from the ' north of the Tweed,' can appreciate the deep impression that the mournful intonation of the Scottish accent produces, when recited with propriety and feeling, as was the case on this occasion. Memory takes me back to the sonorous, tremulous, prolonged, and melancholy sound of the poet's voice as he uttered the last two fatal lines, when the hearers hung with tearful attention upon the sensitive lips that trembled with emotion.

During the above recitation, Baron d'Este and Miss Scott had ceased their musical entertainment, which had been going on apart from the company,—the Baron endeavouring to show Miss Scott how in Germany they introduced, in guitar performances of martial music, the imitation of the beating of drums. This the young Baron did with great spirit and effect, and Miss Scott seemed in ecstasies with him and his accomplishments.

When they resumed their guitar music, and seemed absorbed in difficult pieces of harmony, Sir Walter cast his observant eyes towards them with a look of paternal pleasure, and whispered to Mrs. Hughes,—

> ' Music ! miraculous rhetoric, that speakest sense
> Without a tongue, excelling eloquence.'

All the company were listening to the Baron's

extraordinary performance upon the guitar, and being uneasy as to my return to Melrose, I thought it a good opportunity to retire, but Sir Walter held me by the hand, saying he had never deemed it hospitable to turn a friend out so late in a country-place like Abbotsford, that a bed had been already prepared for me, and I must make myself at home. Lady Scott uniting her entreaties that I would remain, I resigned myself, ' nothing loth,' to the cordiality and intellectual enjoyment of this magic circle.

Sir Walter inquired of me if I knew the curious old ballad, or rather he might call it tragedy, of *Bewick and Graham* — to which I replied that I had never heard of it before. He then said he would try to amuse me by repeating what he could remember of it.

BEWICK AND GRAHAM.

Old Graham he has to Carlisle gone,
    Where Sir Robert Bewick there met he,
In arms to the wine they are gone,
    And drank till they were both merry.

Old Graham, he took up the cup,
    And said, ' Brother Bewick, here's to thee,
And here's to our two sons at home,
    For they live best in our country.'

' Nay, were thy son as good as mine,
        And if some books he could but read,
    With sword and buckler by his side,
        To see how he could save his head;

' They might have been call'd two bold brethren,
        Wherever they do go or ride,
    They might have been call'd two bold brethren,
        They might have crack'd the border side.'

The Laird Graham takes offence at what Bewick says so disparagingly of his son, pays his reckoning, and rides home in a passion, telling his eldest son, Christy Graham, the offensive epithets applied to him.

' He said thou wast bad, and call'd thee a lad,
        And company to his son cannot be,
    For his son Bewick can both write and read,
        And sure I cannot say that of thee.

' I put thee to school, but thou wouldst not learn,
        I bought thee books, but thou wouldst not read,
    But my blessing thou shalt never have
        Till with Bewick thou canst save thy head.'

Now Christy Graham, being urged by his father, objects to fight a duel with his dearest friend; but the old man insists and throws down his own glove, saying, ' Here is my glove, — thou shalt fight me.' Thus compelled to give

battle he meets his friend Bewick and chal-
lenges him—

> ' Away, away, thou Billy Bewick,
>   And if care, man, let us be,
> If thou be a man, as I trow thou art,
>   Come over this ditch and fight with me.'

> *　　　*　　　*　　　*　　　*

> Now they fell to with two broad swords,
>   For two long hours fought Bewick and he.

One being struck down, the other, having vowed
not to survive his friend,

> First bequeathed his soul to God,
>   And upon his sword lept he.

Both dying were buried in the same grave.
But —

> Now we'll leave off talking of these bold brethren
>   In Carlisle town, where they were slain,
> And talk of these two good old men,
>   Where they were making a pitiful main.

> And now up spake Sir Robert Bewick,
>   ' O man, was I not much to blame?
> I have lost one of the liveliest lads
>   That ever was bred unto my name.'

> With that up spake my good Laird Graham,
>   ' O man, I've lost the better block,
> I've lost my comfort and my joy,
>   I've lost my key, I've lost my lock.'

'Such sad tragedies,' said Sir Walter, were not uncommon in these rough times of border hardihood. The ballad is written in the quaint old style of the time ; but I have no recollection of the name of the author. The Laird Graham, I suppose to be of the Netherby family, and you, I suppose, will be descended from the original stock of Sir Robert Bewick, or, as my friend Surtees would say, you are originally of the Tyneside Bewicks. I think there is a romantic legend respecting some of your name, that I learned when at Rokeby, and which if I remember right, has a fatal catastrophe attached to it ; but it contains some attributes of the same high spirit, and, if I may so, of obstinacy and pride, as the character of Sir Robert Bewick himself. You will, no doubt, remember the ancient story of your family on the banks of the Tees, as I heard it there, better than I can, Mr. Bewick, and will favour us with a short recital.'

I then told him what I had heard, as forming a tale we used to denominate *Aunt Sarah's Legend.*

'My family is an ancient one, and was located long ago on the Tyne, where it had large estates, some of which we might have been enjoying now, but for the independent spirit of one of my ancestors. My great-grandfather in his early manhood became acquainted with a very beautiful but nearly portionless young lady in his own neighbourhood. Her beauty and modesty quickly won his heart; but his parents were sadly disappointed at the inequality of the match, having formed very different views for their son, and his father, in the height of his indignation, declared that he would disinherit him if he persisted in attaching himself to the portionless beauty. Opposition, as was perhaps to be expected, only added fuel to the flame, the father's conduct was declared to be " tyranny," and to escape from it the young man persuaded his beloved to marry him privately. The fiery father, when informed of the union, could not control his indignation, and carried out the threat which he had previously uttered.

'The youthful pair do not appear to have yielded to despondency on this event, for my ancestress was as proud as she was beautiful. They determined to leave the neighbourhood that had been their home; and gathering together the little property they could call their own, comprising a small library of books, some pictures, and a very little money, they removed to the banks of the Tees, where their descendants continue to cherish a spirit of self-dependence and decision more conducive to their happiness, perhaps, than the possession of inherited estates.'

Sir Walter and his friends gave a kindly attention to this little story, and Sir Walter playfully christened it, ' All for Love.'

When ten o'clock had arrived, the hour of separation for the night, the distinguished host told me, ' they always made it a rule when in the country to retire to bed at that early hour, and in the morning breakfast would be on the table at nine, so that until then your time is at your own disposal, and we shall then be glad to see you.' Everyone took his night-taper, and we dispersed to our several chambers, Sir Walter shaking hands and wishing every one a hearty good-night. Then attending me to my room, and turning up the gaslight, he said, ' You see, here is the gas lighted ready for you ; you can keep it burning all night by turning it down, thus to the size of a pin's head ; and if you wish for light during the night turn it up again. I dare say you will find everything comfortable and proper, but should there be anything want- ing, pray ring the bell.' Then casting his ob- servant eye about the room he wished me 'good night and a sound sleep,' thus offering to me as a stranger the marked attention and hospi- tality of a true gentleman, with that frank simplicity that characterised him.

It may be imagined that sleep did not come to me very early. I lay on my couch in wakeful ecstasy, ruminating on the highly interesting events of the day. Can it be, thought I, that I am really in the lair of the lion ? Am I then in the mansion of the charmer—under the mystical roof of the alchymist ?—the supposed concocter of those extraordinary productions that are exciting such world-wide interest, admiration, and curiosity ? Is it here that the yarn is spun and the woof elaborated in such perfection, with such successful secresy that the mystery even gives zest, and· the uncertainty produces speculation as to who is, and who is not, the being that possesses such wonderful power of production, so original, and of quality and excellence so varied. These works came upon the world of literature as a new pleasure of the time, and were devoured with such appetite that they could with difficulty be supplied fast enough, or in sufficient quantity. All ranks and qualities of men were reading them as they appeared, and it was then that all men's minds were occupied with the question, who was '*the great unknown*' writer of them; and although many eminent individuals were named, yet it came generally to be allowed that no one was so likely to possess claims to such varied powers as Sir Walter Scott.

As I thus lay sleepless and meditating, I thought upon the strange but fortunate chance that had brought me in contact with the three distinguished authors of the period, Knowles, Hazlitt, and Scott, within such narrow limits of place and time that I could almost fancy I had been in their company together. I have said *chance*, for it was by mere accident that Mr. Hazlitt pointed out the picturesque hills at Melrose, and desired to be taken there; and this place was so near to Abbotsford, that I was induced to walk over, and was afterwards invited to remain the guest. These three gifted men were remarkable for their original genius, as well as for their party politics in a stirring epoch of our history. Scott was a professed high Tory, honoured by the King. Knowles wrote *William Tell*, every line of which breathes the spirit of liberty, and he was then the proprietor of *The Glasgow Free Press*. Hazlitt was a fiery Bonapartist, and something more. The first and last wrote their lives of Bonaparte, how diverse the world already knows.

It was long before I slept. I could not but reflect upon the unaccountable phases and vicissitudes that occasionally fall to the lot of man. Here I was, thrown into the lap of elegance and luxury, of every domestic enjoyment. I cast my thoughts back to the late troubles and anxieties of my London life, with my arduous exertions and struggles for success and fame. Alas! these hopes and exertions, assisted by the want of means, the dire misfortunes and utter ruin of one friend, and the base want of feeling and breach of honour of another pretender, had failed; so that the misery and the desperation of my situation had become insupportable. I now lay on the downy bed of luxury, amidst the elegance of domestic indulgence, and surrounded by all the concomitants of honourable distinction and the rewards of successful genius. The contrast was too great; my tears flowed, and I breathed a prayer of thanksgiving to the great Dispenser of all good. My short sleep was the most profound and felicitous that had visited my pillow for many a long night.

Morning came; and after breakfast I made a sketch of the building for Baron d'Este, which he was desirous of having to show to his mother in Germany, who had been, I understood, a friend of Sir Walter's in early life.

I now became very anxious to return to Melrose to show Mr. Hazlitt my drawing, and Sir Walter very kindly took great interest about it, brought me an old portfolio to carry it safely, and in reply to Lady Scott, who wished to send it by a servant, said, smiling to me, 'I warrant you, Mr. Bewick will be something like myself, he would rather not lose sight of it, but take it in his own keeping,' to which I thankfully assented. And now every one came forward and cordially shook me by the hand,—Sir Walter attending me to the door. There pausing, he drew me aside, and asked if Mr. Hazlitt was at Melrose? I replied in the affirmative. He then inquired, with some expression of curiosity, and in earnest tones, though with delicacy, 'What he was doing down here?' There was hesitation in his tone, as if some doubt existed whether he ought to have asked the question. However, I had nothing to conceal, and frankly told him that Mr. Hazlitt was on his marriage tour, and also of his then writing a paper for the *Edinburgh Review.* Sir Walter observed, with great apparent sincerity, that 'Mr. Hazlitt was one of our most eloquent authors, and a man, as far as he could be allowed to judge, of great natural and original genius; that it was a pity such great powers were not concentrated upon some important work, valuable to his country, to literature, and lasting to his fame.' He then pressed my hand in his and kindly urged me to be sure and call upon him when he returned to Edinburgh.

I hastened with the drawing to Melrose,

thinking of all I had to recount to Hazlitt, of Sir Walter's high opinion of his genius, and his friendly expressions towards him as an author, which I was sure would be most pleasing to him ; and of the hospitality and kindness I had received from all parties. In fact I thought I had a pleasant budget of interesting information about Abbotsford and its lord for him. What was my surprise and disappointment to find the bird had flown ! My eccentric friend had quitted Melrose for the south, and there was a kind letter explaining the reasons for his departure, with a present, as a memorial of our meeting at this romantic place, of the two volumes of Lady Morgan's *Salvator Rosa and his Times,* with Hazlitt's notes and remarks, made on reading for his critique upon the work for the *Edinburgh Review,* which he wrote whilst here.

It so happened that we did not meet again for some years after, and when, where, and how we came together once more will be afterwards recounted.

I forgot to mention that Sir Walter Scott put into my safe keeping a small parcel nicely tied and sealed up, directed to his publishers, requesting me to deliver it myself *safely* as soon as I arrived in Edinburgh. His manner and expression were serious and impressive as he held the parcel in his hand until the last moment of my leaving him, when he again desired me to be careful of his little packet, as ' it was of consequence, and he relied upon me.' I made myself certain that I was the bearer of some portion of ' copy ' of a forthcoming Waverley Novel, and felt the importance of my situation as being implicated in the great mystery. On my arrival in Edinburgh I waited upon the publishers, and found one of them seated in the shop, under a window, with Captain Basil Hall, examining together some ' proofs ' very attentively. I no sooner said I was the bearer of the packet from Sir Walter Scott than they both lowered their proofs and took a regular Scotch stare at me, wondering what and who I could be ; and probably the Captain might wonder what part of the Scotch novels I had to do with, for suspicion and mystery spread to everybody but those really in the secret.

CHAPTER X.

MR. BEWICK had now acquired great skill as a copyist, and while at Gartmore, the guest of Mr. Graham, he had made a copy of a ' Rembrandt,' for which that gentleman had given 4000*l*. The person who had sold the original obtained a loan of the copy, and was so charmed with it, that he steadily refused to give it up, saying that he had always regretted parting with the original; but this copy was so nearly equal to it, that it in great measure reconciled him to the loss of his picture, and he concluded by begging Mr. Bewick to name his price. He did so, and it was paid at once, but Mr. Bewick never saw his picture again.

The fame of Bewick's success in this copy reached Glasgow before the artist himself. At a dinner-party there, which included several gentlemen who took an interest in art and artists, a discussion arose on the style and colour of Rembrandt, and the materials used by him to produce his effects of light and shadow, and the strong impasto on the surface of his pictures. The discussion was suggested by the wonderful sketch by Rembrandt in Glasgow University; and a very spirited argument was maintained between two of the party, the one asserting that he could not have produced such an impasto without the aid of wax or some similar material, while the other contended that it might be done with pure colour and linseed oil, and that Rembrandt used nothing but these simple materials, which accounts for the manner in which his works stand the test of time. The opponent offered to lay a wager that it could not be done, and Bewick undertook to make a copy, using nothing but linseed oil and pure colour. He had almost finished his task, and being anxious to study the effect, he had put his copy in the frame and the original on his easel, when two of the professors came in, and having looked carefully at both, said, 'Well, Mr. Bewick, we cannot tell one from the other, this is so perfect a *facsimile* of the original.' This remark decided the wager, which was cheerfully paid, and thus was exploded the idea of vehicles. This copy afterwards deceived a very great judge of Rembrandt's works in London. This gentleman, when he saw it, was convinced it was an original work of the great artist, and offered to purchase it as such. When assured that it was only a copy, he expressed his astonishment at the artistic skill displayed in so faithful a reproduction.

'Whilst in Edinburgh,' writes Mr. Bewick, 'General Graham, at that time Governor of the Castle, drove me to his seat at Gartmore, in the Highlands, to see a fine Rembrandt. The place was a most lovely one; the approach being lined by an avenue of Portugal laurels, twelve or fourteen feet high. Here I remained a fortnight, during which time the General permitted me to make a copy of this fine work, and showed me the most courteous hospitality, taking me to see the different views and fine scenery in which this neighbourhood abounds. Here were eagles with their nests perched on the magnificent trees. The coachman, a daring fellow, attempted to climb these gigantic trees, and succeeded in bringing us a nest of young ones. Presently the old ones returned, and their shrieks and batterings became so fearful that it was thought advisable to leave them their young.

'During my sojourn at my native place, where I had been ordered for change of air, I was agreeably surprised by the honour of an invitation from the Earl of Eglinton to witness the magnificent entertainment got up by that chivalrous and high-spirited nobleman. Notwithstanding my then delicate state, my spirits rallied when I thought of the opportunity now afforded me of witnessing in reality the grand sight which I had so often pictured in my imagination, when reading the ever-delightful and graphic descriptions of the tournament given by Sir Walter Scott in his *Ivanhoe.*'

From Edinburgh Mr. Bewick went to Glasgow, where he made an exhibition of his works, and added several new portraits to his gallery. It will be remembered that Dr. Birkbeck was the founder of Mechanics' Institutions, and that his first institution was established in Glasgow. For this institution Mr. Bewick had painted a portrait of Dr. Birkbeck. He had been requested to be present at one of their meetings, by a deputation which had waited on him in London; and when, being in the city, he complied with their request, and was introduced as the painter of their founder, all the meeting rose *en masse* and cheered the artist, who was lifted off his feet on to the lecture-table, that all might see him, while the names of Bewick and Birkbeck resounded through the hall.

When Bewick left London he had no intention of extending his tour further than Scotland, but an accidental suggestion, thrown out at a dinner-party at Glasgow, induced him to pay a short visit to Ireland also. His intention at first was only to take a short trip to

Belfast and the neighbourhood; but he was so pleased by what he there saw of the Sister Isle, that he determined to extend his journey to Dublin. To one so observant, a visit to Ireland could not but prove advantageous, presenting to him new forms of scenery and new types of character. There was a good deal in the nature of Bewick which enabled him readily to appreciate the finer qualities of the Irish character, and the sympathy thus awakened procured him ready admission to the homes and hearts of those whom he met there. Travelling on the top of the stage-coach at a time when railroads were undreamed of in Ireland, he doubtless witnessed many strange exemplifications of national life and character, with which he afterwards adorned his sketch-book. His gallery also was greatly enriched by the portraits of the able and genial men with whom he became acquainted in the Irish metropolis. Lord Norbury, O'Connell, Maturin, Shiel, Curran, Lady Morgan, and other celebrated natives of the Emerald Isle, were thus added to his portfolio.

———————

Note of a Visit to Ireland.

While we were chatting over our punch at a dinner-party at Glasgow, some one proposed a run over to Belfast by steamer from Greenock, as there was opposition and fares were nominal. A party was formed, of which I was one. We examined at leisure the town and neighbourhood of Belfast, scrutinised and visited some of the inhabitants to whom we had introductions, or with whom we were acquainted; among others, a Mr. or Dr. Gray, a very intelligent clergyman and father of Mrs. Hogg, the wife of the Ettrick Shepherd. The whole of the party were so far delighted with the Emerald Isle, and it was proposed to continue our tour to Dublin. We placed ourselves, therefore, on the top of the coach, that the best view of the beautiful country might be had, and we galloped all the way in the finest style that the coaching times could boast of, for the roads, the country, and the horses were superb; the merry guard playing a selection of Irish melodies all the way upon his key-bugle—pigs, donkeys, ducks, and chickens flying before us, with crowds of ragged urchins — lame, blind and halt running bare-legged round the coach to catch the halfpence thrown from the top to excite their cupidity. The journey from Belfast to Dublin was all fun, obstreperous frolic, and joyous hilarity. Guard, driver, and horses, all young, seemed to be alive with the spirit of Irish waggery, that amused and astonished some of my cautious and sedate Scotch friends, who could not help laughing with the rest, but called out at every risk of an overthrow —'Have a care, man, and do not at this frightful rate break our necks, *so far frae hame.*' A merry, care-nothing sort of laugh from coachee, and the delicious notes of *Paddy Carey* from the key-bugle of the guard, were the only responses to the cautious prudence of my Glasgow friends; and we rattled away, changing horses at every posting-house, where the jeers and wit and fun of mine host, and all his pack of stable-men and boys, kept up the farce, and the merry laugh rang round as the guard gave his ' All right,' and we started off again at full speed, the bugle sounding chorus to the shouts and the hearty cheer of the free, gay spirits we left behind us. Surely it was a novelty to the natives of Scotia to witness this business done in such masterly style, off-hand, with drollery and smiling humour, as if it were the mere frolic of youthful pleasantry, and we were going to the wedding of *Ballyporeen,* or some of those sportive Irish fairs where the 'boys' would play off some of their choicest sprees with their shillelahs, and 'perty sport' of breaking heads.

Thus we galloped up to Bilton's Hotel in Sackville Street, Dublin, covered with a liberal coating of Irish dust, and ready to devour whatever of edibles might be set before us ; and to do justice to this establishment, I must report that no hotel was ever better served than Bilton's in 1824. My Scotch friends were profuse in praise of the abundance of silver with which we were served ; and they remarked it was well they came there, saying that they only had selected Bilton's because he was a Scotchman, and they seemed proud of their countryman's success, and took care to make it known to the host that they were from ' the Land o' Cakes.'

After having seen all that our guide-books and an occasional *cicerone* deemed interesting in the metropolis of the *Emerald Isle,* my friends returned to their quiet homes and to their business habits at Glasgow, leaving me behind to see a little more of the gay society and the intellectual celebrities that adorn this polished and elegant city ; for I hoped to combine enjoyment with the interest of adding to my portfolio the heads of some of the eminent men I might be fortunate enough to meet in society. Thus I was introduced to most of the persons distinguished for intellectual or literary ability in the Irish capital ; and from most I succeeded in obtaining consent to sit for sketches or finished drawings, life-size ; and I brought away with me an exceedingly interesting collection of portraits of men of fame and character, such as Chief Justice Bushe — Lord Norbury — O'Connell — Maturin — Shiel — Curran — Carmichael, with Lady Morgan, and her charming sister Lady Olivia Clarke, with whom and Sir Arthur Clarke I had the pleasure of passing a good deal of my spare time, for she gave me, and my sprightly and talented friend, Mr. Curran, a general dinner invitation, whenever either of us was disengaged. In these delightful hospitalities, in society so accomplished, refined, and enjoyable, a few weeks glided quickly away ; and I have to express my acknowledgments and gratitude for the courtesy and friendship I everywhere met with, amidst this lively, hearty, and talented people. Do not let me forget that it was because I was there as a young *artist*, that my reception was open-handed, manifesting in the people of this brilliant capital an appreciating intelligence and estimation of the *agrémens* of ART. And I do hope that I was able to convey to my entertainers a sense of the gratitude that I felt for their attentions, and an assurance of the high consideration, esteem, and affection, I shall ever entertain for them.

The first remarkable Irishman whom I at-tempted to portray was the Rev. Charles Robert Maturin, the author of *Bertram, Melmoth,* &c. I had read his works, and was anxious to secure, not only a faithful likeness of him, but, as far as lay in my power to give it, *the character of his mind*, as it might appear either in his general appearance, in particular configuration, or in his expression when excited by feeling or passion. And accordingly I tried to engage him, whilst he was sitting, in subjects analogous to his strange turn of mind, and to the gloomy tendency of his wild imagination.

From reading his works, and from what I had heard of the idiosyncracy of his very peculiar and original genius, I had formed in my own mind a vague but defined notion of what he was like ; and my expectations were raised at the prospect of seeing him in his own house,—where it might be supposed he would be found in all the picturesque surroundings one is apt to associate with the author of works of such mysterious gloom and burning passion. What was my surprise and disappointment when, coming to him by appointment, I found him waiting for me dressed up for the occasion, a courteous and finished gentleman, pacing his drawing-room in elegant full dress, a splendidly bound book laid open upon a cambric pocket-handkerchief, laced round the edges and scented with *eau-de-Cologne,* and held upon both hands ; a stylish new black wig curled over his temples, his shirt-collar reaching half-way up his face, and his attenuated cheeks rouged up to the eyes ! It was a perfect *make-up*, and my chagrin was accordingly great. I had expected to find him in a costume which would have been such as to aid the poetical character, in something Byronic and picturesque, something suggestive of the personification of a wild and romantic hero, cast in the sombre light and shade of mysterious thought or ascetic asperity. I had expected that the author of *Melmoth* would have received me as an author in his true character ; not in the elegance fit for a lady's boudoir, or with the etiquette of the court of George IV., but seated in his dark studio, where the walls and ceiling were black,—the light only admitted from one pane of the window above, which would have fallen upon his fine intellectual forehead, on which

the wafer might be placed which indicated to his
family that he was engaged in communings
with the spirits of his imagination, and
that the chain of his cogitations was not
to be interrupted by any call to meals,
but that a perfect silence must reign in his
household while the afflatus was upon him.
Indeed I was told that on these occasions all
domestic matters were conducted by signs
only, speech or noise of any kind being pro-
hibited.

Before commencing the portrait, I explained
to Mr. Maturin what it was I wished to obtain in the drawing,—that I only desired to
represent his natural character, and to embody
his mental traits. Upon which he seemed
satisfied, and begged I would just do as I
wished with him. Whereupon I began to
disrobe him of his neckcloth and collar, and
of every accessory likely to detract from his
individual character. When the drawing was
finished, I was rather alarmed lest his family
should be disappointed that I had not dressed
him up in the style in which they no doubt

had put him into my hands. However, upon seeing it, they all expressed their unbounded satisfaction at the perfect resemblance, and Mrs. Maturin was affected to tears; their beautiful daughter sympathising with a grace and simplicity truly affecting. I was struck with the elegance of this family; while their appreciation, lively affection, and interest in Mr. Maturin, seemed to lend an additional charm to the peculiarities of a genius so original. He appeared delighted that his family thought the drawing so like him, expressed himself proud of it, and begged to be allowed to present me with a copy of his *Five Sermons on the Errors of the Roman Catholic Church*, just published.

I could not but view a gentleman and scholar endowed with such rare intellectual powers as Mr. Maturin, with his interesting family round him, with feelings of commiseration; he only *an assistant curate*, with so small a pittance for his Christian labours as would scarcely suffice for the most ordinary mechanical labour, often embarrassed, and in pecuniary difficulties that must have oppressed and goaded his sensitive mind. Surely there must be something shamefully at fault when the good things of the Church are so unequally divided. An educated gentleman and scholar ought to be provided with necessaries for himself and family in decency and respectability, and not allowed to pine in the misery of want, and die in premature decay. Such a state of things, so prejudicial to the Church itself, makes reasonable men blush, while they hope for a reformation so evidently necessary to its stability.

The next attempt I made upon the genius and character of Irish spirits were the two friends, Richard Lalor Shiel and William Henry Curran. These two gentlemen were then living together in the same house in Dublin. The first, it may be remembered, was one of the most brilliant and eloquent men at the Irish Bar, and afterwards in the English Parliament—some time Master of the Mint—retiring, on account of his health, as Ambassador to Florence, where he died rather suddenly, having achieved a brilliant reputation by his genius as a poet, his eloquence as a speaker, and his wisdom as a statesman. At the time my drawing was done he was the successful author of *Evadne*, a tragedy, and other works, and I sketched him as a poet just as I found him in his study. Mr. Curran is still living, and continues to do honour to the Bar or the Bench of Ireland, of which he is one of the ornaments. He is the author of a very interesting life of his father, the Right Honourable J. P. Curran, who is said to have been 'the most celebrated wit that ever graced the Irish Bar.' It was delightful to witness the gentle and social friendship existing between these two men, with what kindness and sincerity they mutually asked and received advice on points of difficulty in their profession, and on what a generous footing they seemed with each other. They gave a dinner-party, to which I was invited in order to meet some of the merry spirits of the time; and the feast was graced by the sprightly humour and vivacity that was sure to characterise a reunion of intelligent Irishmen, most of whom were of celebrity or distinction. Sheridan Knowles being then in his native place was one of the invited. There was also Comerford, the famous miniature-painter, whose great hobby at this time happened to be the invention of the steam-engine ; and as he sat near to me at dinner his conversation, which was lively and vivacious, turned upon this the most extraordinary discovery of the period. He discussed his valves, pistons, wheels, and boilers, and in the midst of some general laugh of the wits of the table, his steam would explode, and he would look out of his engine-shop, as it were, like one waking and peering out of a dream, and ask ' What was that, I wonder?' and when I had repeated the cause of merriment, he would add his after-laugh to the roar that had excited his attention. Knowles was in great good-humour, and in a fine vein of conversational hilarity. Wit and mirthful intelligence, with touches of the racy Irish brogue, in imitation of well-known characters, enlivened the pleasantry that flowed in continuous streams of facetious waggery down both sides of the table.

Leaving the elegant entertainment that we had enjoyed so much at a late hour, my friend

Knowles seemed not quite satisfied that we should part for the night without having a little cozy conversation together; and for this end he invited me to join him in a treat, as he said, that could be had nowhere but in Dublin. Then seizing me by the arm, he led me to a well-known resort, where, entering by a glass door, I could not but express my delight and astonishment at the brilliant gaslights and the perspective of a reception-room that seemed at least half a mile long, with innumerable tables, most of which were occupied by guests engaged in the night's entertainment of feasting and drinking. Having taken our places at a table by ourselves, the author of *Virginius* rang the bell, and the ready waiter stood before him. ' Now, my good friend,' exclaimed the author, striking the table with theatrical effect (which startled the said waiter) ' it is thirteen years since I was in my own country, therefore treat us well; show to this English gentleman, my friend, what noble shell-fish you can boast of in Dublin; let us have the best you have in the house.' The waiter, all smiles and delight at such a complaisant countryman, replied in the richest brogue, 'An shure yer honor may dipind upon having the best that's to be had either in the house or in all Dublin city.' And here, at this new and novel feast we remained, enjoying ourselves, and beguiling the hours with sweet converse until morning, 'when daylight doth appear,' quite forgetting that we had previously been fed upon dainties in abundance, garnished and spiced with the 'feast of reason and the flow of soul,' that might have satisfied reasonable demands for one day, at least. But the air of Ireland is redolent of spree, fun, enjoyment, pleasure, wit, and humour; and lively repartee seems to be the food and relish of Irish existence. Bon-mots sparkle and beam in smiling faces. A beggar asks charity with a charming smile, and closes his grief in humorous lamentation. Knowles asked me if I was much annoyed by the Irish beggars? I answered 'No, I contrive to get rid of them generally by sometimes speaking in French, sometimes in a gibberish between German and French; and then they stop at once, and leave me gazing in mute disappointment, not because they have not succeeded in getting relieved, but because they cannot understand what I mean, and it goes beyond their wit to reply to it. Some would say to the others, " Ah ! he's foreign, and the likes of them niver have a rap to spare ; they only give us blarney." Yesterday, for instance, I accompanied Sir Arthur and Lady Clarke and their family to the " Strawberry-beds." The beggars crowded after us. Lady Clarke had my arm, and the rivals for charity were a teazing pest to me the whole way there ; but I hit upon a plan to send them behind to Sir Arthur, by telling them to go to papa, who carried the money. Of course they flew to him, clustered about him and his family, hung upon his flank, tormenting him with their cries, " For the love of God !" " Bliss yer honor, and all yer perty young ladies." " There's a beauty, dear ! do tell the gintleman to bestow one ha'penny upon a fatherless mother and her two infant childer." " Ah ! yer beautiful curls and yer killing eyes, young lady ! do help a poor unfortunate cripple, born so, and niver able to do anything barring asking for charity." " Sure, yer honor, honey, you'll bestow one ha'penny upon a starving family," &c. All this kind of solicitation was uttered in the raciest vein of persuasive eloquence ; but papa became annoyed, and complained that we in front ought to take some share of the honours of being thus courted in the streets, for he had given away all the "change" he had in his pocket. After our dessert of delicious strawberries, just plucked from the sloping banks where they grew in wonderful luxuriance, the enjoyment ended by a game of romps in the garden, an exciting and favourite amusement in this part of the world.

My friend Knowles and I occasionally met in society during the short time he remained in Dublin, which was very pleasant to me, as I was a stranger.

The next portrait I attempted was one of Comerford, and he was so gratified that in return for the compliment he made a small drawing of me, to show what he also could do with the port-crayon, gracefully telling me that he would keep his drawing in remembrance of the pleasure he had in sitting to me, and the honour of my acquaintance and friendship. Thus artistical courtesies were agreeably exchanged, and whenever we met I received the most cordial attention from this gentleman.

I was also fortunate enough to have the opportunity of making a characteristic drawing of Mr. Hamilton Rowan, a politician of the old school, and a 'patriot.' He was a scientific amateur, and sat to me in his laboratory, dressed as a student, and if he had let his beard grow, would have made an excellent alchymist for a Teniers or Rembrandt. As it was, his strongly marked features and distinctive character made a striking and remarkable portrait. Mr. Rowan brought his daughter to be introduced to me. She was tall and graceful, and as she advanced with a bewitching smile, I thought her one of the most beautiful women I had ever seen. She reminded me of Guido's 'Magdalene,' a style of beauty that would have been a rich treasure to a painter; and the observation was strikingly impressed upon my mind, What soul appears in the expression of these Irish women of high caste! What native elegance and grace! 'It is the mind that so informs the tenement of clay.' I observed the same feeling, grace, and sensitiveness of manners in Mr. O'Connell's daughters, who, when he sat to me for his portrait, which was early in the morning, before breakfast, came into his study, after walking in the Square, and saluted him, as was their usual custom. While thus sitting for my gratification, he employed his two amanuenses, — sharp fellows, — in writing down to his dictation, his 'opinions' upon two different and distinct law cases. Whilst the one wrote down the words at one side, he dictated to the other, and thus alternating, employed two quick pens at the same time, occasionally adjusting himself to my requirements, and courteously requesting me to correct him should he forget himself and be sitting in a wrong light or position. It was while he was thus engaged that his daughters came into the room to bestow their usual morning salutation. They both greeted their father with a grace and good-breeding truly beautiful and affecting to witness, and the affectionate smile of delight that spread over the features of this extraordinary man as he embraced the two slender figures of his children, awakened in me the wish that I could with propriety have seized the expression of rapturous love, and fixed it there in my drawing, instead of that character for bold unflinching eloquence for which he was remarkable, and which it was my duty to portray on the present occasion.

I made a drawing of Lord Chief Justice Bushe, characterised by a noble and appropriate seriousness, that promised to award due justice to every cause brought before him, without prejudice or favour.

I likewise took a characteristic portrait of Judge Torrens, called, as a lady told me, the handsome judge, I suppose the handsomest man of the Irish bench or bar at this time. His manners, like his features, were gentlemanly and refined, and in his intelligent eye beamed eloquence, soft and placid.

I had an opportunity of drawing my Lord Norbury, the punning judge, or the hanging judge, as he was sometimes called, from the circumstance of his being the greatest punster of the time, and that he had probably consigned to the hands of the hangman a greater number of unfortunate individuals than any other judge living or dead. Lord Norbury, as may be supposed, was quite a character, and enjoyed a reputation for humour and fun, even in the most grave and serious exigencies, his puns and bon-mots circulating freely in the gossip of the town and the newspapers of the day. His lordship invited me to dine with him,—there were five or six other gentlemen there. He placed me close to him, being deaf, and did his best to be complaisant and courteous to me as a stranger. He conversed about the fine arts, and punned about my chalks, my lines, head and tailpieces, at which everybody laughed, except the monstrously grave old butler standing behind his lordship's chair like a mute, doing nothing and saying nothing, but standing bolt-upright in grave pomp, directing occasionally by signs the other fellows who spun about the table. This old butler was as great an original as Lord Norbury, but a far more important person. His whole attention was concentrated upon his master, and they seemed both utterly unlike anybody else, and quite suited to each other, as if they had been born in one house, at the same time, and rocked in one cradle. Although in different spheres of existence, each occupied his position with originality and seeming satisfaction. I sketched the head of the master, and I wished I could have done the same with his servant; but an idea of the latter could only be given by presenting the whole figure, as, from the crown of his head to the silver buckles of his shoes, he was one masterpiece of eccentricity. His face and every feature were of the most crooked Irish type conceivable, every line 'out of drawing,' whilst the expression of assumed consequence was the most grotesque and ridiculous imaginable. The hair on his head was white as snow, carefully combed and arranged in plaits or cords, like dimity, from a point at the top, hanging like a large white tassel in thick threads, and cut in a uniform line all round his head; his eyes were like those of a fish, showing the white quite round the pupil, with a peculiar inhuman stare; the nose turned to one side, as if it had had a dab when it was modelled; the mouth was one straight line, like a cut or slit; and the fleshy, fatty muscles of his cheeks quivered upon the slightest movement or agitation. His voice, too, embraced the power and variety of the trombone and clarionet,—though it was only heard once on this occasion.

The dinner was excellent, and the wines, in great variety, were passed round in the quick spirit of the country. His lordship was facetious and merry, blowing out his cheeks and puffing, as he laughed and told his jokes in his peculiar way, setting the table on a roar. When he had proposed some health and finished his glass, the ancient butler moved from his statue-like position, and stooping with his mouth near his master's ear, shouted in the rich brogue of his country, at the top of his changeable voice, 'Your lordship has had enough wine.' The word 'enough' enunciated with such firm expression left his master no choice; and he with great felicity kept up the joyous hilarity with an empty glass, lifting it up and requesting us to drink the health of some favourite dignitary, saying, 'Now, gentlemen, fill your glasses; I beg to propose to you a loyal toast,' &c., which being done he would set down his glass with a hearty thump upon the table, as if he had in reality drunk the health that he had so cordially proposed; but his lordship never touched wine after the mandate so authoritatively given by his faithful Mentor, who, his important duties being terminated by this last warning, retired with 'measured steps and slow;' and as I glanced at his back, it was lucky that my Lord said something that gave me an opportunity for relieving myself of the risible excitement which his ridiculous figure produced. Liston could not have imagined anything more provocative of laughter. The coat! what a 'misfit!' it seemed to have been made for *the Irish giant;* and as he swayed from side to side in his gait, it showed every fold and wrinkle. His 'smalls' and his stockings seemed to me to form the large or small forms of laughing mouths—and his shoes, creak, creak, creaking! echoed the laughter. I did his lordship's mirth great justice, for I laughed most heartily and outright, without being able to contain myself within moderate bounds. And when I saw this 'broth of a boy' stop at the door, turn methodically round to the company to see that all was right, and with serious respect bow his head to his master, shuffle his feet and close the door upon himself, I perceived that the day's duty of an Irish butler of the old school was completed ; his office had been performed with satisfaction to himself, and I suppose to his noble master likewise. I should have liked to ask for a sitting from him for a sketch, had I not felt doubts as to how the question might have been understood, as he seemed so sensitive and punctilious a person. There is no doubt that both he and his forefathers for generations had been serving-men to the house of the Tollers from its foundation.

When old 'Square-toes' had retired, his Lordship observed to me, 'Your friend, Sir Arthur Clarke, is always gladly received wherever he goes, if he only takes that charming wife of his with him. She is his passport, sir. Although he is clever, and a good social little person, yet his fascinating better half takes precedence of him : such is the effect of beauty, talent, soul. These in superior degree would be the only ground for my hesitating about a handsome and clever wife. I should not like to be cut above by one of the other sex, to be overlooked, although she should be my own wife. I might feel pride, perhaps jealousy, that other men admired what was my own, still I should like to cut a caper above her, and keep her in her place.

'That Maturin, poor devil! is a moody dog; I never can raise a smile in him, and, I suppose, he never could laugh in his life, except perhaps it might be at that scarlet dame of Rome whom he hacks and tears at with such seriousness and power. Egad, gentlemen, that poor curate Maturin possesses enough genius to make two bishops, and yet they hardly allow him bread and cheese. Surely if he had generous food and a glass of good wine he would write all the better, his fancy and imagination would be in more healthy tone, and the world would be more felicitous to him. We should not be having those dreadful spectral visions that haunt his wild and starved genius. I often commiserate a man like him, of great capacity and intellectual endowment, who is placed in a situation where he cannot by his superior powers enforce preferment. It is lamentable to think of. There is no one knows what noble works might be produced under other and more favourable auspices. We will drink Mr. Maturin's health, if you please.

'There is young Curran, too, a sensible fellow and prudent; he, you know, is of a laughing stock, *Curran-t* wit flows in his veins, and I like him, loved his father and all his wit and fun, and many a laugh we have had together; his humour was the richest, and his stories were the best told of any joker I ever knew. Sir, it all came from him spontaneously, without, as it were, his knowing of it; and as we say of a poet, "he is born," so it was with my old friend Curran, wit was born in him. Life at the bar now is tame and flat, indeed, compared with what it was in my time; there used to be a set of "boys" then that would stick at nothing to carry on the game. See now, how serious we are become when the religio-political obtains. But, gentlemen, do not let me digress into state affairs, let us drink to the memory of Curran, the wittiest of the witty.'

A gentleman here began to tell something of Moore and *The Twopenny Post-bag;* but Lord Norbury stopped him by saying, 'I beg your pardon, Mr. ———, but I never wish to sympathise or even laugh with a Radical; do excuse me, therefore, for interrupting you; those Byrons,

Moores, Hunts, and such-like small beer, are all canting politicians, from some personal interest or personal pique; they are not indeed the patriots they would wish to be thought, no more than our Dan O'Connell is, and we all know what his patriotism is,—it's blarney.'

It is impossible for me to convey an idea of the drollery with which the great punster uttered the last Irish word, which he gave in the broadest Connemara—the mirthful lines about the angles of his mouth curling and twitching and pursing his laughing face—his eyes running over with the sportive fun natural to him, expressing far more than the words he had said, while he ended with a knowing nod to one of his friends opposite to him.   Thus this banquet was kept up to the end in hilarity and enjoyment.

A short time after this I met Lord Norbury riding down Sackville Street, and as I did not at first recognise him, I wondered what strange figure it could be, and thought surely this was the strangest specimen of horsemanship ever seen.   His round plump body was buttoned up tight, and seemed like a large cricket or football, the two short legs wagging, and spurring, and balancing this globular form upon the saddle, where he did not seem by any means to possess a safe 'seat,' if seat it could be called. No doubt the horse would be a safe one, otherwise I should have expected an easy 'spill.' The groom rode behind on a spirited animal, and carried his master's great-coat buckled round his waist. As his Lordship turned towards me I perceived him puffing and blowing out his fat round cheeks as if suffering from some internal spasmodic pains, his arms and legs in a constant action, working to get along faster than his Rosinante seemed inclined to go. My Lord lifted his hat and stopped me to ask if I would 'just do him the favour to show the Chancellor and his Lady the drawing I had made of his beautiful little favourite grand-daughter (I think she was) which I had done for him?' and with which he expressed himself mightily pleased.

Of course I went to the Chancellor's, where I saw the Lady, and showed her not only the drawing in question, but that of Lord Norbury and the others that I had done. The Lady expressed herself delighted, and commented freely upon the resemblance and characteristics of each. She said, ' You have not only obtained striking likenesses of these remarkable persons, but produced the character of their minds and the peculiar idiosyncracy of each. You have not flattered my friends with the smile of inanity so common in portraiture, and which I dislike extremely ; for grave men upon the bench, as judges for instance, ought to appear with the seriousness proper to their position, and the importance of their judicial functions. As for dear Maturin, it is the man himself, his mind, his mysterious gloom. He has just penned *Melmotte*, and taken away the warning wafer from his forehead, so that we may speak in his presence without the fear of disturbing his romantic imaginings. There is O'Connell, too. Does he not seem to " browbeat " a witness ? ay, and judge too ; how exactly you have hit the man and his character, fearless of God, man, and— may I say it ?—devil and priest. I like his talent, but I do not admire his principles, if he has any. Now here is the Chief Justice ; how capital ! He is a man of strict and impartial justice, severe, but searches for the true, the right, regardless of consequences. And there is my handsome friend Torrens; what an intelligent face and beautiful eye! Curran and Shiel too, all men of "mark and likelihood," of genius. Look at the author of *Evadne*; his eye is poetic, it beams with eloquence, and as his beautiful thoughts flit and shoot they are embodied in as splendid language as ever came from the lips of the Grecian orators. The man of genius is to be adored; his inspiration is divine. And now I turn to the delightful companion of my early years, Olivia, the charming Lady Clarke, whose bewitching smile, soft loving eyes, natural powers of mind and engaging accomplishments, captivate every heart. Oh! those dear days when we were both young, who could equal us at a game of romps, or beat us at sharp cutting wit or smart repartee? What fun we two have had together! Her gifted sister, Lady Morgan, you have not got; her Ladyship is from home. She is the brightest star we have in all Ireland. Indeed, she shines with a splendour unequalled here, as well in her works as in her conversation. Let me return to Lord Norbury, that dear old humourist! His likeness is one of the best, it is himself as he looks in his judicial robes.' And after politely thanking me for the treat I had afforded her, she wished me good morning. So this pleasant interview ended.

To Sir Arthur and Lady Clarke I have to express my sincere obligations for their constant hospitality and attentions during my sojourn in the Irish capital. A stranger, even with particular introductions could scarcely expect so much courtesy, and the expression of so much spontaneous friendship; and the hearty cordiality with which these attentions were accorded to so unpretending a person as myself, demand from me the expression, however feeble, of my sincere acknowledgment.

I made a finished drawing of Lady Clarke, the writer of that fund of Irish humour and inimitable comedy, *The Irishwoman*, as also a sketch of Sir Arthur Clarke, distinguished for his comprehensive work on *Bathing*, and other publications.

No one who came within the circle of Lady Olivia Clarke's society but must have been aware how varied and attractive were her talents and accomplishments. Her personal beauty, her graceful, courteous, and winning manners, with something of an arch but artless and original style, impressed every one admitted to her acquaintance in her favour. It is well known amongst her intimate friends that this lady possessed a remarkable and varied power of imitation and mimicry, and she would make up and sustain a character even for the whole of an evening — face, figure, costume, language, and peculiarity, so perfectly assumed that those of her own family, her own sister even, would not be able to discover the deception. Her Ladyship's taste for music, together with a finely modulated voice, rendered her a desirable acquisition to the social circle, an entertaining and interesting companion. She was frank, free, and unsophisticated, possessed of all the tact and elegance of an accomplished woman moving in the best society.

I had done the drawings of Sir Arthur and Lady Clarke, but not of Lady Morgan, who was in London at the time. She returned, however, in time to give me an opportunity of making my portrait of her.

I also made one of Mr. Carmichael, the eminent surgeon, and his brother, both professed phrenologists. These, with Sir Arthur and Lady Clarke, and a large number of ladies and gentlemen, made up a pic-nic party for me to the 'Dargle.' We filled several carriages with every kind of provision, wines, attendance, &c. We found already on the spot another party of wild Irish, merrymaking, dancing to music in a small columned temple upon the pinnacle of a high rock, by the side of a waterfall. Wild I may call them, for they were excited to the highest pitch of romantic enthusiasm. The servants soon spread tables upon temporary tressels, on a flat smooth piece of green turf at the foot of the waterfall, fine old trees flinging their branches over our heads as we sat at our repast, the murmuring sound of the waterfall by our side, and the merry music above. It was a scene for Watteau, Spencer, or Poussin. Surely, never was a place so favoured for poet or painter. The air itself, balmy, pure, and brilliant, was inspiring, and in the midst of the gaiety, the beauty, the luxuriance, and the poetry of Nature, I confess to being overcome by a fit of silent contemplation, and I fear I may have appeared but a stupid and lifeless companion.

The champagne went its rounds, but the landscape so charmed my mind as to render me insensible to its influence ; and I sometimes found myself standing alone, viewing from some changed point of sight the exquisite picture, my friends laughing and calling me to the viands. Such enjoyment of the soul so rarely falls to the lot of man that to drink deep of its inspiration is soothing and all-absorbing, and you insensibly give way to these heart-thrilling impressions, enthralled, as it were, by the beauty of the scene and the romantic combinations of nature. The first time I heard that classical artistic little melody of Moore's ' A Temple to Friend-ship,' was from the charming lips of Lady Clarke on this occasion ; and the feeling and expression she contrived to throw into the simple but elegant words struck me as the perfection of the ballad style. I beg to be excused for repeating the ballad here, for my memory of it as I heard it then is to me very pleasant. ' A thing of beauty is a joy for ever,' as my late dear friend Keats used to hymn to me.

A Temple to Friendship.

'A temple to Friendship,' said Laura enchanted,
'I'll build in this garden ; the thought is divine '—
Her temple was built, and she now only wanted
An image of Friendship to place on the shrine.
She flew to a sculptor, who set down before her
A Friendship, the fairest his art could invent,
But so cold and so dull, that the youthful adorer
Saw plainly this was not the idol she meant.

CHAPTER XI.

ON his return to Scotland, Mr. Bewick at once proceeded to Abbotsford, having been requested by Sir Walter Scott to pay him a second visit, which he thus describes.

———

On my arrival at Abbotsford, I found the house full of company, a constant succession of arrivals and departures; and the whole time I remained it had the appearance of an open house. Indeed, one day Miss Scott made an exclamation on the announcement of a new and unexpected arrival, 'Oh! dear, will this never end, Papa?'

Sir Walter quietly remarked, ' My dear, I am too glad to see any or all of my friends, let them come, " more the merrier ; ' " and he walked off smiling to meet his new guests. It was curious to observe the air of mystery and reserve, the curiosity everyone felt about something that could not be named—and never was named, that I heard, in the presence of any of the family. It was like being in an enchanted castle, where everyone that entered became conscious that, at the uttering of one word, some spell would be broken. That word was 'Waverley,'—and people went about peering and spying, as if some mysterious nook or corner, some secret window or turret-room, might reveal to them something of what they so ardently desired to know.

Sir John Malcolm came to me in the library one morning before breakfast—no one else was there—and *sotto voce* asked, ' Pray, Mr. Bewick, is there such a thing in your room as a Waverley Novel ? I have contrived to be in every room in this house except yours—even into Miss Scott's room ; and I have not found the semblance of *one* volume, and this is the only house

I gave been in, anywhere, that I have not met with them.' On my replying that there were none in my room, Sir John, with an expression of having made a shrewd discovery, said, 'Ha! is not this a strange circumstance? It goes with other reasons I have to convince me who is the real author. Sir Walter no doubt *is* the, "great unknown," and it will be proved so;' and he laughed. Sir John Malcolm, the author of a History of Persia, was a handsome, intelligent, and frank soldier, and when dressed for dinner, with his star and ribbon, looked the Governor-general to perfection. He informed Sir Walter that the King (George IV.), when creating him and his two brothers baronets on the same occasion, expressed himself well pleased with all of them, and gracefully complimented each with some particular allusion to his services.

Mr. and Mrs. Lockhart, and their beautiful little boy, were staying at Abbotsford at this time; and after dinner, when dessert was served, the little fellow was introduced. He always ran to Sir John and leaped upon his knee, the Baronet's star being the attraction to the child.

This ornament filled his eye, and dazzled his imagination. He would touch it and kiss it, then admire it and handle the ribbon, while he, sat and gazed at its brilliance in delight. The owner asked him, in kind and endearing tones, placing his hand upon his head, 'if he liked that beautiful star?' The child seized hold of his hand and looking up in infantile joy, replied, 'Oh, yes, Sir; it is beautiful.' 'Would you like to have one of them?' 'Indeed, I would; but when am I to get it?' 'Oh,' replied Sir Walter, 'they are to be had, they are growing upon the hedges—upon the trees—ready to be plucked.' The child looked at his grandpapa with an expression of incredulity, and Sir Walter added, 'You must try to get hold of one.' The boy shook his head, and looked over to his admiring and smiling Mamma with an inquiring expression, as if doubtful of the truth of such fruit growing on the hedges where he had not seen them. The father, too, deigned to smile, the only time I ever observed him relieve his fixed features from that impenetrable reserve that chilled as it repulsed you.

Sir Walter turned to me and said, 'Sir Joshua Reynolds seems to have been a great lover of children, and the children must have liked him too, if we may judge by their expression in his beautiful pictures of them. For my part, I do not know how it is; I like children very well, but they never come up to me, they always seem shy of me,—I can make nothing of them, they never seem to enjoy my company, and soon run away. With boys of a certain age, when I was a boy, I managed very well, for I was never at a loss for a good merry or wonderful story for them. With dogs, too, I do very well; they take to me, and I understand them, and can be friendly with them; some old acquaintances, too, I can even love, so to speak.' I expressed my surprise at this, as really Sir Walter Scott always seemed so playful, good-tempered, and mild, that one would have thought him the very person to have pleased children of all ages. Children, like some animals, seem to have an instinctive comprehension of human expression; and, although Sir Walter had a fine expressive smile in his eye, there might, perhaps, be something in his mouth not exactly corresponding with it, or equally assuring to infantile sensibilities. ' As for himself,' he said, ' he could never make out the reason of children being shy with him ; it had often occupied his thoughts, as he in truth was very fond of them. There was Garrick, he could make up his face, personate the frolics and peculiar antics of boys, even go through a game at marbles with them in the streets, and they did not make out that he was rather an *old* Boy until the game was over, and he stood up in his character of man.'

Sir John, like our distinguished host, was a capital story-teller, and would charm the whole household from tea to bed-time with long Persian stories,—told with infinite humour and varied expression, action, and tone of voice. He would begin with a short preliminary address, asking Lady Scott if there were any other persons in the house that might be likely to wish to hear his story, and that were not then present. It would be well to inform them that he was ' going to begin,' as there would be no possibility for him to repeat what he had to tell ; it was too long. He was then requested to wait a few minutes, and some of the party would run out and presently return with more eager listeners. One young lady, I remember, was brought from her sick-bed wrapt in blankets, and laid on the sofa. When all were collected, Sir Walter would take his lowly seat upon a footstool by the fireside, and, in silent delight, listen with watchful eagerness to the tales of another 'story-teller,' rubbing his hands and chuckling with delight, like a boy of twelve listening for the first time to the exciting narrative of *Robinson Crusoe*. No one enjoyed more than he did the propriety, skill, and easy manner with which Sir John excited every listener,—how he enchained their attention, raised their sympathy, or made them hold their sides with laughter. His varied expression and gesture were capital, and nothing was wanting but costume to have taken Sir Walter back to the olden time of Eastern story-tellers and paladins. The tales were divided into *miles*, and when a *mile* was reached the story-teller stopped to inquire if he might be allowed to rest there, or if it was wished he should continue another mile? All expressed their desire that he would be pleased to continue. Lady Scott in particular was in ecstasies, and paid Sir John a compliment, adding, 'Do go on, Sir John, if you please.' The stories were something in the vein of *The Cobbler of Bagdad*, and seemed capable of being spun out to any length by the invention of the story-teller. It was a fine entertainment, good as *Mathews at Home*. While at Abbotsford I made a drawing of Sir John Malcolm, and no one can look upon the picture without remarking his dignified and soldierly bearing.

Mons. Alexandre, the French ventriloquist, came while I was there. He began his wonderful imitations by setting to work to plane the French polished dining-tables. The attitude, the action, the noise, the screeches and hitches at knots, throwing off the shavings with his left hand, were all so perfect that Lady Scott screamed in alarm, 'Oh! my dining-table, —you are spoiling my beautiful table, it will never be got bright again,' &c. Sir Walter pacified her by saying, as he walked up to her, 'It is only imitation, my dear; it is only make-believe, he will not hurt the table.' She replied, 'Impossible, what! don't I hear the shavings come off and drop down?' Alexandre worked away, producing all the peculiar noises, and the sound of the checks caused by the different grains and knots of wood that the instrument appeared to cut through—dashing off the perspiration occasionally from his forehead, and imitating the manners and tricks of cabinet-makers at their work, until Lady Scott must convince herself that no harm was done to her table, by going to examine and feel the polish! exclaiming, 'Is it possible *dat* you have not cut the table? I cannot believe! dat is wonderful! it is not cut!' and everybody laughed.

Here too was my Lord Minto, the head of the house of Elliott, with his chaplain or secretary, and servant. His lordship was a short, unassuming person, dark and sallow, very unpretending, dressed in a plain suit of black, with a white neck-cloth in the most primitive tie. His chaplain, too, was a primitive character,—saturnine, and rather disposed to be severe upon whatever he deemed of modern innovation. He spoke little, and what he did say was sententious, and not to be questioned. His black hair, straight and shining, was combed down upon his forehead, and then cut in a formal line, as if by the edge of a barber's bason. My Lord's servant, too, was a rare character, also dressed in black, with shoulder-knots. He was present with other men in livery to wait at dinner, and contrived to place himself as far from his master, and as near to Sir Walter, as he could; and there he stood, with his napkin under his arm, stock-still; never changed a plate the whole time, but entranced by the humour of the host —and Sir Walter was unusually vivacious and jocose—he tittered and shook his sides, enjoying all the conversation that was going on, and was evidently neither born nor bred a serving-man. Sir Walter cast a quiet side-glance at this original when he heard the unusual tittering by his side. I happened to catch his eye at this moment, and he looked to me as much as to say, 'This novelty now deserves sketching.' The young man seemed so riveted to the spot, that it appeared as though he would have to be handed out of the room, with the last plate, by some of his fellows when dinner was over.   He was absent enough to have been a great genius.

The quiet simplicity of manner, and the absence of showy qualities in Lord Minto, I liked extremely.   I had the privilege of conversing with him for a short time, and found him, though in some respects peculiar, a very well-informed man.   Our talk was partly about the principal artists of the day, and the more remarkable works which they had produced.

Sir Walter asked me if I had seen his own room.   I said I had not.   'Oh, then step this way.'   I followed into his private study, and was greeted by the slight growl of a large dog lying on the hearth-rug.   'Oh, poor Nimrod—he knows you are an artist—for ever since his likeness was taken, he carefully runs away from all the artist race.   Poor fellow ! well, go away then, there ;'—and he shut the door, and I was in the *sanctum sanctorum* of the all-creating author of *Waverley*.   The room was plainly furnished, with a table and a couple of chairs, and bookshelves all round, full of books *in use*, not in ornamental bindings like those in the large library.

Wilkie came the next morning and prepared for a sitting. I had previously obtained Sir Walter's consent to make a drawing. Wilkie arranged his sitter and his easel as he wished, and placed Sir Walter in a broad light, in front of a large window, without closing up any part of it, as he said he wanted little shadow on the face, for he had in his mind the picture of Goldsmith by Reynolds, and thought there was a great resemblance between the two authors. This rather surprised me, as I expected that such a man as Wilkie would have struck out something of his own—an original impression of the individual character, rather than have followed or adopted anything, even from Reynolds.

Sir Walter sat in his usual costume, green coat, yellowish waistcoat, and black neckcloth; his feet one over the other, with his walking-stick between his legs, both hands resting on the top of it (this stick was a keepsake given to him by his friend, Mungo Park, when they last parted). Sir Walter seemed well practised at sitting for his portrait, and, although conversing all the time, contrived to keep his head in one position. The house was full of company, and they all crowded to the library to witness the sitting. Wilkie seemed annoyed by the movement and conversation going on. He bit his lip and fidgeted about uneasily, and had not advanced very much at the end of the sitting. My drawing was life-size, and lucky it was for me that I had overcome the nervousness of working in a crowd, having drawn a good deal in the British Museum when there were hundreds of gaping spectators. The visitors, therefore, did not annoy me in the least, and I worked away as rapidly as possible. The great painter, hearing some lady say my drawing was very like, came to see how I got on, and said, 'Ah, very like indeed!' after which everybody exclaimed, 'Yes, indeed, Sir Walter himself!' The 'sitting' ended, Sir Walter explained that he could not sit more at that time, being engaged next day with the Duke of Buccleugh to a greyhound-course, but he would be glad to give Wilkie sittings in London when he came there, and would let me finish my sketch in Edinburgh. I was called away, however, to other 'scenes,' and my drawing remains in my possession exactly in the state it was.

When I left Abbotsford I showed Sir Walter my Dublin treasures ; among others the drawing of Maturin. Sir Walter was very much struck with it, and nervously said, 'Ah ! poor Maturin, it is just the man I should take for the writer of *Melmoth* and other heart-stirring works ; yes, Sir, he is a true genius.' His eyes then filled with tears, and he said to me in a low voice: 'My heart bled for him. Yes, Sir, a man with such talent, with a large family to educate, ought not to be so neglected, and only allowed a small pittance to maintain them all. I know from a friend the great difficulties to which he is put ; my eye dropped a tear when I was told of them. I soothed my feelings by sending him an enclosure for sixty pounds, at the same time taking care not to let him know whence it came.' This was a noble trait of a generous, warm heart, and I felt I could have embraced Sir Walter for it.

A few mornings after this conversation I received a note from Mrs. Maturin informing me in the most affectionate and touching language of the death of her husband, and begging me to let her have the drawing I had made but a short time before of him, it being the most faithful and characteristic likeness ever made of him. I handed the note to Sir Walter, who was very much affected and said, ' Well, Sir, you cannot refuse the poor lady this small comfort.' I readily made a copy, and sent it to her; Sir Walter enclosing a five-pound note in the letter I sent in answer to Mrs. Maturin.

CHAPTER XII.

AFTER leaving the breakfast-table we sauntered on to the lawn to look for the best view of the house to sketch, and Sir Walter pointed out a part which he said always pleased him. As we strolled on, he asked me 'if I had ever met his friend Hogg in Edinburgh?' I said, 'No, Sir, but I should like to see him very much;' to which he replied, 'Yes, and sketch him, too,' and shaking my hand, said, 'I will send Mr. Gordon to you. He will show you the stables, and there you will find my grey pony, on which I go greyhound-coursing. Take him, he will find the way for you; he is a most sagacious creature.' When Mr. Gordon and I arrived at the stables the pony was gone, some one had preceded me, and I found I must walk. The morning was fine, the air clear and bracing, and everything looked cheerful. So, nothing daunted, I set off accompanied by Mr. Gordon, who walked a little way with me and kindly showed me the road to the Ettrick hills. After a short time we parted, he to Abbotsford, I to the Ettrick Shepherd.

After many turns and passing through tracts of moss and heather, I found my way into pastures filled with Cheviot sheep, the sight of which told me I must be drawing near to this Border bard of mirth and song; and at nightfall, by a clear moon, I espied a house on the side of a hill, brilliantly lit up. This was a cheering sight to me. I thought here I shall find my host or learn what distance I am from his cottage. Accordingly I knocked at the door, and it was opened by a real 'Highland Mary.' I asked in the plainest way I could if Mr. Hogg lived there. 'Mister wha did ye say, Sir?' 'Mr. Hogg; if he lives here, tell him I come from Abbotsford.' With this the host, hearing a parley and the sound of 'Abbotsford,' came forward and very heartily invited me in. On my telling him my name, and giving him the password 'Abbotsford,' he led me into his parlour, filled with company and smelling of whisky toddy (no bad thing after a long walk in the clear mountain air). He invited me to partake of their Highland fare, and I was surprised when a young gentleman stepped forward, and, offering me his hand, said, 'You do not remember me, Mr. Bewick?' I stared in amazement on hearing my name and such a friendly greeting. 'I see,' he continued, 'you do not remember me. I saw you in Belfast at the house of my father, Dr. Gray; and this is my sister;' and taking me to Mrs. Hogg, he introduced me to her. I was soon initiated into the jollity of the party, for this was a Christmas party, and a right merry one.

After his friends had left, Mr. Hogg, anxious to show me attention, drew his chair near me, saying, 'Now, Mr. Bewick, what have they going on at Abbotsford?—full of company, I suppose, eh? My friend Walter is a fine fellow, and a clever one too. How well he carries on the secret of those Waverley novels! I dinna think ony but his self could manage it.' I looked at him with surprise, and said, 'So you really think Sir Walter the author?' 'Yes,' he replied, 'I dinna ken any other body could write them. I'll tell ye a good joke I put upon him. I have these same Waverley novels, ye ken, placed in my library, and I invited Sir Walter to come and see some of my rhymes. A thought had come o'er me that I would try him by altering the word *Scotch Novels* to *Scott's Novels*. Well, when Sir Walter came, I took him into my library, and he, in his usual way, was always looking to see what I had new. I went round with him and keepit a keen look-out. Coming to the novels, he stopped quite still, read the name two or three times, and then turning to me with a very knowing look said, " Jamie, your binder has made a mistake here?" " No mistake at all, Sir Walter;" and he let it pass, as he could not deny the truth. I had on the outside of the volumes *Scott's Novels*.' Hogg laughed one of his boisterous laughs, crying, 'I tricked him that time.'

Next day I asked Mr. Hogg to sit for a sketch of his head; and when I had done it, I asked him to write his autograph at the bottom, which he did, but immediately said, 'But this is nothing of an autograph; I will give you a better;' and he then produced the rough draft of his song, with the note attached to it.

CAMERON'S WELCOME HAME.

AIR.—'*Rattling Roaring Willie.*'

Oh, strike your harp, my Mary,
    Its loudest, liveliest key,
And join the sounding correi
    In its wild melody;
For burn, an' breeze, an' billow,
    Their sangs are a' the same,
And every waving willow
    Sounds 'Cameron's welcome hame.'

Oh, list yon thrush, my Mary,
    That warbles on the pine,
Methinks her strain so airy
    Accords in joy wi' thine;
The lark that soars to heaven,
    The sea-bird on the faem,
Are singing frae morn to even,
    'Brave Cameron's welcome hame.'

D'ye mind, my ain dear Mary,
    When ye sat on my knee,
Till bonny Auchnacarry*
    Brought tears to your young ee?

---

* The name of Lochiel's Castle, the wildest in Christendom. I saw it in blackness and ashes before a stone of the new building was laid. Many of the venerable old trees

The flame was red, red glaring,
  And marr'd the beams o' day,
And aye ye cried despairing,
  ‘ Our hame's now gane for aye.’

I said, my ain wee Mary,
  D'ye see yon cloud sae dun,
That sails aboon the carrey
  And hides the weary sun?
Beyond yon cloud so dreary,
  Beyond and far within,
There's ane, my dear wee Mary,
  That sees this deadly sin.

He sees this ruefu' reavery,
  The rage o' dastard knave,
He saw our deeds of bravery,
  And He'll reward the brave.
Though a' is lost but honour,
  And nought stood round but Death,
I still had hopes that Heaven
  Would right poor Scotia's skaith.

The day is dawned in heaven,
  For which we a' thought lang;
The good, the just is given,
  That kens the right frae wrang.
My ain dear Auchnacarry,
  I hae thought lang for thee!
Oh, sing to your harp, dear Mary,
  And sound its bonniest key.

---

in the avenues were also standing, scathed and half consumed
with fire, as memorials of the horrid barbarity of the conquering army.

When I was prepared to depart after making a drawing of him, the Shepherd, desirous to show me some particular attention, mounted me upon one of his very high horses, upon an old worn saddle. The horse was to be left at a certain friend's house on the road, who would return it to its owner. By the time (ay, long before) I had come to this friend's, I was literally skinned, for the saddle was a very oddly-made one, a fine antique of the good old times. There was a buckle here, a projecting nob or strap there, and the leather was worn through everywhere, so that the edges cut me like knives; and whenever my body or limbs touched this piece of antiquity, it showed me that I had skin on those parts, although I was told by a grave philosopher that I was 'going through the world without skin at all.'* The motion of the horse was such that I am sure that of the camel must be a fine ambling walk in comparison. A horse-dealer would not have called it *action*, for it was the oddest jog up and down, and might have rocked Hogg's infant, with the nursery song, 'Here he goes up,

* Mr. Bewick had a peculiarly fine skin.

up, up, and there he goes down, down, down,'
&c. I could not have refused the kind offer of
the Shepherd, had I even known of the extraordinary pace of his Rosinante and the sad effects
of these antique saddles, for he really appeared
so delighted to mount me, that I leaped up upon
this high-backed animal with that ready consent which animates you when you know you
are doing something to gratify a friend.

In the evening Sir Walter was anxious to
see my drawing, and hear an account of my visit
to his Border friend. He was delighted with
the drawing, and laughed heartily at the likeness, exclaiming, 'Just the man, Sir. The very
man.'

Shortly afterwards my visit drew to an end;
but on my departure for Edinburgh Sir Walter
asked me to step with him into his library, when
he presented me with a note, saying, 'There,
Mr. Bewick, that is an introduction to my friend
Lord Jeffrey, the Arch-critic and Lord of the
Session; show him the drawing you have made
of me.' For this mark of attention, I tendered
him my sincere thanks.

On arriving in Edinburgh I waited upon

his lordship, and after talking of Abbotsford and Sir Walter, I took the opportunity of showing the drawing I had made of the latter. Jeffrey, after looking at it, said, ' Yes, Mr. Bewick, you have caught the happy, good-natured smile in his eye, and the benevolent contour of his head; I hope you will be favoured with another sitting to finish the mouth a little more. I consider this a difficult feature in Sir Walter's face, but I think it a good likeness.' After these remarks I took the opportunity of asking him to allow me a little of his valuable time, that I might make a similar drawing of himself. After a little consideration and counting his engagements, he told me, if I would come to breakfast with him next morning, he would give me an hour for the first sitting, and the same time the morning following. I thanked him, and told him I should not require more than two sittings. ' Is it possible, Mr. Bewick,' he said, ' that you can make a finished drawing in so short a time ? ' I then took my leave, breakfasted with him the following morning, and had the first sitting. His expression, vivacious and volatile, required to be caught on the instant, as it vanished in the next; but I was fortunate enough to catch it, and so was able to give a striking likeness of the shrewdest critic and one of the most eloquent men of his day.

When I was in Edinburgh in 1824, Wilkie came there out of health and in great anxiety. I called upon him, and saw him in his bedroom. He was rather dull and out of spirits, but seemed in his cool way glad to see me. Of course Haydon's recent misfortunes seemed to hang, as it were, between us, and there was some hesitation on both sides in beginning the subject. He looked as if he was conjecturing how I stood towards my late master, and what were my feelings with respect to him. After staring for some time in blank suspense, he muttered in a tone of seemingly settled conviction, ' After all, Mr. Bewick, *selfishness* is the *best*.'* I made no reply, and he added earnestly, drawing a long breath, ' You see, Haydon ought to have entered the Academy. Ay, he ought to have gone in, —he would have been a great acquisition; what a Professor of Painting he would have made! what powerful lectures we might have had!

* It must be remembered that Wilkie at this time was suffering from misfortune, anxiety, and disappointment.

how the school of painting would have been extended and improved! But then, ha! he must have had all his own way, or we might have had poor Barry over again, and that would never have done in our days,—no, no. However, we might hope for better things, for he has great tact. I asked him if he thought Haydon was justified in his complaints of the treatment he received from the Academy about 'Dentatus?' He replied, 'Oh, yes! yes, he was ill-used—badly treated in that matter, but he should never have heeded,—passed it by, and got in. He might then have pursued a deep scheme of retaliation, if he had liked, upon the very parties who behaved so shamefully on that occasion; for he has vast powers, stores of varied acquirements, and a command of language that none in the Academy at present can combat with. Besides a career of success alone is the best answer to make, both to enemies and to men who are envious of superior powers. Success gives a wonderful stimulus to man's natural powers, and re-assures, as it were, the efforts of genius; whilst trouble and misfortune tend to unnerve a man, and damp the ardour necessary to carry him on to great results. But you see, Mr.

Bewick, I am myself of the Academy, and it is a rule that "birds are not to foul in their own nests," so, if you please, we will change the subject.' Then he added with decision, ' Haydon has great power in his art; there is nothing in our times to compare with parts of his "Judgment of Solomon,"—that is truly a great work,—well gone through in all its parts,—nothing slighted, nothing little, and it combines tenderness and delicacy of feeling with real power over his materials and his art. Ah, it is grand! with affecting sentiment, and would have done honour to Rome or Venice. But large historical pictures, such as Haydon's, have this disadvantage, — that they are beyond the scale of private purchase; those of the size of Martin's are more readily disposed of. You see Mr. Martin has always contrived to make his pictures profitable, either by sale, by exhibition, or by engraving them.'

' Yes, but Mr. Haydon could not engrave his pictures himself, and they were attended with great expenses compared with Mr. Martin's. You are aware what the expense of models alone will be for a picture like " Christ's Triumphal Entry in Jerusalem," and Mr. Martin told me that he never had a model in his life for any picture. Consequently that was an expense he was saved in the execution of his works. Haydon was, so to speak, reckless in this part of the business, and would pay exorbitant sums for some of the models for his heads. For instance, the Jews screwed out of him whatever they demanded; and even then he was obliged to cover up the figure of Christ, otherwise they refused to sit to him at any price. He would pick up a beggar in the street, and for fear of losing him would bring him home in a coach. Of course his own man, Salmon, sat for the figure; then there were draperies, armour, &c. The female figure—hands, feet, and so forth—all costly, for he did not paint without both drawing and studying every part of his picture first. Every nostril, every finger-nail, will be found to be a complete study.'

'Ah! yes,' returned Wilkie, 'models are expensive, and I am surprised Martin can do without them. It is so much saved in the expense, to be sure, but his figures are wanting in nature and variety; and his works are a kind of scenic painting only; for if one's imagination is surprised by perspective infinity, by repeated objects fading away, as it were, to distant no-thingness, by mountain upon mountain, and sky and mountain again, and lo ! a fainter bit of sky, and fainter bit of mountain above those again, why, it becomes the romance of painting, and needs no models. It is totally imaginary, and has nothing in common with natural objects. Give Martin a thousand pounds, and he could not paint a great toe the size of life. He wants no models like Fuseli, Nature would put him out.'

'Haydon was six years in bringing out his picture of " Christ Riding into Jerusalem," and he had accumulated such a weight of debt upon him, that although he cleared £3000 by the exhibition, yet its not being sold left him still in debt, and by the time he brought out his next picture, his " Lazarus," the cost of that work, and the precipitate conduct of one of his creditors, and he a pupil of his own, com-pletely ruined him. The works are not sold, and have been seized for debt, while he himself is thrown into the Bench — a loss and a disgrace he will never be able to recover.'

'If you paint pictures of a certain size, and send them to the Academy, they will be sure to get good places, and probably sell. Size and merit command a good place.' Then gazing through the window, and with a long-drawn desponding sigh he muttered, 'Pity—what a pity!'

We were both lugubrious enough, but I enlivened him a good deal by showing him the drawing, life-size, of the beautiful Lady Olivia Clarke, that I had done a few days before in Dublin. He said, 'What a charming face! and the dress-bonnet, with black and white pendent feathers clustering and drooping about her head, are graceful in the extreme.' He asked 'who she was, the pretty creature?' and I told him her name, informing him also that she was a writer of comedies, a sister of Lady Morgan, and a fascinating, bewitching person, possessing the power of mimicry to such perfection that she was able to deceive her own family and most intimate friends by personating well-known female characters, which she would sustain during an evening without being discovered or suspected, and that I had heard her sing her own compositions with great naïveté, grace, and expression.

I then put before him another head of

beauty. 'Ha! who is that handsome creature?' he asked. 'What an eye!—what a
beautifully-sculptured nostril!—what elevated,
noble expression, full of the fire, the soul of
genius!—and what a form!—what a bust!' I
told him that she was a niece of my Lord Mont-
eagle, and a writer of novels, and that it was to
the kindness of the venerable Mrs. Grant of
Laggan that I was indebted for the privilege of
enriching my portfolio with this fine head. He
seemed quite cheered by the presence of the two
Irish beauties, so different in style and character.
His eye sparkled and lighted up, but no one ever
saw him really warmed. Our interview closed,
and I did not see Wilkie again for some short
time, until we met unexpectedly at Abbotsford.
He was visiting Sir Adam Ferguson close by,
and I was making my second visit to Sir Walter
Scott. It was on this occasion that Wilkie
began his small oil portrait of Sir Walter, on
panel, about two feet long.

CHAPTER XIII.

SCOTLAND had been a great boon to Mr. Bewick at a very critical period of his life, but while he was there his income barely covered his expenditure, and he had conceived an intense desire to visit Italy, that he might see and study the works of the great masters of that country. In 1824–5 he returned to Darlington, and having now a considerable local reputation, he easily obtained commissions, and began to see his way to the realization of his desires. At this time he married the amiable lady whose name will henceforth appear constantly in his correspondence as the recipient of his letters or as his beloved companion. It was her earnest desire that these letters and autobiographic sketches should be given to the world as the fittest monument of the husband she survived hardly four years, and whom she loved and honoured after he had passed away, as she had loved, honoured, and tended him during the forty years of their happy union.

Sir Thomas Lawrence, President of the Royal Academy, had conceived the idea of illustrating his Presidency by presenting to the School of the Royal Academy a series of full-sized copies in oil, of Michael Angelo's Prophets and Sibyls in the Sistine Chapel at Rome; and hearing of Mr. Bewick's great skill as a copyist, and of his earnest desire to visit Italy, he offered him one hundred guineas for a large copy of the Delphic Sibyl in the Sistine Chapel. The artist, seeing in this offer a means of realizing his wish to study the great works of Italian art in Rome, went immediately to London to see Sir Thomas Lawrence. All seemed favourable to his wishes. At his own request his commission was increased, and leaving his young wife with the mother he so tenderly loved, he left his native place to visit that land of art whose shrines are the goal of every artist's pilgrimage.

In Italy he had the happiness of again meeting his friend Sir David Wilkie, but the story of his life and experience in that country will best be told by the letters he addressed to his wife. From this correspondence the reader will perceive how conscientiously Mr. Bewick discharged this new commission as well as every other duty that he undertook. He prepared himself for the study of Italian art, and for the execution of the task on which he was specially sent, by rendering himself familiar with everything about Italy, by surrounding himself, so to speak, with an Italian atmosphere. He studied the language, he read accounts of the country, he made himself familiar with the manners and customs of the people, and he pored over the maps which delineated the physical features of the peninsula.

A voyage to Italy was in those days a much more lengthened and formidable task than it is now when railways take us over the Alps into the very bowels of the land. By all but the most wealthy the journey had to be undertaken by sea, and the voyage was made in a sailing vessel, generally by no means remarkable for speed or comfort. Bewick was accompanied by a young gentleman named Le Mesurier, and on joining the vessel in which he was to sail, he was happy to learn that the captain and pilot were both natives of Newcastle or Sunderland.

Mr. Bewick sailed in a small sloop of 150 tons, crossing the Bay of Biscay, passing through the Straits of Gibraltar, going along the coast of Spain and Portugal, and running the risk of being made prisoner by some Barbary pirates, a danger to which he laughingly alludes, but which was often attended with serious consequences in those days.

London, June 21st, 1826.

MY DEAREST BESS,—I write to tell you how I am going on. My time has been occupied principally in seeing the sights (as they are called) of London—or rather that part of them named exhibitions. The exhibition of Somerset House is the first to be spoken of, not from its superior claims on the score of merit, but because it is the most crowded both with pictures and with people, and is little less than a lounge for all sorts of gaiety. In this exhibition there are more bad pictures than good ones, and it becomes really tiresome to search out the few which are worthy of notice, and the only relief a man has in such a case is to let his eyes drop upon a natural beauty close by him. This is certainly a relief from the disgust excited by a bad picture of an ugly woman or disagreeable old man.

The most striking portrait in the collection is that of Mr. Canning, by Sir Thomas Lawrence. There is one of the King (by whom I don't know). That is wretched; the sign over Mr. Scott's door is as well painted, and more kingly in appearance. It offers a striking contrast to the masterly work of Canning. Mr. Haydon has two pictures in this exhibition, neither of them very good. I was disappointed in them. Mr. Wilkie is at Venice, and has nothing. The best landscape, or what comes nearest to pleasing nature, is by a Mr. Constable. The great Turner has two. Neither is to my taste, but still they are grand. Mr. Briggs, a relation of

Mr. F. Smith, has two of the best historical pictures, and a Mr. Etty one of the Choice of Paris, the best of that class. Mr. Calcott, Mr. Collins, and Mr. Mulready have good pictures. I will not tire you, however, with a catalogue of what you have not seen, but go to another exhibition, which was more select, and of course more complete and gratifying. I mean the exhibition of pictures entirely in water-colours. Here there is *nothing* to offend either judgment or taste, and you leave the room delighted. It is pleasing to observe how Mr. Robson shines; he has some beautiful drawings of lake and mountain scenery. The next exhibition is the British Institution, where His Majesty has allowed his collection to be placed for a short time. There are pictures of the very first class, by old masters, Titian, Rembrandt, Teniers, Cuyp, Reynolds, &c., &c. I happened to go at the fashionable hour on the second day. The company were all gay and fashionable, and a crowd of carriages and servants was waiting in the street. I next visited the interior of St. Paul's Cathedral, ascended as high as the top of the dome, passing through the Whispering Gallery, where the closing of a door sounds as loud as the report of a gun. We were so tired by climbing so many stairs that we did not see the Great Bell, the bell that is only sounded at the death of any of the Royal Family, when its tremendous bass voice is heard all over the city. St. Peter's at Rome is one-third larger than St. Paul's. The Parliament House I also visited. This morning there was a grand requiem sung to the memory of one of the Canons at the Catholic Chapel. The musical composer, Von Weber, Braham, Miss Stephens, and all the principal singers, joined. The music at the Catholic Chapel was very fine, but the ceremony altogether was not so imposing or so grand as I expected, and I propose to myself the pleasure of hearing and seeing much more splendid Catholic ceremonies on the Continent. Kindest remembrance to all friends, and believe me truly,

Your faithful

W. BEWICK.

London, June 29th, 1826.

MY DEAR BESS,—I have written two letters to you since the one I sent by post, intending to send them by Mr. Sams. His parcels go by sea, and therefore I send this by post.

I have been a good deal with Mr. Bandinel, who is extremely kind in giving me letters of introduction to Lord Burghersh, our consul at Florence, and also to the consul at Naples, with other persons of consequence on the Continent. He takes great interest in me, and goes with me here and there to make inquiries, &c. I dine with him to-day, and after dinner we intend to go on the water in a boat. He takes great delight in rowing, and particularly in passing other boats, which he does with great rapidity, his boat being so light and well shaped. I have had one excursion with him, and it was delightful. A summer's evening sail up the Thames is one of those treats that can only be appreciated by those who have enjoyed it, and which I purpose myself the felicity some time, ere long, of giving you, as I intend you to meet me in London on my return. Indeed, whenever I see anything curious, or that gives me pleasure, I always wish you were with me; and I only seem to enjoy it half without you. However, we must hope for the future.

I breakfasted this morning with Sir Thomas Lawrence, who has been kind enough to give me a commission to execute for him in Rome, and likewise begs of me to write from that city about an extensive work that he has long wished to have done, and which he will propose to the Academy in London. Sir Thomas will give me a letter to obtain easy accommodation for this purpose in the place where those fine things are. I dare say you will all feel gratified with this unexpected show of kindness from Sir Thomas Lawrence, considering the situation in which my connexion with Haydon has placed me with the body of the Royal Academy, of which Sir Thomas is President; and I must observe it augurs very well, and is no doubt promising. 'It is a good thing to have a friend at court.'

Tell my mother that Sir Thomas had written an answer to my letter, but for some reason or other did not send it. He gave it to me this morning, saying, 'I would find that he had not been so negligent or uninterested about me as I might think.' The letter is curious, and of course, I must preserve it.

I have just seen Dr. Birkbeck, who, according to his usual benignity, is extremely kind, and gives me an introduction to Prince somebody, whose name I do not remember. I shall see him on Sunday morning, and if an opportunity offers, will speak to him about Bob. The Doctor is so engaged in his profession, that it is difficult to speak with him. I waited an hour this morning, with a number of other visitors, before I could see him. Dr. Birkbeck says that he saw Jonathan Backhouse here, and that he told him I was settled at Darlington, practising my profession. Strange thing that he should tell him about me, and not even call to see me, all the time I was at Darlington; but Dr. B. says 'they are curious.' Give my best love to all. I think I shall set off from London about Monday first. I have seen George Harrison. He is dressed in tip-top fashion, and has a Chancery suit pending with George Allen for property belonging to his mother. He does not seem to have anything else to do.

Ever yours truly,
Wm. Bewick.

The two letters that I mentioned, I will enclose in Mr. Sams' parcel by sea.

The weather here is extremely sultry and
oppressive.   What will it be in Italy ?

London, July 2nd, 1826.

MY DEAREST BESS,—I have just been on
board of ship with my companion, a young gentleman, a son of Mr. Le Mesurier, late Rector
of Haughton-le-Skerne, who is going as far as
Rome with me. We have determined upon going
by sea, it being the most pleasant at this time of
year, as also cheaper and less troublesome. The
vessel is quite new, this being her first voyage
to the Mediterranean. She is made for fast sailing, and has certainly the best accommodation
I have seen for passengers,—a beautiful large
cabin, with only two berths in it, one at each
side, like couches, with moreen hangings round
them. We are provided with food, and porter,
beer, and spirits, for the sum of forty guineas
for two. They usually charge twenty-five to
thirty guineas for one person; so that this is
thought very cheap. The passage is calculated
to be about a month or six weeks, but we have

been told this morning that thirty days will be the extent—as far as Genoa. After stopping a short time at Genoa, we go to Leghorn, where I intend to buy myself a straw hat ; from Leghorn we go to Rome ; and from thence it is my intention to proceed at some time or other to Naples, for which place I have letters of introduction. Should you wish to write before you hear from me, you can direct to me at Messrs. Freeborn, Smith, and Co., Rome, where I shall get letters on my arrival. Mr. Le Mesurier is a young man just from Oxford. His going with me is quite accidental, and a hurried journey, as he knew nothing about it when he left Oxford. On Friday last he came to London, and his uncle persuaded him to go with me. He is quite a young man of fashion, and about twenty. I intend to write to you from Genoa or Leghorn, and tell you all that seems strange and amusing. I have had an interview with Mr. Hamilton, late of the Foreign Office, and late Consul at Naples ; he gives me letters to Sir Wm. Gell at Naples, and others there. Mr. Bandinel, who is now Under-Secretary of State at the Foreign Office, gives me permission to send my letters to him, for any of my friends in this country. There is another gentleman who is very anxious to go to Italy with me, and will, he says, follow me in a fortnight. The name of the vessel that I go by is the *Columbian Packet*, Captain Saddler. Mr. Bandinel's address is James Bandinel, Esq., Foreign Office, London; should you wish at any time to apply to him for any information or business that I may write about.

On Board the Columbian Packet.

July 7th, Friday.—We are to be in the Downs this day, and the pilot will take this letter on shore for the post-office. I am looking at maps, learning Italian, and reading about the country. My father will see in his geography the long voyage we are taking. We expect to see Spain and the coast of Portugal, through the Straits of Gibraltar, and crossing the Bay of Biscay we hope to see the scene where the famous and ever-memorable battle of Trafalgar was fought. Our Captain and Pilot are both from Sunderland or Newcastle, and there is one of the owners on board who comes from the county of Durham; so that on the first day we dined five persons all from the same or adjoining counties. We came on board on Tuesday Mr. Bandinel has given me a Bible and a Shakspeare. Young Le Mesurier is fond of poetry—Lord Byron, &c. &c. ; I find him a very good companion. We were on shore at Gravesend yesterday, getting fowls, pickles, gin, &c. Gravesend is a very poor place, the streets are narrow and dirty, and the shops are like those of a village, except the spirit-shops, which seem to thrive best. The women are anything but pretty. Whether we go on shore at the Downs or not, I don't know ; if the Captain wants anything, we probably may. Our vessel is 150 tons burthen, and has ten hands on board. I find my bed too short, and my pillow very hard. The mattress and pillow are stuffed with short hair, the waste from brush-makers, or something of that kind, so that I have not slept well, but have been caught dreaming aloud, calling out so loud that the Captain came to ask me 'What was the matter ?' when I awoke in the greatest agony, and was glad to find it *but a dream*. I shall most certainly write to you on my arrival at Genoa, where I anticipate most delicious gales, wafted from orange, pomegranate, and citron-trees. The best way for you will be to write down on a paper whatever occurs that you wish me to know; and then, when you send to me, you have only to refer to the paper, and there will be no chance of your forgetting anything. Yours truly,

W. BEWICK.

On Board the Columbian Packet,
August 15th, 1826.

MY DEAR FRIENDS AT DARLINGTON, — I write this in the Gulf of Genoa, about four miles from the city of that name. It is a beautiful day, a slight breeze ripples the water, and we expect to be in the harbour in an hour or two. It is with difficulty I tear myself from the magnificent view before my eyes to make something in way of a note for England, for fear that anything should prevent my doing so after getting on shore, as I have no doubt that you will feel anxious to hear from me. Therefore, I prepare this sheet for the post-office, to be the first thing for me to expedite on my landing. Calms and contrary winds have detained us so long that we have had what is thought rather a tedious passage. However, we have had no rough weather, neither have I been sick. The only thing I can complain of is the extreme dulness and monotony of a long sea voyage. Your bones ache with lassitude and *ennui*, you tumble and toss and roll about. A game of chess is dull, draughts are stupid. Shakspeare is too much, Milton hard to understand. Your Italian grammar you cannot bear to look at, and you lie on your back watching the changes of the clouds, the twinkling of stars, the crack-ing of the cordage, the flapping of the sails, and the music of the rigging. But it is rather a pleasant thing to be going at the rate of eight or nine knots an hour, your vessel swinging over the water. We rounded Cape St. Vincent at this rate. It was fine, and a beautiful sunset. The Captain was in a good humour for the first time and cracked his joke, and pointed out the spot of Jarvis' triumph.

But time wanes, and I must speak of the present. It is certain that no human being could fail to enjoy a sight so enchanting as the one before me just now, a city of about fifty palaces, with villas and rural seats spread over the rich wooded mountains of the Apennines, extending for upwards of twenty miles each way along the line of coast. At this distance it gives you the idea of dominoes pricked into a ground of moss, and you see by the telescope the immense palaces of marble, with windows innumerable, such as we used to draw from fancy when boys. My brother John was famous for these castles of fancy. This is a fairy scene indeed!—what a situation!—what advantages of water, mountains, cultivated banks and hanging gardens! The brown and barren mountains, see how they pierce the sky and grasp the clouds. What strange dragon-like form is that which creeps along the side of that steep, yet sloping mountain, casting its shadow far athwart the ravine below? Then the city walls wind crooked, zig-zag up and down,—here the road ascends to Lucca, Pisa, and Leghorn. But now I leave this distant view and prepare to show myself a healthy subject—not an improper caution. The bill of health is produced, and we land. What joy! such we judge liberty to be after captivity.

August 16*th*.—Since writing the above I have been ashore, and as I have told you that this is the city with its fifty palaces, I must now correct myself and say that it is a city of palaces, noble buildings, enriched and beautified by painting, gilding, and marble of different colours. By moonlight many of the buildings are splendid, in point of effect and picturesque display, for the pale moonlight renders defects that time has made upon the decorations less distinct, and therefore you have the beauty of light and shadow, extended proportions, and other characteristics in perfection. The moon is full to-night. I have been gratified and astonished. I go in the morning to see the interior of some of these Palazzi. There is here a very good family, that of Mr. Le Mesurier, cousin to my companion. He is a merchant, and very attentive and kind. A young gentleman of the name of Wakefield is visiting them from England, and he will accompany us to the south. It is expected we go from this on Monday first or Tuesday; and although I intend to remain in Florence a week or two, yet as a letter will be a fortnight in coming from England, you had better write to me at Rome (Messrs. Freeborn, Smith, and Co.) I will write on my arrival there, if not from Florence.

The ladies here wear no bonnet in the morning, but a piece of muslin like a scarf, that certainly looks extremely graceful. They carry large fans, which they use constantly, as do the gentlemen also. I lodge at a very good hotel, where I have a very nice room with crimson silk draperies and white cotton, and on the ceiling are three Cupids in the sky, with flowers, and wreaths of laurel. The floor is brick, no carpets in this country—good houses have marble or painted stucco. I have just seen, in one of the palaces, the interior of a room, called the 'Golden Saloon,' from its being almost entirely covered with gilding—pillars, doors, walls, ceilings, all richly carved and gilt, with a painting in the ceiling and mirrors where there is not gilding. The mere decorations of this saloon cost forty thousand pounds sterling. It is principally gold upon *lapis lazuli*, with all kinds of rich ornament. Hanging from the ceiling are cut-glass chandeliers, which the mirrors, reaching from top to bottom of the room, reflect

and repeat *ad infinitum,* and you fancy yourself in an immense suite of halls, extending as far
as the eye can reach.   This has a fine effect.

I am very anxious to hear from you to know
how you are, and if Robert has got another
situation, or what he intends to do.   Has my
father looked into the geography yet ?   Tell him
we passed close round Spain, and saw Cadiz,
Gibraltar, Cape St. Vincent, and might have
been taken prisoners on the Barbary Coast, and
'sold to slavery,' but we were not.   We were
frightened a little, however, by a strange sail that
gave us chase, but it turned out to be a French
corvette that wished to know who we were and
what, and so fired.

Ever yours affectionately,
W. Bewick.

Should any letters come for me they need
not be opened, but you can tell me where they
come from, and I can send you word if you are
to forward them to me.   The streets are very
narrow here ; they scarcely allow two carriages
to pass between wall and wall, and the houses
are very high.   Some parts of the town put me

in mind of Edinburgh, but in this respect only.
In other respects the much-boasted Edinburgh
falls short, and the houses look like so many
stables compared with the houses here.

The following letter, giving an account of
Bewick's journey to Rome, shows that he
not only possessed the talents of an artist, but
also that spirit of observation which enabled
him to form, from the facts and circumstances
that came under his notice, very accurate and
discriminating judgments on the position and
prospects of the country through which he travelled. In a very limited space we have here
a remarkably comprehensive view of a considerably portion of Italy in the early part of the
present century—a view which to those who are
acquainted with that country, and can compare
its past with its present state, is exceedingly interesting and instructive.

Florence, Sept. 15th, 1826.

My Dear Bess,—I should certainly have
written to you before this, had I been certain
either of remaining here at Florence, or of pro-

ceeding to Rome. But although I have been here about a fortnight, I have lived in doubt all the time. On my arrival, I was told it was dangerous and highly improper to go to Rome at this season. This made me delay, and I thought, if I could employ myself for a month or so here, it would be safer. I accordingly determined to copy a picture, and obtained permission to do so at the ' Pitti Palace ; ' but unfortunately, after giving myself a great deal of trouble and vexation, and losing about eight days in getting this permission, I found, to my surprise, that they only had one scaffolding (to enable one to get up to the picture), and this *one* was engaged for a month ; so that my idea of stopping here is quite done away with, and as I am assured that there is no danger what-ever at Rome, now the rains have fallen, I have determined to set off on Friday the first, and to remain at Rome during the winter. I should not have gone so soon, but a friend of mine with his family of *nine* went on Tuesday. He had received letters assuring him that on account of the season being so favourable, and the late showers, not the slightest apprehension need be entertained. I should tell you that in and near Rome, the inhabitants (and yet more strangers) are liable to a complaint arising from the *malaria,* during the summer season. This is what frightened me,—but now I am assured there is no danger whatever.

You would hear from me at Genoa, at least, I wrote a letter and put it in the post myself. I have since that time travelled through a most delightful, rich, and varied country, particularly the part from Genoa to Pisa, which is the most picturesque that the eye can behold or the imagination conceive. In ascending the Apennines, by an excellent new road, winding through *forests* (I may call them) of olive and chestnut, interspersed occasionally with the other varieties peculiar to the country, we passed the most beautiful villages and cottages, perhaps only more beautiful to an artist from their being placed in such fine situations and built in such picturesque styles — not to speak of external ornaments of painting, &c. ; for in this country every cottage, barn, or palace must have its exterior decorations of painting, sculpture, or earthen ornament,— and these often evidence good taste and excellent fancy. Then again the vine in this part does not grow in small bushes as in France and some parts of Italy, but is trained from tree to tree in festoons, the most luxuriant you can imagine; the large purple bunches (about the size of yourself) hanging in luscious profusion; tempting the thirsty traveller to a dangerous risk, for it is dangerous to eat fruit just plucked in the sun.

You will think it very odd at Darlington that, after I have abused the people here for being such thieves and robbers, there should be no occasion for fences to the gardens and grounds. But so it is nearly the whole way that I have travelled. A fence has seldom obstructed my inclination to take fruit of any sort. Peaches, nectarines, plums, walnuts, figs, almonds, and grapes, in variety and profusion, have tempted me at every turn. The large ' water-melon,' green outside and red inside, is plentiful here. It is a little larger than a *Bailiff's* head, very juicy, but tasteless. The other melon, which is called here *poppone*, is white outside, and of a richer flavour. The general appearance of the country is that of one immense orchard. There are no green fields of grass (ah! how delicious is the recollection of a grass field!)—of turnips, potatoes, or even corn; for the whole country is planted with fruit-trees, having cabbages, or a few potatoes, between the rows of trees. Occasionally you will see a small plot snatched as it were for corn, or millet, perhaps half an acre at a time, not more. Even the steepest hills and highest mountains are formed into terraces, each terrace containing its due quantity of fruit-trees. Land thus cultivated must require much labour and attention, and cannot be parcelled out into large farms, as nearly all farmers cultivate their farms by their own family.

At first, I thought that the houses which peeped through the trees in the valleys, and covered the sides of the mountains, were villas belonging to gentlemen, or the country-seats of those connected with a large city. But no! There is scarcely an acre of land but what has its farm-house,—and you are astonished frequently at descrying a snug, romantic cottage perched in wild sublimity on the rocky summit of a mountain half hid in clouds, without any apparent road by which you can ascend to it. On the way from Genoa to Pisa, you travel at no great distance from the sea. The road often winds up an almost perpendicular mountain, and sometimes you look down on chimney-tops below you,—sometimes on the sea. Then the road descends again to the water's edge, the carriage-wheels sinking into the sand, and you are taken over mountains, across rivers without bridges, and so on till you enter Pisa. Here your coachman cracks his whip, and drives at a furious rate, crossing the river Arno by a stone or marble bridge. The rumbling of the carriage, and the jingling of the bells on the horses, are quite astounding; and when it is known that *Milord Inglese* is driving to the sign of the 'Hussar,' he has a dozen fellows following him, keeping up with the speed of a four-horse drive.

From Genoa to Florence, I had two companions, who, with myself, formed the party occupying a fine carriage with four excellent horses. At a place on the road called Rappello, we had very good beds, but unhappily tenanted, and the mosquitoes too buzzed about; and although I had a mosquito curtain, I could not sleep for the other vermin. At last, my head fell on the pillow from sheer weariness, and I slept soundly until morning, when I found Mr. Le Mesurier stung all over by mosquitoes, so that I was afraid he had got the measles. For my part I did not feel these disagreeable tormentors till I came to Florence; but at this moment I am covered with red spots, like the chicken-pox. At the Galleries to which I go, I generally observe the English visitors with their foreheads pimpled by this insect. However, I can bear this tolerably well; but I must tell you it is quite disgusting to see the people, even the finest ladies, as coolly spit upon the carpet, should there be one, as if they were using a perfume bottle. By the by, carpets are uncommon here. Those that are used are made of list of different colours, which form the weft into stripes so irregular that, when the seams are made, the colours are all different, white joined to black, and red to blue, and so on. There is no such thing as paper for rooms. They are all either painted with landscapes, figures, and ornaments, or in the best houses hung with rich figured silk damask, which looks beautiful. Their beds have no poles, and the tester hangs from the ceiling. There are few fire-places, although I am told that in winter it is colder than in England. Amongst other wants to the comforts of the houses here, are the bells. You have to call to the servants by name if you want one.

I will write you from Rome, as I expect letters from you there. As there are no letter-carriers here, you may as well direct your letters, William Bewick, Esq., *Poste Restante*, Rome. My travelling companion to Rome is an old but respectable priest, and an acquaintance of Dr. Gradwell's, to whom I have a letter of introduction from Mr. Hogarth. The ladies here dress well, exactly like the English, even to the rainbow ribbons. They generally have fine figures, and walk gracefully, and with dignity. They are, I think, rather tall and full grown, and tie themselves very tight at the waist. They are not pretty, but have expressive countenances. Their eyes are large, black, and languid, with long black eyelashes; and they stare very much at a new-comer. I have been told, by an English lady here, that they are very fond of Englishmen, but not of Englishwomen. Compliments to Mr. Smith and family, Dr. Burn, Mr. Graham, and Mr. Botcherby.

Mind you tell me how you are! and all news; write upon thin paper, as the postage is according to its weight. I will write to Mr. Smith from Rome. It will be about five weeks before I get an answer to this letter at Rome.

Affectionately yours,
W. BEWICK.

From Florence, Sept. 15th, 1826.

In reference to the artist's remarks on the manners of the Florentine ladies, it may be observed that, although they were no doubt perfectly true at the time they were written, they are no longer applicable to Italian ladies, either of Florence, or of any other city of the Peninsula.

THE END OF THE FIRST VOLUME.

LIFE AND LETTERS

OF

WILLIAM BEWICK

(ARTIST).

EDITED BY

THOMAS LANDSEER, A.R.A.

VOL. II.

CONTENTS

OF

THE SECOND VOLUME.

CHAPTER I.

CHAPTER II.

VOL. II.   *a*

CHAPTER III.

CHAPTER IV.

CHAPTER V.

CHAPTER VI.

CHAPTER VII.

CHAPTER VIII.

CHAPTER IX.

LIFE AND LETTERS

OF

WILLIAM BEWICK.

———

CHAPTER I.

THE following letter to Mr. Chatfield gives a very minute account of Bewick's temporary sojourn at Genoa, and of the impressions produced upon him by that city.

Rome, September 21st, 1826.

At Genoa, I arrived wearied with a six-weeks' voyage by sea. Here I remained for a week, delighted with the splendour of the palaces that compose the greater portion of this rich city. I was not less pleased, and more excited, by the distant view of the city and its environs from the Gulf of Genoa. Perhaps, it might be owing to its extent and novelty (as seen from 'on board a ship' with a telescope) that it excited the interest I felt; for it is a strong feeling that curiosity perhaps dictates, when a person is transported from his native land, is for the first time boxed-up in a vessel, and sees little all the way but the waves and the sky; the Barbary coast, Gibraltar, and perhaps Cadiz, at a great distance. A strange town, with strange buildings, strange people, and strange noises of bells, must be, and is, very striking to one who has lived as it were—for a month or five weeks on the sea—amphibiously, and seeing nothing but a porpoise, a dolphin, or some ugly monster. Had I come by France, effects would have been gradual, and not so perceptible.

In Genoa there are comparatively few good pictures or works of art. At the Hospital *dei*

Poveri there is a bas-relief of a dead Saviour and Madonna. The head of the former is beautiful, and tranquil in expression, and the hands of the latter equally to be admired for their exquisite form and grace. But the rest is poor and unequal, and cannot certainly have been by this great man. It is of an oval shape, and only contains the two heads and two hands. The head of the Madonna in expression and drawing is dreadful. There are many things here that are said to be by Michael Angelo, that are not only doubtful, but impossible.

Of Paul Veronese there is a large picture, the Anointing Christ's feet, from which there is a print. It is painted (as are all the large pictures of this master) in a bold, large, and grand style. In painting it, the oil seems to have been absorbed quickly, as the touches are dragged very much, and done with full, large brushes, — perhaps these bold, striking lights were painted after the picture was dry. The head of the principal female has its toning taken off, and it looks raw and pinky, though beautiful—more beautiful than most of the heads by this master. There is a weeping expression about the cheeks and eyes that is affecting. Some parts of the picture are vulgar and unmeaning, and some parts quite a study for style. This is in the palace of the Grand Duke, which contains many bad pictures.

In the Palazzo Brignole there are some excellent Vandycks; one, a whole-length, on a grey horse with a broad long tail, is capital for its breadth and simplicity of effect. It is the portrait of the Marquis Antonio Julio Brignole, where the whole picture is made subservient to the head, which is brilliant and Titianesque, and shines out from a darkish, blue-grey sky.

The Prince of Orange, too, is by the same hand, and is very fine.

The portrait of a young Venetian nobleman in a black dress over armour,—a rich gold-handled sword by his side, upon which his left hand rests gracefully, his right taking his hat from a table covered with crimson velvet ornamented with gold. A crimson curtain is behind, with a bit of landscape and twisted column at the right corner. He stands firm, yet graceful, and has the true nobleman look. His frill comes up to his chin and round his throat, like some of Titian's heads, but the whole picture puts you in mind of Velasquez. Indeed, the general character of their minds and genius does not seem to have been dissimilar.

'The Jews tempting Christ,' by the same artist, is in good preservation, and with others exhibits an excellent old characteristic head, looking through short spectacles.

In this collection is a celebrated Carlo Dolce, 'Christ in Agony on the Mount,' with gilded rays ingeniously softened into a blue sky, and the blood dropping from his forehead on the grass, which is discoloured by it. It is the size of your two hands, and on copper, highly valued by the Genoese and others ; but I confess that I have a distaste for the works of this hand (upon which I could enlarge a good deal), and cannot reconcile myself to this picture, even when the ladies were extolling its high finish (which I do not deny), its beauty, its affecting expression, and everything that is wonderful *in* it, and not in it.

Rubens, always striking, is here himself and his wife by his own hand, voluptuously indelicate, but splendid in colour and in style. He seems to have painted it in happy moments of slight inebriation. In the background is a bacchanalian figure holding a goblet of wine, and Cupid below completes the salacious idea. Rubens himself looks princely, is in armour, with a fur cap and feather.

But the finest thing in this collection is the portrait of a Chancellor in black robes, with open lace-worked collar hanging upon his shoulder. It is the thin head of a deep thinker, —listening and thinking; his dark intellectual eye looking through a pale reflecting face, with a serious severity of expression that rivets your attention. The head reminds me of the present Chancellor Manners of Dublin, who has one of the finest heads for a judge I ever saw. Perhaps, not so severe as this by Rubens, or so vigorous.

Was ever anything more like life?

But you are tired of the pictures at Genoa, which cannot boast of numerous *good* ones. There is a curious picture of the stoning of St. Stephen in the Church of St. Stephano alle Porte—the upper part of which is said to be by Giulio Romano, and the other by Raffaelle, the principal head having been destroyed by French soldiers. David has restored it unsuccessfully, as it is of a different colour and stone from the rest of the picture. The size is about ten feet by eight—on wood, and rather hard. But now I have done about pictures, I must say something about Genoese women, and so forth, to fill up my letter.

When an Englishman lands on the quay of Genoa, the variety of distinct smells of fruit and filth is very striking. One is surprised, too, by the odd foreign figures, the queer voices, the strange dresses, and the unusual expressions. A small, sallow, puny face is seen sunk in an immense hat, or, on the contrary, a large fleshy face like Liston's with a little brimless bonnet stuck on one side. The conversation, too, is so energetic, so loud, and there is so much action, the propriety of which, not knowing one word of the language, you cannot appreciate. You hurry through the narrow streets, passing people that seem to labour at each step, and are all fanning themselves, without distinction—men and women, young and old. Then you come to the corner of a street where they are preparing the picture of some Saint or Madonna, with lamps, and garlands, and crimson curtains, to be lighted up at night in great style, sometimes with illuminations and fireworks. And there are grand doings, where the women make assignations and the men meet their lovers. Then there is the horrible singing of casual voices, instead of the fine music which you expect in Italy. Nothing disappointed me so much as the singing of the general run of women. Instead of hearing full, capacious voices, harmonious if not educated, your ears are astounded with small, confined, pipy voices, powerless and squeaky; but I have no doubt that in society there may be some very different. The only powerful voice that I met with at Genoa (and she was allowed to be one of the best) was a Mrs. Barrie, an English lady, residing there.

At Genoa I heard of a sort of ' Beau Nash,' who, having a pretty good fortune, and being a well-whiskered fancy hero, amused himself by making his person as remarkable as his conceits and egotism were disagreeable and ridiculous. The Governor gives occasional grand balls in the winter, and generally sends his cards to the English in regular form, specifying, I believe, that it is a dress party. This Mr. ——, thinking of course the Genoese are so much inferior to him as an Englishman, treats them all with indifference, and accordingly goes to my Lord the Governor's ball dressed in top-boots, Belsher cravat, green riding coat, and white smalls, and dances away with his head upright and as dignified as if he were my Lord, with a *chapeau de bras* under his arm. He is fond of horses, and is, in fact, a groom, seldom seen out of his stable in the day, except when riding. He has a great deal of good things to say of every person known in Genoa, so that he entertains the ladies highly; for his wit, and the amusing way in which he tells his jokes, although personal, never fail to be his passport wherever he goes. He has besides a careless, fearless manner that serves him well; is a boxer of the first ring, and shows superior qualities as a rider.

The women of the country dress their heads without bonnets, and have a veil they call *mezzano*, a piece of muslin six or nine feet long, which they throw over the head, sometimes covering the face, and sometimes showing a little of the black hair, parted on the forehead, with occasionally a flash of the brightest and softest of eyes. This mezzano is worn with the greatest simplicity, and gives a grace and beauty that is truly magical; and if it chances to be worn by a beauty, the charm is irresistible. When the head turns the least, or tips to one side, what lines—what composition it gives! We see this in Raphael's pictures often. Although this muslin drapery or head-dress is worn by all classes in the morning, yet ladies of fashion and quality do not drive or promenade in the 'Aqua Sola' without the distinctive addition of a bonnet, which is made either of silk, gauze, or straw, exactly as they are worn in England at the present day. Indeed, there are so many English here that the fashions are soon transported. Black silk gowns are much worn, and being tied very tight at the waist, show the figure in all its fulness. It is the fashion here to be *embonpoint*, and the ladies feed themselves so that they become unnaturally stout. It is likewise the case at Florence and Rome. Their walk has more of majesty than any that I have seen. What an air! Milton must certainly have had the Italian women in his mind when he described the majesty of Eve.

Between Pisa and Florence there is a little beautiful town called Spezia, famous for its harbour, which is said to be the finest in the universe. I do not introduce the name of this place here for the purpose of mentioning its famous harbour, as I know nothing of these matters, but to observe to you that I saw one of the most beautiful women that ever was created, a divine face, in a servant-girl. I gazed at her for ten minutes with strained eyes and gaping mouth. She was in a shop talking to an old woman, and seemed rather pleased than otherwise at the attraction she exercised. What a model for a painter! In passing through Pisa I saw the Campo Santo with great interest, and regarded these works as the foundation of a school of design that prompted Raphael's great genius, and gave hints even to Michael Angelo.

I sketched a piece of the Holy Land that was brought from Jerusalem, and is kept sacred in this holy receptacle, likewise some plants that were growing on it, and some bits from the falling tower,—could I do less as a traveller?

I will write to Mr. Mayor, and tell him about Florence, as a continuation of this, which he will show you.

Although the following letter, to a certain extent, goes over some of the ground which the author had previously described, it is too interesting to be omitted :—

Rome, Sept. 28th, 1826.

MY DEAR SIR,—Four or five months have now elapsed since the merry party from the Tees were separated on the Thames ; and by some of that party, no doubt, many, many merry and happy hours have been laughed away in harmless mirth and pleasantry. It is a pleasure to me even at this distance—in so austere, so grave, so elevated, and so splendid a place as Rome—to remember the tricks and eccentricities, the buoyant enjoyments, the enthusiastic exultations, of the West End of Darlington,—not to forget the marine adven-

ture and the 'Kitty awake' (as it was called)—
the *aqua vita* turned so miraculously into
vinegar (sour as *wargis*), like Billy Lacka-
day's small beer in the comedy. This brings
me to mention my very tedious and unsocial
passage from London to Genoa, a passage of
six long weeks' duration, often becalmed for
four or five days, sticking in the water like
a log of wood, motionless, with nothing but a
cloudless sky above, and the tiresome and painful monotony of a dazzling, glassy surface of
water below—no object except, perhaps, the
head of a sleeping tortoise at some distance,
to break the immense expanse of shining waste,
—sky-bounded. We had few books calculated
to amuse us at sea. Veneroni's Italian Grammar
and Exercises, with two or three more equally
serious, became stupid, and are likely to cause a
distaste for the same studies for some time to
come. 'Aboard a ship' is not a 'seemly' place
for study, except for a sailor, who is all the time
in his element; but how few sailors study!
If you recollect, you brought with you from
Darlington 'An Essay on the Principles of Human Action,' or perhaps 'An Exposition of the

Sacraments,' which I believe you scarcely ever opened—perhaps from social excitement, a delightful hilarity, or more probably *ennui*, which, however, is a thing never known—a feeling never understood at the 'West End,' but banished like the plague or malaria, every means being taken to avoid or prevent it, as it should be ; for what could we think of existence, wanting the beautiful simplicity and virtue of innocent enjoyment? But now I am prosing, and, if you please, we will change the subject and talk of something else.

I sit down to write, as much to endeavour to amuse you as to fulfil my promise of writing, without knowing where to begin, or what part to take, the best to meet my intentions—for my memory is glutted with objects so various, of such different interest, so important in the history of the world, and either of such vast magnificence in themselves, or of such interest in the associations they excite. Indeed, if we speak of Rome alone, at every step, every turn we take, we come upon some scene hallowed with its charm—possessed with its talisman, associated with the classics, important in history, or looking majestically through the eyes of venerable antiquity. On this subject, I must say, there is no end. However, as I know you are fond of excursions, and delight in the wonders of art and the beauties of nature, I will try to speak of what I saw at Tivoli, having made a visit there with a friend so late as yesterday, and the scenery being now fresh in my recollection, strong 'in my mind's eye.'

Although Tivoli is only three hours' drive from Rome, yet the road is so bad, uneven, and dusty, and the country so wanting in interest, that if you were not excited by the expectation of something at the end of your journey to repay you for all the hard thumps, and rubs, and shakes, and the constant action ' to and fro,' and from side to side, I am persuaded that most people would stop at the 'sulphur river,' which, smelling as it does, perhaps, ten times as strong as Middleton Spa, would complete the *finale* of disagreeables, and render the ' stop short ' here memorable to the sensitive. The whole road (about eighteen miles), crossing the miserable and melancholy ' Campagna di Roma,' traverses a flat, uncultivated swamp, abounding in thistles, nettles, and every indigenous wild plant that adorns an abandoned or neglected soil, which, although having every appearance of capability, remains not only useless to man and animals, but, at certain seasons of excessive heat, is baneful and dangerous to the health and existence of both.

On our journey yesterday, I observed a long line of dense fog following the winding course of the Tiber, not like our mists upon similar rivers in England, thin, vaporous, and milky (as on the Skern), but a line of clouds, formed into regular and distinct cumuli—floating close, and extending only fifteen feet above the ground, so that we could see the tops of trees over their outlines ; and on crossing the Tiber at half-past seven in the morning, a few miles from Rome, this fog was so thick as to prevent our seeing the figures of men and cattle that were meeting us upon the bridge, not more than forty or fifty feet from us. Had it not been for the noise of our carriage rumbling over the old arch some accident might have occurred (which although it might have

come well in at this place as a 'bit of the romantic,' still we can do very well without by
leaving it to the imagination); the bridge being
narrow and admitting but one vehicle at a time
to cross it. It is a genuine antique, untouched
by the hand of the *restaurateur,* and the road is
paved with irregularly-shaped, large flat stones,
as was the custom in those days; their appearance
when joined together resembling the map of
England divided into its counties, each stone
having its accidental or circumstantial division, which forms the exact counterpart to the
boundary of the adjoining one; each line running
as fantastical a course as the 'county line' or
the windings of a river that sometimes serve for
that purpose. The surface of this pavement is
as unequally worn and torn as the outline of
the stones is irregular, and subjects you to much
exercise in leaps from your seat and thumps
against your shoulders. I might here observe,
that this taste for irregularity was possessed by
the ancient Romans in other matters than pavements, for in their inscriptions on marble we see
the writing undulating in crooked lines, running up to one corner, or down to another, some

letters large, some small, words crowded and confused, and running one into another, or the contrary, the letters wide apart, large, and of unequal proportion. This apparent eccentricity sometimes excites a smile, and you would scarcely believe that a workman who had to labour over the cutting of a letter with tools, should not first mark out what he had to do, so as to get each letter and word in such a proper lineal situation as to be read with ease and facility ; and this seems so simple and self-evident, that the irregularity could not be unintentional, but must have been the result of some perverse taste or fashion of the times, which was gratified by these crooked epitaphs and unruled lines.

Tivoli stands upon a rocky eminence commanding an extensive but barren view across the Campagna, bounded in the extreme distance by the Grand City ! St. Peter's, breaking against the horizon, towers in the sky like a huge giant,—

> ' Whom transcendent glory raised
> Above his fellows ! '

The inn at Tivoli is like most Italian inns ;

it is characterised by a want of comfort and cleanliness, and all those nice little attentions to the wants and convenience of customers that make an English inn so pleasant and so tempting to visitors. This inn, although in a situation that is scarcely to be equalled as a temptation to the admirers of beautiful, romantic scenery, has nevertheless such indifferent accommodation that, if you are disposed to stop, you must look for private lodgings —which fortunately may be had. The town being considerable, and the scenery being attractive, strangers come and reside during summer and autumn, and the natives find it worth their while to fit up apartments to receive such visitors, who, being generally English, pay them well, or are expected to do so. Our breakfast at Tivoli was quite in the primitive style. Bread, eggs, and wine, with grapes and fresh butter, made up our fare ; and that we might have something nice for dinner, we ordered a pigeon-pie ! —a pigeon-pie ! Could I avoid thinking of the exquisite, tender delicacy of such a dish at ' the West End,' for instance ? I confess that, in my romantic and classical walk, with objects of the greatest interest, beauty, and novelty before me, the idea of 'this pigeon-pie' was ever crossing my mind; and after walking three or four hours, climbing rocks and zig-zag roads, judge my disappointment when the pie was served on the table, with a dark-brown crust, thick, hard, and heavy, of a saturated drab-colour inside, with only *one* pigeon, for *two* hungry young travellers! It was what is called 'a standing pie,' and had a strong paste handle passing crescent-like from side to side like that of a tea-kettle. Could I but laugh when this piece of pastry was put on the table, with so much ceremony too, the cook looking in to see how it was received! It looked, indeed, so thumbed, so clumsy, so dark, and so odd, unrelieved by any of your modern attempts at ornament, that it could only have suited a person of very 'plain taste.' Yet our host thought, no doubt, that this was one of his 'crack dishes,' for he sent up to tell us what the expense of such a pie would be before he made it. This smacked of honesty, and showed that he did not wish us to be deceived.

From the window of our dining-room we had a beautiful view of a sweep of the river above the 'falls,' with rising banks topped with picturesque houses and turrets, with cattle, and figures of Italian peasant-women (washing clothes in the river), and one small fall of water, which serves as 'a prelude' to the scene. The constant roar and noise of falling waters, and the hollow sound of subterranean cataracts, make a wild and curious music to your repast, which, whilst at one moment it excites your imagination to poetic sublimity, subdues you again to calm reflection, or rouses impassioned thought.

From the same window (in the inn-yard) are seen the remains of a beautiful little circular temple, called 'the Temple of the Sibyl,' in tolerable preservation, and in proportion, symmetry, and situation exquisite; and if not the one copied by Claude, it is very similar to that introduced in many of his works (a circular temple with Corinthian pillars). Close to this, and nearly touching it, are seen portions of another temple of a square form, and dedicated to Vesta, but now formed into a church by modern brick walls, as unseemly as the idea is barbarous, and almost exceeding the story told of an Englishman who bought a round temple for the purpose of removing and placing it in his garden in England. The proper authorities, hearing of this circumstance, very judiciously ordered the money to be refunded to this tasteless Gothic barbarian, who would have robbed the rocky pinnacle of its temple, as he would have deprived the violet of its perfume, or the lily of its beauty, for the gratification of his own grovelling selfishness.

But let us descend to the bottom of the rock and see the 'first fall.' You hear it boiling and dashing its spray against the damp rocks. Half-way down the zig-zag path are seen two sons of nature (with moustachios wild), perched on a perpendicular eminence, sketching, with rapid hand and eye severe, the falling Anio, which, spitting its foaming mass, one hundred feet, sheer from its rocky bed into the dread abyss beneath, joins its other portion, long time lost, and tossed from rock to rock in subterranean darkness, as it rushes, howling and roaring, on its dreadful way, bringing animals or man disjointed or dashed piecemeal to the bottom, where you now are standing, wet with the spray, and deafened by the horrible noise. The cavern whence issues the subterranean fall is called 'the Grotto of Neptune,' and is extremely curious from its dark mysterious effect. In the morning, the prismatic colours are seen vividly reflected in the spray at the mouth of the Grotto. The fall here derives great advantage from the rocks, which are beautiful in colour and surface, and rise high and majestic in form. Next there are the Cascatelles (of Bernini the sculptor), who, bringing part of the river across the town of Tivoli for the use of its inhabitants, to drive their mills, and for other purposes, has thrown this part of the water over natural rocks in a singularly beautiful and striking way, so that from different points of view you get the most interesting and picturesque combinations. For instance, from one point, you see on the left, high up, the tower of a church; then in perspective you have the beautiful remains of the Villa of Mæcenas, or Villa d'Este; below these you have three waterfalls in perspective, the large one near to you falling and dividing itself in a most beautiful way, and the other two long streams rushing down a rocky slope; and again, in the distance, you can see Rome and St. Peter's. Another picture is seen the contrary way, looking up the river, taking in these falls differently varied, and the Villa of Catullus against the side of a hill which forms the boundary of the picture. The Villa of Horace might be taken in from another point. So that four or more capital pictures might be got, not only of beautiful and romantic scenery, but of objects that excite classical associations. Now we cannot have such objects united with the falls either of Tees or Clyde, both which appear to me tame and bare after Tivoli. I have not seen Terni, but I am told it is superior to Tivoli in grandeur and extent.

On our return from Tivoli, we visited the ruins of Adrian's Villa, which is calculated as much as anything to give a splendid idea of the magnificence of the ancient Romans. The masses and piles of building, consisting of the

Imperial palaces, theatre, baths, barracks for the Prætorian guard, stables, &c., occupy about as much extent as the town of Darlington. The situation, too, is beautiful, and the grounds are embellished with large pines and cypress-trees ; but the plough now finds its way into the halls and courtyards, and turns up pieces of marble and lumps of wall, that cover the surface wherever you go. The remains of the Baths of Caracalla (which are near Rome) give an idea of buildings upon a larger scale, and are· magnificent in themselves, exciting (as the relics of greatness generally do) at once astonishment and melancholy.

I might continue to any length with the ruins of ancient Rome now existing, but of guide-books and tours of Italy you have plenty, describing everything that is, and much that is not. I must now close this confused packet by asking what I am to do for you ? Here are Tivoli, Terni, Frascati, Ruins of Rome, all subjects of intrinsic value and deep interest. Let me do you something a little larger than the last.

I have had an interview with the *major-domo* of the Pope, and have succeeded in getting permission to study in the Sistine Chapel, from those stupendous works of Michael Angelo. You may judge of the scale of the objects when I tell you that the canvas I have ordered for one figure of a Prophet is eleven feet high, and this only takes in one figure from the top of the head to the feet, and the prophet is sitting.

It is my most anxious wish to obtain copies of all the best of Michael Angelo's works that are in this chapel, as they are decidedly superior to anything of epic composition in existence ; and indeed they are so tremendous in power and grandeur, that no one has hitherto attempted so arduous an undertaking. I must erect a scaffolding from forty to fifty feet high to enable me to finish them. Then, again, there was some difficulty in obtaining permission just now, which my letter from Sir Thomas Lawrence cleared away, and I found no obstruction to my wishes. I have a beautiful figure of Eve, and two other smaller commissions, to do for Sir Thomas in this chapel.

To Sir Thomas Lawrence.   Rome, Oct. —, 1826.

SIR,—You were kind enough to request me to write to you from Rome, so soon as I should have seen the Sistine Chapel, and put in progress the copies you did me the honour to commission me to make from those stupendous works of Michael Angelo. You likewise spoke of a select set of copies of these glorious things, which had long been the object of your solicitude, as you wished to propose them to the Royal Academy.

The idea of getting large copies of the Prophets, Sibyls, and some others, seems to excite expectations of pleasure in the breasts of every one; and the thought of the Royal Academy of London possessing such copies would be much for the interest of the British school, and on a task of such a nature I should enter with all the enthusiasm that the magnificence of the subject would inspire. The expense of such a set of copies would be comparatively trifling to an institution like that of the Royal Academy. At any rate, in the projection of a new building, it might be of importance to bear them in mind.

Through the influence of your letter to Sig. P. Camuccini, I have obtained permission to study in the Chapel; but as I can only be there for three weeks, by reason of ceremonies that take place in it from the end of October to the beginning of April, it will be enough for me to rub in carefully the proportions, colour, and effect from below, and then finish them from a scaffolding which I am promised in the spring, when I can have three months without interruption of any kind.

There has been some noise lately about persons having taken tracings from the 'Last Judgment,' and imaginary injuries were mentioned. So that I found, in a conversation with Mr. Morris at Florence, that permission at all would be difficult, if not impossible, to obtain. It appears, however, that the *major-domo* is only directed to be more particular in consequence, and that propriety of conduct must gain indulgence for the future.

Of the portion of the 'Last Judgment' that has been cleaned by the simple process of rubbing with bread, there are two or three opinions about. Some say it is spoiled, others that it might have been. The colouring of the flesh in the angels, coming as it does against a deep blue sky, takes much of the richness of Titian. The figures seem no longer attached to the background, but are suspended in the air, floating along the azure blue with masterly foreshortening, and, in this part, certainly not without grace and an attention to aerial perspective that is not perceived through the obscure opacity that wraps as a cloud the other dingy portions.

Allow me to return my sincere thanks for your kindness in sending me the two letters, and believe me ever,

Your obliged, and obedient servant,

WM. BEWICK.

I have commenced with the upper part of the Sibylla Delphica for you on a canvas six feet high, which takes in the figure below the knee, the two hands with two boys behind. It is on a scale larger than life, but not quite so large as the original. The head has much of beauty as well as powerful expression; and you may depend upon my endeavours to make the copy worth your recollections of the sublime original.

The Prophet Jeremiah, too, is begun, the full size of the fresco, on a canvas eleven feet high. After finishing the outline with dark colour, the size and grandeur of the proportions were quite striking when near the eye. In these figures each head is upon a scale of about two English feet.

CHAPTER II.

IN the latter part of this year, as may be seen from the previous letters, we find Mr. Bewick in Rome, and, amid all the novelty and interest of the scenes by which he was surrounded, eager for news from home. The marble palaces, the gorgeous processions, the magnificent art-collections of the Eternal City, could not efface the feeling with which he looked back to familiar Darlington, and the relatives he had left there. By this time he was diligently at work in the Sistine Chapel, where, partly from mischance, and partly through his own imprudence, he contracted an illness which must have interfered greatly with the manual practice of his art.

Wilkie, too, was in Rome at the same time, and visited him. This great artist, who was in a very indifferent state of health, must have had a high opinion of his friend Bewick, for we find him urging him to attempt the production of some large and important painting for exhibition in London. The following letter to his sister gives some account of his life and doings in Rome, but says little or nothing of the impressions made upon him by that city and its magnificent remains of antiquity.

Rome, Dec. 11th, 1826.

MY DEAREST BESS,—I received your letter yesterday, so that it has been two months coming to me, for it is dated 10th of October. I suspect it has been in the Post-office here for five weeks, in consequence of your putting 'Post Restante,' upon it, which I must beg you not to do again, but direct for me at Freeborn, Smith, and Co., Rome, and the letter will come direct without being detained. You do not mention if Mr. Smith has received a letter from me, nor if Tom had got his. I have been very impatient at not hearing from you, or some of the family, so long. Your two letters are the only ones I have had since I left England, except some from London; and a letter from Darlington is very acceptable at this distance. You might write twice as much in your letter if you wrote closely and took time; begin a few days before you send it, and write a little every day, so that you will forget nothing that would amuse or interest me at this distance. You must forgive me if I write ill-naturedly in this letter, for I am not in a good humour, nor inclined to be good-natured. The reason is, that I have a pain in my right hand that tortures me at every turn of the pen; and it concerns me much when I have to tell you that for two months I have not been free from pain in some part of my body, for whilst I was working very hard, and perhaps perspiring in the 'Capello Sistino,' the windows were set open to get rid of the smell of the paint, and most unfortunately, in consequence, I caught a rheumatism, which, beginning at my left shoulder, has jogged on from part to part, until it is now in my right foot and right hand. These are, I hope, the last places it can creep to, and I trust now soon to be able to resume my labours. When it came to my knees I could not sleep at nights, but passed a most wretched time. I write with considerable difficulty, my right hand being swollen and very painful. The doctor has ordered me to put half-a-dozen leeches upon it, which I shall do to-morrow. My mother will know well what an attack of this kind is. Thank God, I am now almost quite recovered, which it gives me great pleasure to tell you.

The weather here has been for some time wet and damp, and we have had one shower of hail — the hailstones as large as filberts, and coming against the windows like marbles. There has been no snow in Rome, but we see it on the mountains. The winter so far has been like our spring at Darlington, rather cold, but no ice, and I have four roses in a glass in my room as beautiful as in summer. In conse-quence of my cold I have been but to one party this winter, which was given by the Countess of Westmoreland, and was very gay. The English here, who in winter are numerous, keep up a style of fashion and gaiety which becomes the reputation they have of being very rich and ex-travagant, and indulging in unnecessary luxuries, and the Italians say, 'that we have carpets even upon our stairs,' which is a luxury they cannot see the good of, besides that it costs so much money.

Mr. Bewick remained settled in Rome during the year 1827, extending his circle of acquaintance, enlarging his knowledge of life, and to a certain extent entering into the gaieties of the city. His introductions procured him admission to a society in every way congenial to his taste, Rome being the centre, not only of a considerable colony of artists, but also of persons of rank and fashion, the majority of whom took a deep interest in artists and their works. Much attention was paid to him by families of distinction, and he gladly availed himself of such opportunities as he had of becoming acquainted with the world of rank and fashion. If a too ready attention to the claims of society is considered, on the one hand, inconsistent with the laborious practice of art, on the other hand it has the advantage of enlarging the artist's knowledge of life, and rendering him familiar with the manners and customs of a class on whom his success is so largely dependent.

Mr. Bewick unfortunately still suffered from the attack to which allusion has been previously made. For several months he was compelled to submit to the treatment of a patient, and appears to have suffered greatly from rheumatic pains, the consequence of the exposure to atmospheric influences to which he had unfortunately submitted. Still, though his right hand was greatly affected, he was able both to work at his easel, and to enter into the pleasures of society, though doubtless he could do neither with so much devotion as in other circumstances might have been expected of him.

The following letters to Mrs. Bewick continue the record of his life in Rome :—

Rome, January 29th, 1827.

My dear Friends at Home,— Your two letters with the bill came safe. They had evidently been opened and sealed up again. This, I suppose, was done at the Post Office at Darlington, a practice long common there, which, no doubt, will ere long receive its due punishment. You say that I have told you nothing about Rome, but as you can read in guide-books and travels more than I could tell you in a letter, it will be more interesting to write you anything connected with myself, which such books cannot possibly tell you. Besides, out of the few months I have been here, three have been consigned to racking pains, swellings, and rubbings with ointments, wrapping-up with flannels, bleeding, bathing, and physicking, and the devil knows what of disagreeables; for I have had a landlady with a glass eye, and if ever there was a fiend in the shape of a woman, this is one. She annoyed me constantly, although she had nothing to do with me, for I had my own apartments and my man-servant, but still she continued to draw from me daily a torrent of invective better unspoken. I have now got out of her house, a little Irishman having taken the lodging of me; and I am glad to say she has already received such a tearing, and swearing, and stamping from this little Irishman, that she will not like to come much where he is. He says she is extremely humble and good-natured since he kicked her out of his studio; but he knew how she had annoyed me, and was determined to take the first opportunity to pay her off; for he is a fine-spirited little fellow, and, like his countrymen, easily put into a fury of passion. The reason of my moving was that I could not do anything for myself, not even cut my own meat or tie my cravat; and I found it necessary to go where I should be taken care of and nursed. So I took the lodging which I first came to, and made a bargain for board and everything; and I must say that it is owing to the care and attention of both landlord and landlady that I am able to write this letter, for my right hand has not been uncovered for a month, and it is with some difficulty that I guide the pen, my fingers not having their proper strength or flexibility.

As to painting or drawing, I have not done anything since my right hand has been covered up, so that I have seen little of the winter's gaiety in Rome. Last week Lady Westmoreland sent her carriage for me, to give my assistance in the preparations she is making for a grand dress-ball, which will take place on the 12th of February. All the ambassadors and great people from all countries are to be present; and there will be music and dancing, and all kinds of splendour and gaiety. You will say that I cannot dance, or play music, or sing; and what can I be wanted for? I will tell you. During the evening there will be exhibited what are called *tableaux*, which are no more than people dressed up to represent the different characters in some celebrated picture. They are placed behind a gold-frame in the positions and with the expressions of the picture. A green cloth is put all round the frame, and hides the light or anybody that may be behind. Then a piece of thin black gauze is thrown over the front of the frame, and the effect is perfectly beautiful. There are several of these pictures made during the evening, in which the noblemen and ladies, and people of fashion, stand for the characters; I mean such as have faces and figures adapted for it. The character that I have to take has been twice rehearsed. The subject is a young warrior, dressed in steel armour, and his page is buckling on his shoulder-piece. A young lady of exquisite beauty is to be the page. Her lovely face and delicate hands will be set off to great advantage by my grim visage, for I am to frown most abominably. Lady Westmoreland calls out, 'Frown, Mr. Bewick! frown, Sir! You must look cross for once, for this is your page only—you must not think she is a pretty girl.'

This is the first piece that has been tried, and those who were placed as judges exclaimed, ' Beautiful ! wonderful effect ! ' and so on. One gentleman, a sculptor, not thinking at the time how it was produced, called out, ' How wonderfully like nature !' Another, a painter, came very close with his friend, and, not knowing that the lady was an Englishwoman and understood their conversation, said, ' How very like flesh her face is !' and then thinking she was an Italian added, ' A devilish pretty girl that page is !' While we were standing so, my page whispered to me that she should not be able to stand still or keep from laughing if those people were to talk, so I gave the signal, and the folding-doors were closed. Just as this was done and I was putting off the armour, we were told that a lady had arrived to see us, and the picture was made up again. After this I walked into the party with the armour on. As it was taken off, the ladies laughed heartily at the odd figure that the removal of each piece made me look, some comparing the process to the shelling of a lobster, others to the peeling of an orange.

The lady who arrived late, and whose taste seemed to be held in high esteem, requested to be introduced to me; and she told me that she belonged to Newcastle, and knew T. Bewick, the ' celebrated engraver.' This lady is Mrs. Chenie, widow of General Chenie. I have paid her a visit, and was shown some of her drawings and paintings, which are quite exquisite. She is a true artist, and is drawing and painting every day of her life. She is, besides, a most accomplished woman, and lives in high state here with her family. Her daughter dressed herself in her Carnival dress to show it us. The Carnival (which you will read of in books of travels) takes place here in about twenty days. They will have me dressed in a splendid Greek costume to go to the masque-ball given by the Duke di Bracciano during Carnival. The Baron Stackelberg is to lend me this costly dress; and although this is a sort of thing that I do not like, yet I will go, because I shall see a great deal that is new to me, and curious, and in fact it is one of the things that everybody comes to see.

Now to answer your letters. I am sorry to hear of Mr. S.'s fever, and of my mother being ill. You must nurse her and take care of her, for there is no one, next to yourself, that I more esteem or love. I am glad you had such a pleasant and quiet Christmas, and that you drank my health on my birthday. You never mention Sister Ann, I suppose she never writes to Darlington. The Christmas here was very gay, but I saw nothing of the gaiety. The processions and illuminations are very fine, I am told. The people here, particularly the women, are very idle and dirty, and half their time seems to be spent in festas, and holidays, and religious ceremonies, that are of very little good, I am afraid, if any. At ten o'clock at night Rome is as quiet as Blackwell, and everybody asleep, except those who have parties. There are no rows or quarrelling in the streets, no drunkenness, and no watchmen or guards of the night.

Your letter came too late for me to keep your birthday; however, I will keep it with a friend or two. I wish you were here to mend my pen, for your letters were written so nicely, and, though close, I had no difficulty in reading them. An Italian gentleman, seeing one on the table, observed how beautifully it was written, and with what small characters. As to my return to Darlington you know everything depends upon my health. I cannot determine upon anything until I am quite well. I am quite persuaded that the atmosphere of Rome does not agree with me, but people say everybody is ill at first arrival, and that after this I shall not feel it.

I long to taste your mince-pies. We have no cakes here except plum-cake, which is bought at the shops. I have excellent wine for two-pence-halfpenny a bottle. Bread is about half the price that you pay. For a capon or large fowl we pay about fifteen or eighteen-pence; but then they are larger than yours. Then we have wild boar's flesh, which is delightful, and cocks-combs'; and they make me every day five or six different dishes to dinner, although one of them would be enough. But I sometimes make a clear board.

Mr. Wilkie is still here, in delicate health, but not ill. Two dinners have been given to him as testimony of his talent, one by twelve English students, and the other by all the Scotch people in Rome. The second arose out of pique at the first dinner. I was one of the twelve of the first entertainment, and now there is a feeling of ill-will between the Scotch and English. An English lady has written the following lines on the Scotch dinner :—

> ' To give Wilkie a dinner the Scots have decreed,
> So in praises and eating he 's honour'd indeed ;
> But to order his pictures they never found need—
> 'Tis enough that he 's born on the north of the Tweed.'

It was Wilkie's own assertion that he never had received one commission from Scotland.

I am glad you keep up your French and music ; remember me to all friends.

It is pleasing to learn of that fine benevolent gentleman the Rev. Dalton, of Croft, and his amiable family being so highly spoken of for their attention and kindness to the poor people in the parish. I find I have told you nothing about Rome—its grandeur, its ruins, and its filth ; but I will tell you something in my next letter if there is room for it.

Yours,

WILLIAM BEWICK.

From Rome, January 29th, 1827.

During the Holy Week Mr. Bewick's attention was almost unavoidably distracted from the labours which usually occupied his time by the novel spectacles and magnificent ceremonies of which Rome at that period is the scene. The magnificent displays which take place in the Sistine Chapel at that time compelled him to remain idle for some days, and thus he had leisure to gaze with others on those pompous shows by which the Church of Rome exercises so great an influence over certain minds. On Easter Sundays St. Peter's Church is a spectacle of unexampled splendour; and an observant artist could not but be struck by the ingenuity displayed in the arrangement of ceremonies naturally so well calculated to carry away the feelings of the unreflecting worshipper. Nor was he less disposed to take his part in the pleasures which follow those ably directed manifestations of devotion. His health now considerably improved, he was able to enter into the amusements of masquerade and Carnival—species of entertainment which, with his hearty, joyous disposition, he was in every way disposed to enjoy, as

we may see by the following letter he addressed
to his sister :—

Rome, April 13th, 1827.

MY DEAREST BESS,—I only received your
letter three days ago, although it is dated so
far back as Feb. 26th, and I think you had
better direct to me at No. 30 Via del Gambero,
3 Piazzo, Rome,—and then, perhaps, I may get it
sooner. Your letter amuses me much, although
I think you might have written more. Mary,
too, is very kind in adding her mite of amusement to me. I see you all in Darlington when
I read your letters, and am glad to see you so—
all in good health and spirits — as I suppose you
are when you say nothing to the contrary. I
am glad that I can say, too, that I am quite well,
can cut my dinner and clip my moustachios
with my right hand. I have been working at
the Sistine Chapel, but stopped for some days
on account of the Holy Week, during which the
chapel is occupied with daily ceremonies. Palm
Sunday was the beginning—the blessing the
palms by the Pope—which, although not so
splendid and pompous as the ceremonies on

Easter Sunday, yet was interesting, and the singing beautiful, but Easter Sunday eclipsed everything in splendour and magnificence. The whole body of the Church of St. Peter's, and the square in front, was one immense crowd; and when the Pope came out at a window in front of the Church to bless the people, it was such a sight as I never saw. There seemed to be a world of people, and although the weather was rainy, all Rome and the country around appeared to be there; the umbrellas, too, adding much to the effect. Every eye was raised to the window, and when the Pope came all the soldiers and individuals there took off their hats and fell down upon their knees in the most profound reverence to receive the blessing; this, too, in front of a building the extent and magnificence of which is the admiration and wonder of the world.

In the evening the whole of this building, even up to the cupola and cross, was to have been completely covered and illuminated with lamps, and at a short distance, at the Castle of St. Angelo were to be displayed some splendid fireworks. All this the bad weather has prevented. The ceremonies at Easter are splendidly beautiful—the dresses of the Pope and the Cardinals are magnificent, and the procession in the Church of St. Peter's exceeds anything of the kind I ever saw or imagined. The Pope, too, looked better than I have seen him. He is brought from the altar on that day into the centre of the church on a chair covered with crimson and gold, which is carried on the shoulders of twelve men, eight more carrying a canopy over his head, all dressed in crimson-figured damask. The Cardinals were in their robes of white and gold, scarlet and purple, some carrying the mitres of the Pope all embossed with precious stones. There were two Greek priests that were quite magnificent. Then followed the Pope's body-guard, all formed of the young nobility, and very handsome men. The Pope, after being taken from his chair, kneels and prays in the centre of the Church, and so do all the people; then the relics of our Saviour are shown from a balcony, and all the people cross themselves; and after this the Pope is taken in procession to the balcony-window in front of the Church to bless the people. He throws from the window two printed papers, which are called bulls, and for which the people scramble and fight to see who can get them.

But I must now tell you something of the Carnival. To tell you the truth, I really enjoyed it—I suppose the more from having been confined so much in the house previously, and I think the excitement and gaiety really did me a world of good, for everybody in Rome, of all ages and conditions, was merry, and the laughing and feasting continued for eight days, with all sorts of fun and antics—the people dressed in all sorts of curious dresses—with all sorts of odd faces and masques of strange expression. The sport begins about one or two o'clock, when all the world comes out into the principal streets, either on foot or in carriages—or to the windows and balconies, which are all covered with crimson or green damask. The principal street, which is called the Corso, and where everything is in uproar and frolic, has a beautiful effect with these long damask cloths hanging from the windows, all full of people gaily dressed, throwing comfits at those below whom they recognise on foot or in carriages. Sometimes hand-battles are fought with these comfits, particularly when two carriages rest opposite each other, and the parties are known to each other. These battles are generally fought by the English. You will scarcely believe that in two hours seventy pounds of comfits were thrown from the carriage I was in, and there were only four of us ; but we certainly fought some hard battles.

One day the carriage stopped opposite a barber's shop, and seeing a poor fellow sitting to be shaved, with his chin all soap, we involuntarily threw our bullets all together in at the door, which was open, and the shop was presently covered with them (they are made, not of sugar, but paste or lime). The barber and the man to be shaved ran away, the latter covering his eyes with his hands, the soap upon his chin, and his mouth full of comfits (for he began to speak when he saw us throwing) ; it was quite a hailstorm. Everybody is mad at this time, and there is no economy or reserve. Some throw kisses made of sugar, and others flowers. This fun continues till an hour before dark, when the guns fire as a signal for the carriages to move off the street.

A horse-race takes place immediately after, and the soldiers clear the road for it. This racing is not like an English horse-race, for the horses are made to run *without riders*, which may appear odd to you. They are started at one end of the street and run to the other, having tin goads, with sharp points to prick and goad them, attached to their sides and backs. The horses are poor creatures, no better than our worst cart-horses, neither trained, nor fed, nor bred for a race. In the evenings there are masqued balls at the theatres, where everybody goes dressed as he fancies, in masque or not. This is the long-expected and delightful time for the ladies, who either go to intrigue themselves, or to watch their husbands or lovers, who are generally known to them, even if they be masqued. This is, indeed, the grand time for making love, and is looked forward to with anxious expectation. You must know that the men and women speak through the mouth of the masque with an altered squeaking voice that rarely can be distinguished, and I was completely deceived myself. A masque came to me and conversed with me some time. I made up my mind who it was, and walked the

whole evening at intervals with him, talking
of a variety of private matters that he seemed
to know, and he kept up the thing so well that
I was satisfied he was an English friend, and
we agreed to sup together with two or three
more.　After all was over, we went to supper,
all being masqued but myself; and while we sat
and chatted, waiting for supper, my companion
told me he was not the person I took him for.
The others all guessed who he was, each taking
him for a different person, and when he took off his
masque we were all completely astonished to find
him quite a different person from what we had
supposed.　The laughter was tremendous, for he
turned out to be an American, a young man all
knew very well without the masque. Yes, the fun
of Carnival is certainly capital. People of all sorts
come to you, torment and teaze you to death,
and say anything they like ; the women perhaps
being worse than the men.

The masque ball that I mentioned to you
given by the Duke of Bracciano was splendid
beyond description, all the beauty and fashion
of Rome being there.　My dress attracted universal attention and admiration ; and I will

describe it to you for your amusement. It was a true Mameluke dress, just brought from Egypt by a French gentleman. The costume was complete and unique, and I have sat to two painters who have made pictures of me in it. The under-dress was a sort of long jacket of rich striped shining silk of a peculiar bright scarlet, with blue and white, and the sleeves tightly buttoned from the wrist to the elbows, with small silk buttons attached to cord. Over this came another jacket of the same material, with loose sleeves hanging open below the tips of the fingers. Then came the wide trousers of green cloth, of a rich russet colour, like a russet apple, made like a very wide petticoat, sewed at the bottom with two holes for the feet. Wrapped five or six times round the waist was a cincture of striped silk, fringed at the ends, in which was stuck an antique silver-hafted, short Turk-ish sword. Then came the short outer jacket, of the same colour as the trousers, all orna-mented with gold, and the long sword hanging by a gold cord. Light yellow morocco boots, turned up at the points, and a white turban, with the throat uncovered, completed the costume.

When I entered the rooms I was stopped by the Duke and Duchess, who wished to examine my dress, as it was so perfectly elegant and rich, and my head so completely Eastern —with my black mustachios, bare neck, and not a bit of hair to be seen on the head — that they exclaimed, 'Superb! superb!' As I did not expect this, you may easily . suppose how glad I was to get out of so conspicuous and trying a situation. But when I had slipped into the more crowded rooms, I perceived that the Duchess had brought the Duke of Hamilton to see my dress. Wilkie was arrayed in a splendid costume, for which I believe he had been at a considerable expense ; mine cost me nothing. There was a capital masque at this ball, an English gentleman dressed one side as a man, and the other as a woman,—the latter he called his *better half.* He spoke with one side of his mouth like a lady, and with the other with a rough voice like a man.

Lady Westmoreland continues to give *tableaux*, and I am in want of money. Send to me by return of post, in the same way as you did before. I dined with a friend on Sunday, on lamb and green peas; lamb is $1\frac{3}{4}d.$ per lb. Remember me to all the family, and believe me,

Yours,

WILLIAM BEWICK.

Direct to me, Via del Gambero, 30 Piazzo, Rome.

The weather has been rather wet for a few days, and I feel my right hand and foot inclined to twinges of rheumatism, but I hope the hot sun will take it away again.

CHAPTER III.

PARTLY, no doubt, through his illness during the winter, and partly through the uncertainties and difficulties that beset the artist in the early part of his career, Mr. Bewick was still unable to depend on his own exertions entirely, and, to provide for the expenses of his residence in Rome, was compelled to apply to his father for assistance. The work on which he was engaged in the Sistine Chapel rendered necessary the erection of a large scaffolding, an expensive work, but which was indispensable to the task which he had undertaken. As the summer months approached, bringing with them heat and the dread of malaria, the English visitors took their flight from Rome, and the now comparatively solitary artist began to find his residence in it dull and weary. But he had come for a certain purpose, which he believed to be essential to his success as an artist, and till that purpose was accomplished, he determined not to return to England. Gibson, the sculptor, was one of the most valued friends whom Bewick made in Rome. The painter always speaks in the highest terms of his brother artist, and Gibson was no less sincere in his appreciation of Bewick, as will be seen in more than one place in the course of this correspondence.

Rome, June 2nd, 1827.

MY DEAR FRIENDS AT HOME,—It is nearly two months since I wrote to you, telling you that I was in want of money, and as I have not had an answer, I have drawn a bill upon my father for twenty pounds, which will come to Darlington for his acceptance, and you will arrange with Backhouse's people where it will be made payable : I suppose, at Hammersley's, in London, will be the best. I should have waited your letter with patience, but that my winter's illness has not only wasted my time, but cost me a good deal of extra expense; and again, I have had a very high scaffolding put up at the Sistine Chapel, which has cost me a good deal, but it was indispensable for the works I am engaged upon. I am glad to tell you that my health is perfectly recovered, and that I hope to be able to remain in Rome during the summer, working hard, to make up for lost time in the winter; but you may rely upon it that, if I feel the slightest indications of the fever, I will go into the country immediately, and not return till the danger is quite over. The heat has not been very great yet; indeed, I have felt very little difference between this and London, and I think it equally hot in May. The weather has been very changeable, frequent rains, and cloudy, as in England. This is usual in this climate. I cannot say that I like Rome much, and were it not for the purpose for which I came, I should not stop; but as I have come so far I am determined to do what I came to do, if my health will carry me through, which I sincerely hope it will, now that I have gone so far. The hot weather seems to agree with me the best. It is the wet and damp that puts me out, and I still feel pangs of rheumatism in my right hand when there is wet ; but I have great hopes that the perspiration by the excessive heat of summer may completely rid me of what gives me not a little anxiety. The English visitors have nearly all left Rome, and it is a very dull place.

Mr. Sams, who was here about a fortnight, is gone to Sicily and Egypt, but expects to be at Darlington in about seven or eight months. He was quite a figure here, and was described to me before I saw him in a way that made me laugh. He came to me at the Sistine Chapel, and looked very well, with a white hat and clean gloves. He came up to the top of the scaffolding, and climbed all the ladders with great caution. He gave me three oranges, and wished me all good luck.

I have not heard from Robert, or Thomas, or anybody—neither have I written. What you told me about the expense of postage prevented me, and I think it very prudent, for so long as all is going on well, we cannot but feel satisfied. However, I pray you always to write me all you can about them—and my sister Ann, you must not forget to remember me to her. I suppose Mary is quite accomplished upon the pianoforte, and other lady-like qualifications. I am glad to hear she was the belle of the ball, and that you yourself enjoyed it so much. By-the-bye there is a young Italian lady here who has composed an opera, the music of which (to my taste) is very sweet and melodious. She is called for upon the stage every evening after the curtain drops, and is applauded by all the gentlemen— the ladies seem not to be moved—perhaps they are a little jealous. She seems very modest and lady-like, and it is remarkable that this is the first opera that has been written by a lady—it is no less curious than true. Ladies write novels, poetry, and history, paint pictures, and make statues, and act plays, but never write music or compose operas. This last is a great undertaking, so many instruments to attend to, and such variety of expression required.

Two young friends of mine, who came about the same time as myself, have been extremely unfortunate here. One I knew before in London. He came to the Cappello Sistino to draw with me, and I suppose the whole thing, being so grand and so extensive, overpowered him. After finishing one drawing, he went to bed in the evening, and felt something at his breast. Presently the blood flowed out of his mouth in a most dreadful way ; and when the doctors were sent.for, they said he had broken a blood-vessel, which they thought arose from over-anxiety. He is now a great deal better. The young gentleman is a Scotchman, of most respectable parents and connexions. He has been, and is now, confined to his room, his mind having become deranged ; and all I could get him to say was that he had acted imprudently, and spent all his money at Florence, and could not submit to explain matters to his family. He cannot have spent much money, for he was always a most prudent young man, as the Scotch people in general are. It is true he visited the best society, but this costs little.

I have had two busts done of me, one by the first English sculptor here. I shall preserve a cast for you, and send it over, or bring it ; better to send it. His name is Gibson, a fine, simpleminded, clever genius, with a very refined and poetical taste, and devoted to his art. He tells me all that he lives for is to leave some fine works to posterity. He is very attentive to me, and we walk almost every evening, talking of art, and the fine antique statues. There is a fine grotto (called the Fontana della Dea Egeria). This grotto, according to Flaminius Vacca, was consecrated by Numa Pompilius to the wood-nymph Egeria. At the upper end of it was found a recumbent statue called Egeria. This statue is in very good style, but, the upper part being naked, it is easy to perceive that it is a male figure, perhaps a river-god. The grotto, being in ruins, is picturesque. It likewise appears from classic writers that the fountain of Egeria was near the ancient Porta Capena ; but we have no good authority for calling the fountain in question that of Egeria.

There is another interesting edifice, which is about one mile from Rome, called the Chiesa di S. Agnese fuori di Porta Pia. The Chapel of the Madonna contains a beautiful antique candelabrum, and a head of our Saviour by Michael Angelo. Beauty of form and depth of expression are so rarely met with in Michael Angelo, that this may not only be said to be one of his happiest efforts, but the finest instance of power, sensibility, and elevated character to be met with in the heads of Christ. There is a touch of sorrow with dignity, an eye of affliction, deep-sunk, serene, and beautiful. It is most highly finished, wonderfully simple of style, fleshy, and exempt from any appearance of mannerism. It seems just taken from the chisel of the artist, it is so fresh.

You must tell me about the additional piece of garden ground you wish to buy. How is my dear mother, and my father? I suppose he still goes on with the geography. Tell him we have green peas, and beans, and strawberries, and cherries, the same as in his garden, and the country looks beautiful; but there seems to me to be a great want of green grass-fields, which are so luxuriant and so delightful in England. The thorn, too, is wanting in May with its fragrance, but there is instead the perfume of the orange-blossom and the lemon-tree, and other luxuriant flowering trees. The people here regularly go to bed in the middle of the day, now that the weather is getting hot, and the fashionables do not get up in the morning before twelve or one, sometimes two. Visits are made in the evening, and the theatres are not over before half-past twelve or one. Remember me to Mr. Smith's family, Mr. Botcherby, and all those who are kind enough to inquire after me. My brother John, how does he do? And Tom, is there any talk of his getting a wife? You need not send anything to Newcastle.

My dear Bess, yours truly,

W. BEWICK.

In the following letter we find an interesting record of an excursion which Mr. Bewick took to some places in the neighbourhood of Rome :—

Rome, July 22nd, 1827.

MY DEAR BESS,—Your long-expected letter arrived two days ago, and I am much obliged to you for sending me so much news. It gives me great pleasure to hear the most trifling thing that you do, or that is going on at home. You cannot write me too much of this sort of news. With regard to the copyhold or life-rents, as you do not explain to me, I cannot advise you; but you cannot do better than follow your own judgment, and I am quite satisfied if you are on the spot all will be right, for I have great reliance upon your prudence. If the purchase is thought a good one, you can make an investment. The only thing is that I do not know what money I may want, as I am not certain of receiving regular remittances from Sir Thomas Lawrence, and therefore at this time you must not make large purchases, although desirable; but I will leave all to yourself. I am at much more expense than usual on account of the scaffolding, and other outlay connected with the large work I am doing.

You do not tell me how Jane's love affair comes on; and what is Tom doing with his lady love? and dear Molly, how does she do? My father too, has he been busy with his garden this spring? My mother is very kind in wishing me home before the cold weather; but she must remember that I have not been able to do anything during the winter, and that the summer is the only time I can have the scaffolding put up in the Sistine Chapel. Even now, when it was thought that nothing would be done in it at all, I am obliged to leave off for a fortnight, on account of the making of two Cardinals. This not only wastes my time, but costs me ten crowns besides. Thus I hope you will not make me more impatient by urging me to come, when I have so much vexation and require so much patience to enable me to remain to finish, as I am determined to do, if possible. I intend to try to remain in Rome during the summer.

Two days ago I felt rather unwell, and I am so afraid of the fever that I went into the country immediately, to a friend at a village, about twelve miles from Rome, called Albano, which is situated upon the side of a mountain where the air is healthy. I arrived there to a breakfast of goat's-milk and eggs; after which we went to another small village three miles further, called La Riccia, where we found in the *café* three Scotchmen and an Irishman taking refreshments, and speaking English, amongst a lot of Germans, Frenchmen, Italians, and Russians, all chattering their own language, or joining in general conversation in Italian,

smoking, and singing, and laughing,—all uniting in the chorus like true citizens of the world.
What may be still more curious—all were artists,
some in the most grotesque dress, and with
curious figure and face. The Frenchman, with
his cigar, gay, light, and lively, was humming
a French air, and speaking a little French, a
little Italian, a little German, or a little English,
—all with the greatest *nonchalance* and grace
imaginable. The German, with his beard, his
long matted hair, his great straw hat, his orna-
mented pipe, the comfort of his life, and his
bundle of linen, had his sketch-book hanging
over his shoulder at one side, and his leathern
bottle with wine on the other. His long um-
brella for the sun, his portable seat under his
arm, his walking-stick, and his coarse fustian
dress, complete the sketch of this Teutonic
artist, as he travelled over the mountains of
Italy in search of scenery and subjects of
costume.

From this village we went to another called
Gensano, about two miles, to see a procession
of monks and friars, with their pictures, their
candles, and their crosses, &c. &c.—all marching

to a band of music, attended by soldiers with their firelocks. The road to this village was crowded with peasants on foot or on mules, the women sitting astride like the men. There were dukes, princesses, and ladies in carriages; and on entering the place we found a very beautiful and very gay scene indeed. There are two streets that run up the side of a hill from one point. Festoons were hanging from bushes, from post to post, all the way up, forming a pleasing barrier to prevent the people from going into the middle of the streets, which were completely carpeted with flowers of all kinds and colours. Opposite each house there was some device of the arms or motto of the family, arranged in compartments in beautiful figures; and at the end of the streets were madonnas hung round with crimson damask, festoons of flowers, and lighted candles. Each window had a piece of silk damask of some bright colour hanging about five or six feet down the wall, upon which the ladies and gentlemen rested their arms. These, with the ladies in gay dresses, the flowers below, the crowds of people in the streets, and the procession with music, produced, I assure you, a delightful and most picturesque effect. Indeed, every year crowds come from Rome, and vehicles of every description are engaged for this day. There were the Duke of Hamilton, with Lord Douglas, his son and his daughter; the Duchess B——, and the Duchess of L—— and her two beautiful daughters; the French ambassador, and the ambassador for the Low Countries, and many other fashionables. The whole ceremony was concluded by a display of fireworks.

When I returned to Albano to bed, I slept soundly; but having smelt the serpents very strong in the woods in the day-time, I still fancied them near me. I rose early next morning, and having hired asses and a guide, my friend and I set off to go up a high mountain, where there is a small monastery and an extensive view. For the greater part of the way the road is a mere path for one person, and so thickly covered by underwood that I was frequently obliged to lie down on the ass's shoulders, to prevent the branches that crossed the road from injuring my eyes. At many parts of the way we crossed a very ancient road, composed of very large stones. On arriving at the top we found about twenty German students, with their asses, their large straw hats, and drawing materials, all as happy, and brotherly, and social as if they were one family. We found also some Scotch people, who, after being accommodated with wine, &c., were making a wretched parley whether they should give the monks twopence-halfpenny each, or fivepence, and could not agree about it; some finally giving the first, and some the latter.

The view from this monastery is most extensive and interesting. In front, and about twenty miles off, lay Rome, as clear and sparkling in the sun as if it were only a mile distant. The atmosphere here is so clear that you can see a house at a distance of thirty or fifty miles, or more. Then we had two or three lakes at our feet, which were sleeping, as it were, in the old craters of burning mountains, the sides of which we had ascended for miles upon the devastating lava, marking by its sinuous appearance the direction it had taken. Between these lakes and Rome lay the Campagna, sterile, flat, and melancholy, with the sea in the distance,

and Hannibal's camp on the right — a most
beautiful spot for a camp, as it commanded a
complete view of that of the Romans, while it
was itself scarcely perceptible by them. We
returned by another road, if road it might be
called, through a wood of chestnut-trees; calling at a monastery to see some very fine pictures by Domenichino. I made our guide
drink up the wine, and then trotted him home
in high good-humour, singing love-songs in
Italian.

Ever yours truly,
W. BEWICK.

Mr. Bewick did not escape the effect of the
hot season in Rome, which is generally so trying
to the constitution of those who come from
more northern and temperate climates. He was
reduced to such a state of debility that he found
it impossible to continue his labours As a
remedy for the oppression from which his whole
frame suffered, he was recommended to have
recourse to the baths of Nocera. He wisely
followed the advice given him, and after passing
some months there, found himself so much

benefited that he returned to Rome in a comparatively good state of health. The account of his residence there, and of one or two excursions to scenes in the neighbourhood, is very interesting.

Rome, Sept. 10th, 1827.

MY DEAREST BESS,— I returned here on Saturday from the baths of Nocera, whither I was obliged to go in consequence of extreme exhaustion from the hot weather, that oppressed and debilitated my whole frame. Thank God I am now quite well, and as it has begun to rain here I have no fear of further annoyance of this kind, and I am fortunate enough not to have been affected by fever, as is frequently the lot of newcomers to Rome, some of whom suffer severely. The climate at Nocera (upon the crest of the Apennines) is like that in the Highlands of Scotland, and in some other respects the place resembles that country. The people, however, differ widely, the poor peasantry of Italy appearing the most patient and the happiest people on earth ; and had you seen the many instances of unalloyed felicity and innocent mirth that were presented to my observation in these mountains, you would be persuaded that true happiness does not depend on wealth, rank, or fashion, as it is often thought to do.

The society at the baths was very circumscribed, and I passed my time in retirement and quiet. The accommodations for visitors are two palazzi, and the bathers I found to be all Italians. One old gentleman spoke a little English, but it was twenty years since he had been in England, so that he had forgotten nearly all. We occasionally had the peasants to dance and sing, to the accompaniment of the guitar and tambourine; and one evening the Marquis Azzoline gave an entertainment upon the top of the mountain, where there was a farm-house.

All the ladies rode on asses, each attended by three men. The whole cavalcade, lighted by torches, ascended the mountains by a narrow and somewhat difficult road. High up we saw our destination, which was brilliantly lighted by lamps and torches, and appeared like an illumination. The Marquis sent me a very spirited, beautiful horse, at which the ladies were not at all pleased, as the narrow path seemed too bounded for his proud spirit; and after conducting them to a safe road, I galloped forward to announce our arrival, when I was received with loud huzzas by about a hundred peasants and the Marquis. The whole scene was splendid. The situation was upon the top of a high mountain surrounded by other mountains; all of which had large fires of wood lighted for the occasion. The farm-house was decorated with lamps, and on the green was a large table covered with the most delicious fruits and wines. This table was surrounded by and canopied with festoons of flowers and box-wood, interspersed with lamps; and adjoining the table was a semicircle enclosed and lighted for music. The dancers were composed of all the neighbouring peasants; the girls dressed in white, with crowns of flowers on their heads.

At the head of the table sat the Duchess of Lante; and (being a foreigner) your humble servant was placed at the right of her Excellency. At the bottom of the table was the Marquis, with the beautiful Princess Donna Giacinta, and her sister Princess Donna Mariamia. The rest of the table was occupied by a countess and her daughter, a governor, and other notables. After the flowers were removed, the servants brought in all manner of eatables, boiled, roasted, fried, baked, and stewed, with wines, champagne, burgundy, malaga, cyprus, &c. The music played, and the girls danced. A poet recited verses, and songs were sung by the peasantry. After midnight the procession began to move again with torches and merriment, when it commenced to rain in torrents, while it thundered and lightened terribly. The ladies screamed, and some fainted, and thus we arrived at our homes wet and weary.

The heat rash that covered my body is quite gone, and I feel quite strong and healthy, and ready to go to work again. On my way here I stopped a day at Terni to see the fall of water, which astonished me. I think I never saw anything so terribly grand, so sublime, so picturesque. The falls of Clyde in Scotland and the Tees, and the fall at Tivoli, are not to be compared with it; indeed, this cascade is thought one of the most beautiful in Europe. The noise of the waterfall may be heard at a great distance, the first fall being three hundred feet in height. The waters fall on the rocks with so much impetuosity that a great part, being reduced almost to vapour, reascends almost to the top of the cascade, where the rays of the sun produce a beautiful rainbow upon the foaming spray. The remainder forms a second fall, and afterwards a third, and lastly uniting with another small river, these waters roll in foaming billows, with thundering noise, along the deep valley.

In the gardens adjoining this fall is a beautiful villa, where our late Queen Caroline lived a short time, and where she received her friends. The fruit in this garden is delicious. After seeing the beauties of the place we returned to the villa, and ate a lunch of figs, pears, apricots, bread and wine, for which we were all prepared, having walked and toiled up the hills and rocks, some on foot, some on asses, and some on chairs carried by men; all Italians but myself. There came some English parties whilst we were enjoying the infinite beauties of the scenery, but they neither seemed to enter into our pleasure, nor receive any pleasurable impression themselves; but were stupidly reserved, and walked about like so many mutes, saying nothing, but looking and going away again in decent and speechless quiet. I went to see the lake of Terni, but was disappointed. The day was not fine, nor was the scenery so beautiful as I expected. I have received a letter from Sir Thomas Lawrence, with a remittance which will serve me for some time. Have you been to Croft or Middleton much? I hope the Rev. J. Dalton and his amiable family are quite well. What is the news at Darlington? How are dear mother and father, and all my sisters? How are Mr. Botcherby, Mr. Janson, Mr. Mewburn, and Dr. Hodgson, and all friends? Sir Thomas Lawrence has written me a very kind and flattering letter.

Yours very sincerely,
W. BEWICK.

CHAPTER IV.

ROME — ENGLISH RESIDENTS IN ROME — EX-QUEEN OF WEST-
PHALIA — VISIT TO NAPLES — IMPRESSIONS OF THE CITY —
NEAPOLITANS FINE DANCERS, BUT REMARKABLY UGLY —
DEPRESSING EFFECT OF MOUNT VESUVIUS — ASCENT OF THE
MOUNTAIN — POMPEII AND HERCULANEUM — PURCHASE OF
ORIGINAL DRAWINGS OF THE OLD MASTERS FOR SIR THOMAS
LAWRENCE — SIR THOMAS'S DELIGHT WITH THE ' SIBYL ' —
FURTHER COMMISSIONS.

MR. BEWICK had now been considerably more than a year in Rome, but every day seemed to add to the weariness of his residence in it. He must have been suffering from the *mal du pays*, for his time was fully occupied; and while he was thus constantly engaged in artistic work, his leisure hours were devoted to the pleasures of society. He was well received in several houses of distinction; his talents were recognised by his brother-artists, and he had the happiness of making the acquaintance of several persons of high station and considerable reputation, in some cases even securing their warm friendship and regard.

In the letter which follows he gives in a few words some discriminating characteristics of the French, German, and English students, and of the manner in which, in their different ways, they derived enjoyment and benefit from their residence in that city which they all regarded as the metropolis of art. In the palaces to which he was invited as a guest, he had opportunities of seeing and studying the *chefs-d'œuvre* of Italian genius; and of these he availed himself, not only to imbue his mind with the highest principles of art, but to learn, so far as he could, those manual secrets of the early painters on which so much of their success as artists depended. It is pleasant to read, in the midst of all the gaieties in which he took part, and the absorption of his mind by the magnificent examples of art to which he had access, of the deep interest which he invariably took in the affairs of his family at home, in all that had reference to the prospects of his brothers, and in all that concerned that sister who appears to have been his principal correspondent. Whatever might occupy his attention at Rome, the burden of his postscripts almost invariably was,

Write soon, with all the news of home. He had also more than one patron in the north of England; as, for instance, Lady Westmorland, to whom reference has already been made, and Mr. Lambton, afterwards Earl of Durham.

Rome, January 1st, 1828.

MY DEAREST BESS,—I wish you all a happy new-year at Darlington. Rome is as dull and stupid as can be. Nothing but religious services, processions and mummery, to break the monotonous quiet of the immortal city. If it were not for the English who come here in the winter, the parties they give, and the bustle they make with their money and their equipages, Rome to an Englishman would be insupportable as a residence, and wearisome as a sojourn, recollecting, as every Englishman must, the comforts of his own country, and the conveniences and gaiety of London. To a student, Rome becomes irksome, unless he can wear away the long nights in the company of some choice friends, very difficult to be met with here, where people only come and go, and you have hardly said 'how do you do' when you are called upon to say, 'good-bye.' The students who have lived here some time get used to the sort of life, and become indifferent and unsocial, many of them living like friars in a convent. I speak of the English; the French and Germans, and students from other countries, I confess are different. They live in a social, Christian-like way, and smoke, and sing, and laugh together; careless, joyous, and happy. The only home an English student has is his studio, a comfortless room, with one window; the walls being coloured grey with soot and whiting, and as dirty as a work-shop, with a cold brick-floor, no better than our stables. His bed-room is without fire, without curtains, without carpet, so that he is driven to a *café* in the evening, if he has no invitation to a rout or party. Imagine the discomfort of returning home in silk stockings and thin shoes, at one or two o'clock in the morning, to a lodging without fire, without candle (and perhaps without supper), for the Italians give no refreshment but ice and pastry at their parties. Now this is tiresome if you are young and have an appetite.

This winter I have been out almost every

evening at some party or other. The balls have been very gay,— stars, garters, and orders everywhere. That which I most enjoyed was one at the Neapolitan ambassador's in the Farnese Palace. Imagine this ancient and splendid palace surrounded by torches, and guards, and carriages ; the noise and bustle of the servants and soldiers quite astounding. The carriage drives under an immense arched gateway, and we are set down at the bottom of a white marble staircase, wide enough to admit a mail-coach. We ascend, our name is shouted from one livery servant to another, until it reaches the top of the staircase, where stands the padrone or master of the house. To him we make our way through crowds of elegant, fashionable, and beautiful ladies, pay our compliments, and try to see all we can, going from one apartment to another, or dancing. The interiors of the palaces here are magnificent. The saloon of the Farnese palace, of which I am speaking, has the ceiling painted by Carracci most beautifully, and is one of the finest things in Rome as a work of art.

The next ball was given by the Prince and

Princess Doria at their palace. The Dorias are a most ancient Italian family, and their palace is like a little town, splendid in every detail. The picture-gallery was thrown open, and dancing was very spiritedly kept up in it till two o'clock in the morning. The next and most beautiful ball was given by Lady Westmoreland, at her palace — Palazzo Rospilosi. Here there was a profusion of everything; tea, coffee, wine, supper, and every luxury. A very beautiful ball was given by Prince and Princess Lancelotti. The avenues to the palace were all lighted by torches, and the road and walls were covered with a kind of white cloth, and guarded by cavalry. I went with a party of Italians, Neapolitans, and Romans, and the staircase was so crowded with servants that we could scarcely make our way up, and those who announced our names were hoarse with bawling. After about an hour we found the Princess, and I was presented to her. The ball-room was beautiful, the walls and ceiling painted in fresco; but the ices and lemonade were very scarce.

The French ambassador gave a beautiful ball; and several smaller balls were given by

English people of rank and fashion. Lady Drummond and Lady Eyre had each a very nice and select party, and I was introduced to Lady Sandwich, who also gives a ball. There is likewise a charming party every Wednesday at the house of the widow of Lucien Bonaparte, late King of Westphalia, a most elegant and accomplished lady. Her son is with her, Prince Bonaparte, a young man about twenty, who speaks a little English, and is very clever. Lady Westmoreland has given very few *tableaux* this winter. Mr. Lambton is in Paris, he wrote to me from that city. I have also heard from Mr. Bandinel, of the Foreign Office, London, who writes very pleasantly and kindly. I am very glad to hear of Robert, but I have not heard from him. Pray give my kindest remembrance to all. How does Jane go on? and Mary and Tom, and father and mother? I am sadly interrupted just now by the ceremonies at the Sistine Chapel. I am obliged to leave off five days before the ceremony takes place. The young Prince Bonaparte is a splendid horseman, leaping on and off the horse when going at full speed; and he repeated this feat several times when the horses were racing at the Carnival. He is rather short and slim, with a very smart figure, dances elegantly, is fond of speaking English, and often talks with me of horses and politics. The only thing that makes Rome gay just now is the English, who are wintering here, and they appear with their wealth like sovereigns of the world. Mr. Bandinel tells me that business in England is very low. Adieu.

Direct to me at Freeborn, Smith, and Co., Rome. Write soon, and send all news.

His important labours at the Sistine Chapel were often interrupted by a strange cause which prevented him making such progress as he otherwise would. The Pope had an insuperable aversion to the smell of paint, and every time that the sacred edifice was to be the scene of religious ceremonies, Mr. Bewick had to discontinue his labours some days beforehand, and for the time to remove his scaffolding. The constant removal and re-erection of so large a structure entailed a great loss of time, and subjected him to great and frequent annoyance; and it was only that spirit of perseverance which formed so marked a peculiarity in his character which enabled him to carry on to its accomplishment the great work which he had successfully commenced.

Rome, Feb. 28th, 1828.

My dearest Bess,—I have expected to hear from you for some time, and I am anxious to know the reason of your not writing, fearing that you are ill, or that something particular has happened. Pray write immediately, for yours are the only letters I receive here that are at all interesting to me. My brothers never write to me, and as I do not write to any other friends, on account of the expense, it is seldom that I can hear anything in the way of news. Mr. Lambton has sent me a draft for fifty pounds. He signs his letter 'Durham,' according to the title he has just been honoured with; and I suppose I must now speak of him as the 'Earl of Durham.' His influence, of course, will be very much increased, and I should like you to write to Mr. Wilson, to ask him if I am entitled to give a vote for the property at Sunderland, as I certainly should wish to do all I can in return for his attentions and assistance. You need not mention the reason of your asking, because I think Mr. Wilson's friends are of the other party.

In the summer I purpose going to see Naples, Mount Vesuvius, and the interesting country around Naples. The Carnival is over, and was something similar to the last, only I think not so gay or brilliant, which I explain by the fact that nearly all the visitors here are Scotch, and they seldom or never enjoy a thing of this kind. I have not enjoyed it myself so much as last year, and I feel very glad that I entered into the fun so completely as I did the first year. It was truly an enjoyment to me; every one seemed so happy and joyous, and for myself I had just recovered from the rheumatism, and was like one let out of prison. This year, thank God, I have been more careful of the weather—of wet and cold.

I have not been able to go all the winter to the Sistine Chapel, on account of religious ceremonies. The Pope is so particular about the smell of paint or varnish, that I am obliged to leave the chapel, and clear everything out four or five days before His Holiness enters it. I am now once more at work at the Chapel, and I hope in a short time to be able to send something to London. It is curious that Robert has not written to me. When you write, pray tell me all about the family, and write a very long letter. Is Tom in Newcastle still, and John? How is Jane, and how does Anne like London? Mary you must kiss for me! She is my favourite. Tell me how the people at Darlington go on—Mr. Botcherby, Dr. Hodgson, Mr. Mewburn, the solicitor. I hope he is well, and in full practice. You say nothing more of the purchase of the garden ground from Lord Darlington; if you would like to have it, pray buy it.

Rome this winter has been very gay with parties and balls; but parties and balls cost very little here, as there is nothing but ices and lemonade given. Two beautiful entertainments have been given since I wrote to you —one by Lady Crawford, and the other by a Mrs. Starke, a lady who has written a very good guide to Italy—perhaps the best. She likewise gave *tableaux*, that were splendid and quite perfect—one with twenty-eight figures. The ball was attended by masques, and some very good ones ; both gave splendid suppers. I have not yet become reconciled to Rome, and I long to see Naples, its beautiful country and antiquities. You may depend upon my writing you everything I meet with worthy of notice. Does my father still read the geography ? and my mother—pray tell me how they both are. Everybody here smokes tobacco, or snuffs, or smokes cigars, just as at Darlington.

The weather has been most favourable, and it is more like spring than winter. I do not recollect if I told you that I was introduced to Mr. Ellison, member for Newcastle. He has now left Rome—not in very good health—with his family. I will write to Tom from Naples, to tell him what there is new. I have lost Robert's address. If you will send it to me again, I will write to him, notwithstanding his silence, and to Anne the first opportunity. When you write to Sunderland, pray remember me to all friends, and particularly to Mr. Wilson. I see nobody here from Sunderland ; in fact, they are principally Scotch people who are here this year. You tell me nothing of your health. What kind of winter have you had? I suppose as stupid as ever. Desiring you to write me a very long letter,

Believe me, dear,

Ever yours affectionately,

W. BEWICK.

From this period until the month of July we have no other indication of Mr. Bewick's life at Rome. We may infer, therefore, that there was little in it calling for particular notice, and that he was pursuing his usual laborious course, varied only by the gaieties in which he occasionally mingled. The letter which he writes from Naples to his sister manifests great delight in the life and animation of its streets, compared with the apathy of Rome, which he considered a *ville morte*.

Naples, July 12th, 1828.

MY DEAR BESS,—I write this letter looking upon the most beautiful sight perhaps in the world—the Bay of Naples, with a climate the most brilliant and serene. The balmy air fresh from the sea makes it a delightfully healthy situation ; and although I have only been here a day or two, I feel invigorated, and in better spirits than at Rome, where the heat was great, and the air oppressive, foggy, and unwholesome. The whole town wore an aspect of lassitude, increased by the multitude of priests and friars, clad in every shade of melancholy colour. Rome is at best a dead place, and in the summer it is deserted for very good reasons. Here at Naples everything is bustle, night and day ; and the crowded streets, the shops, the noise, put me in mind of London. Here it may be said that the people 'live ;' at Rome they seem only to 'kill time.' Here the soldiers, the bands of music, the drums, the trumpets, the pleasure-boats sailing in the bay, the carriages rattling in the streets, the gaiety of the natives, give an air of life and prosperity to the place, although the people complain very much of poverty and of the want of commerce. The King, the Queen, and the Royal Family, with the Court, drive out every day in carriages with beautiful horses. The soldiers are all drawn out, the trumpets sound, the carriages stop, and everybody takes off his hat as they pass.

The birth-day of the Queen was kept on Sunday with great gaiety. The ships in the bay had all their flags and colours spread, the guns fired, and there was an illumination in the evening. The theatre of St. Carlo—one of the most beautiful I ever saw—was crowded. The seats in the pit are all cushioned, and filled by the most respectable persons; indeed officers of the army and navy are ordered into the pit.

Card-playing seems to be the amusement of the fashionable people here at parties. I was at a party last night, and counted ten tables. No refreshments are given; even at balls a glass of water is all that is asked for, and all that is offered. I have been at two balls, and found nothing else. The people dance very well, but are the ugliest set of men and women I ever saw. Their teeth, owing to the air, are all decayed, and their complexions are very dark. Although the Neapolitans are remarkable for being the gayest and merriest of the Italians, and have most wit, yet I have observed a general dulness and melancholy in the expression of their countenances, particularly if you talk of Mount Vesuvius, when they drop their heads, and speak of it with sorrow ; as if it had been sent by the Creator to punish them for being the greatest cheats in the world, which I believe to be the fact, even in the presence of the burning sulphur, and everything that may strike terror by its appearance, or horror by its consequences. Though the mountain is always smoking, and belching forth its fires before their eyes, and raining its fiery showers almost upon their heads, the Neapolitans are still the greatest rogues upon earth, and the veriest cut-throats.

Mount Vesuvius is smoking before me, making the only clouds that are seen in this sky. In the evening the top of the crater within looks red and fiery, and as if it would send forth its bowels of burning stones and molten fire. I think an eruption must be as terrible to witness as its effects are generally dreadful. The eruption this year was very insignificant, and only lasted a few hours. I heard of a man that either fell or threw himself into this caldron three months ago. This person, a shoe-maker of Sorrento, is still living. He was discovered by an Englishman, who, as he was going to the top at the edge of the crater, heard the groans of somebody below;

and looking earnestly down perceived this poor fellow on a ledge of lava below him, with his leg broken. He had lain in this situation for two days, and the only thing he speaks of is a perpetual flitting of fire before his eyes, and an immense cave of fire and red smoke. Should I go to Sorrento I will endeavour to see this man.

The country all about here is sulphurous, everything smacking of it. I drink sulphur-water in the morning and evening, exactly like that of Middleton Spa, but stronger. The wines and fruit are all said to be of a sulphurous nature, and it is dangerous to take much of them. The water is generally bad. The road from Rome, at least half-way near Naples, is not very good to travel in at night, and I think I never saw such cut-throat places. I could give you some melancholy descriptions, but I need not now. I am safe in Naples. By day there is no fear, and by night the roads are well guarded; but still by night I would not risk travelling. I was fortunate enough to have a seat in a gentleman's carriage free of expense, and travelling at suit-able times. I have written two letters to Dar-lington without receiving an answer, one to yourself, and one to Jane; and I have waited some time expecting an answer from one or both. I have written also to Robert, but have no answer yet. Tom sent me a long letter at last, a large sheet. I have sent two pictures to London to Sir Thomas Lawrence. When I have finished the one for Lambton, I hope to be in readiness to return to you all at Darlington, and then what strange stories I shall have to tell you.

I have been very ill with the rheumatism that I caught near Rome, sketching in a damp situation without a seat. It cost me six weeks of terrible pain, but thank God I am now quite well, excepting that I am a little feeble; but with this fresh and healthy air I hope to return to Rome quite stout to finish my work. You speak to me about a guitar. Naples is famous for making these instruments, and I will endeavour to send you one; they are of four strings, and are very elegant. Jane, I hear, is going on in the old way. Mary is very much improved in every respect. Anne still remains in London, which I am glad of. You will be good enough to give my kindest love and remembrance to my father and mother, and all brothers and sisters.

To my friends at Darlington you will be good enough to give my kindest remembrance, and to those at Sunderland. At Naples, goods of every description are bought of English shop-keepers, and I have met in company several Italian gentlemen who speak English very well. The carriage I came to Naples in had the maker's name, G. Marks, New Road, London, at which I laughed heartily, not forgetting my old friend the painter of so many Mount Vesuvius's without ever having seen one eruption. Yesterday I saw a most beautiful villa, built in the most enchanting situation, overlooking the town and bay of Naples; every thing of the newest fashion with fine prints of Lord Darlington's fox-hounds, Mr. Lambton's, and one of King George III. reviewing troops, by Sir Wm. Beechey. In the house where I live the furniture is principally English; the best of it at least. Indeed so many English people come here that I do not wonder at the mania. They pay well, and are imposed upon into the bargain, because they give themselves many airs.

Believe me yours affectionately,

W. BEWICK.

Direct to me at Messrs. Cotterell and Co., 10 Largo Della Vittoria, Naples.

Mr. Bewick remained some time in Naples, being much pleased by the new phases of life which that lively city presented to him. He made several excursions to places of interest in and near the city, dared the perils which fifty years ago attended the ascent of Vesuvius, and looked down into its crater. Herculaneum and Pompeii had not been so thoroughly exposed to the light of day as they now are, but what was visible of them he examined with the interest of one who saw in antiquities much that might be rendered subservient to his art. While at Naples he not only received a highly appreciatory letter from Sir Thomas Lawrence, but was commissioned by him to look out for original drawings by the old masters—a task in which he anticipated little success, as the French had been engaged in the same search before him, and had collected almost everything that was worthy of removal.

Naples, Sept. 4th, 1828.

MY DEAR BESS,—Your very obliging letter I received gladly, and am very happy to hear you are all well at home. I have likewise heard from Robert, who is in good health, but anxious to pass the examination in London; and as his time will be at an end with his present master very soon, he is anxious to go to London and attend lectures immediately after leaving Boxford.

Since writing to you I have been up to the top of Mount Vesuvius, and I will recount to you at Darlington my journey, and what kind of thing it is. The company I went with were fifteen in number, with seven men-servants and a lady's-maid, and consisted of a Roman princess and two daughters, Mr. and Miss Brown, nephew and niece, and Lady Lubbock, two cavaliers, officers of the King's body-guard, two sons of a noble Neapolitan, one of the King's couriers, a Roman councillor, your humble servant, and a gentleman who undertook to be our director, and who had made the same excursion in company with Mrs. Starke (who has published her travels). The company left Naples at half-past nine in the evening, in three carriages, and arrived at the little village of Resina at eleven, the full moon swimming in the cloudless sky. We drove into the yard of the captain of the guides, named Salvatone Madonna, which was filled with asses, mules, and men, all ready to set off for the mountain. The entrance of the carriages, the uproar and eagerness of the men to obtain riders, caused a noise and confusion that was as astounding and as laughable as a Neapolitan rabble could be expected to make.

From this place we were taken to a *tratorica*, half a mile distant, by the side of the sea, where was prepared a supper that was as useless as it was tormenting, every one wishing to proceed, and no one having any appetite, for we were all anxious to be uponthe verge of the crater before sunrise. However, the maccaroni was upon the table, and I partook heartily of fish and champagne, and mounted my donkey in the crowd below, with eager anticipations of what was to come—of hair-breadth escapes by flood and field, of robbers, assassins, and of all that fiction, history, the experience of the past, and the facts of the present, could suggest to my imagination.

The roads here are all of lava, and you travel on the accumulation of ages, the guide giving you an account of the different strata. Thus we journeyed on, passing through rich vineyards, the watch-dogs barking and giving notice of our passing, and the peasants running to the road to see that all was right with the fruit. We arrived by crooked and unpleasant paths at the Hermitage, a small white house with a chapel, a hermit, and a guard of six or seven soldiers, stationed there for the benefit of Vesuvian travellers. This guard has been placed there since the robbery of some French gentlemen, at the foot of the cone of the mountain, a short time ago. Some of the banditti have been taken and sent to the galleys, and there remain still four or five who have eluded the vigilant search of the guard. These robbers have property near the village. The story was told to me by my guide, whose brother happened to be guide to these same Frenchmen, as we rode past the spot. He was forced with his face to the ground, and a musket at his head to confess who the travellers were, one of them having a star at his breast. The story, told by moonlight upon the very spot, made me look apprehensively around, the situation being a very dreary one, and by night or day admirably calculated for any black or bloody deed, for it looked on all sides a desert formed of masses of lava, black as pitch, sinking into cavities, holes, curious corners, dells, and dry river-beds made by descending torrents.

We passed this part of the road in comparative stillness, for every one had enough to do to look to his ass; and the path, which is as bad as it can well be, seemed as if made for difficulty and danger. We had tea, with roast beef, and fowls, and a little brandy, at the Hermitage, and then we mounted our asses, and rode on, accompanied by two or three of the soldiers, to the foot of the cone of the mountain, where, dismounting and taking large sticks, we prepared to ascend; the ladies being placed in arm-chairs fixed on poles, and carried by six or eight men. The difficulty and danger were really so great that I wonder, when I reflect on it, that no accident happened. Never was such a scene, with tugging and tumbling, the rolling of stones from above, the screams of women, the shouting, bawling and swearing of men—who, instead of invoking the Madonna, or some goodly saint, called upon the aid of maccaroni,—the laughing of some, and the lamentation of others.   The curious and novel appearance of the party from below, seen stretching from the bottom to the top in picturesque and terrible positions, was very remarkable.   Some seemed falling from fatigue, and others were lying on the mountain taking breath, while the men encouraged each other to exertion, —the leader of the guides, dressed in white, standing apart, exhorting his subordinates, while the soldiers with their muskets ran up to the top to see that all was right there, and that there were no lurkers.   All together formed a scene as picturesque and romantic as it was dangerous, and often ridiculous.

When we were nearly at the top the sun began to rise, lighting up splendidly the most extensive as well as the most beautiful scenery that fancy could conjure up.   The Bay of Naples spread out below, like an immense mirror, the surface studded with fishing-boats with white sails, while the breath of morning slightly rippled the blue water.   The city lay circling the extensive margin of this delicious crescent with its cold white houses, and numerous towns and villages seemed to be melting into air in the distance.

A few more steps brought us to the verge of the crater of Vesuvius, and a more awful or sublime sight it is impossible to conceive. The first impression was one of awe and terror. Pictures or descriptions can give but a very faint idea of the grandeur of this immense amphitheatre, smoking, rumbling, and belching forth with hideous noise, its crimson tongues of fire, the earth trembling under you, and menacing every instant an explosion that might scatter your limbs piecemeal over the scene so far below. A convulsion of nature like this is a curious and very interesting sight, and never fails to impress upon the beholder the omnipotence of the Creator.

The top of the cone of this mountain is said to be about three and a half miles in circumference—it looks about a mile. The inside of the crater is an immense cavern, black with fire and smoke ; and in the centre rises another cone formed of black lava, from the top or point of which issue constantly volumes of smoke, rising majestically into clouds above, or enveloping the summit ; and every two or three minutes burst forth with thundering noise a column of fire of red-hot lava, hissing and spitting. The noise may be said to resemble the bellowing of some gigantic wild beast chained below, and the loud thunderous rumbling may be likened to the clanking of his chains. Think, then, what must be the effect of an eruption that devastates the country around!

Well may the Neapolitans look melancholy and hang their heads when you talk of Vesuvius. It is said that an eruption in 472 was so terrible that the inhabitants of Constantinople were terrified; and in another, the clouds of stones and ashes thrown out darkened the sun at Rome, and even some stones were carried by the wind as far as Egypt. That stones from this mountain have been found two hundred miles distant is certain, but that they could be hurled as far as Egypt is hard to believe. The descent to the point where we left the asses and mules was as rapid as the ascent was slow, and took one hour, three minutes, every step carrying you three or four yards down knee-deep in pumice-stone, ashes, and scoria. If instead of putting your heel down first, you were to put your toe, you would fall, and death would be inevitable, such is the fatal facility of the descent.

My kindest and dearest remembrance to all my family, and believe me *truly and affection- ately yours,

W. BEWICK.

From Naples, Sept. 5th, 1828.

Naples, Nov. 11th, 1828.

MY DEAREST BESS,—Your very obliging and excellent letter, dated so long ago as September 17th, I have this day received, and I derive much consolation, not only from the expressions, but from the manner in which the whole is written. It gives me great pleasure that Tom is again well, and gone to his occupation, and that all the other members of the family are in good health and spirits ; particularly my dear father and mother. You never say if Anne and her husband are still in London. The plants Jane wishes me to bring I hope are for her own garden, and the silk-worms for mother will be for the mulberry-trees that are yet to be planted. I am delighted with your opinion of John. Dear Mary, too, is merry and laughing as usual. Happy girl ! I hope she will choose a husband who will deserve her, for she was always my favourite, and her sisters can allow me to say as much without jealousy.

Naples is filling with English people, and it is becoming rather cold. The grapes are all finished, and the vineyards are all being dressed for next year. New wine is brought on the table ; pears, apples, grapes, and roasted chestnuts form the dessert ; and this dessert, which would cost half-a-crown or three shillings in England, will cost for one person three half-pence or two-pence. The grapes are most exquisite, as well as the peas and apples. There is a fruit I like very much called the white water-melon, gushing with the most delicious juice. The orange-trees are bending with their golden fruit, and the lemons are ready for the punch. You buy an orange nearly as large as your head for a farthing or halfpenny. The pomegranates, too, are bursting with ripeness, showing their rich, ruby insides, more tempting in appearance than in taste. The climate here, although a little cold in the morning, is like the spring in England. The people sit with their windows open all day long, and sup in the street by moonlight at night, singing and playing the guitar ; and it is a curious fact that, amidst wine and merriment, you never see any one tipsy or behaving rudely.

Since writing the above I have received a most pleasant letter from Sir Thomas Lawrence, who informs me that the pictures I sent to him have arrived in the river, and that, as soon as they come to his house, he will show them to his brother Academicians, and write me faithfully the impression they make. The letter is excessively gratifying, and if the expense was not so much I should be tempted to send it to you to read. I am just recovering from a cold in my head and throat, that I think I got upon the high mountains near this city, and I have been tempted to buy some pictures here by the old masters, such as Raphael. What can Mr. Sams be doing in Jerusalem?

Believe me, dearest, yours affectionately,

W. BEWICK.

I have seen Pompeii and Herculaneum, where they are still making excavations, and find every day something curious. The town of Pompeii is a most melancholy and interesting sight. You see the houses, the baths, the pavements, the sacred edifices, and the public halls; the prisons, the stocks, the theatres, the sepulchres, and the monuments of public men or private families; statues, pictures of the highest style of art, and of the very best workmanship; buildings and columns left unfinished; nay, here are their fire-places, with the ashes of the fire; the wine dried up in the bottles; corn, beans, and oats unground, flour ready for bread, and even bread and eggs; figs, olives, almonds, cherries, prunes, linen, cloth, bottles, glasses, cups, spoons, chairs, locks and keys, earrings, necklaces, rings, bracelets, pins, needles, inkstands, and pens—all of the most exquisite taste and invention; frying-pans, girdles, saucepans, ladles made of bronze, and lined with silver (tin not being known); lamps and stands, wonderfully beautiful, and vases, hay, ropes; a purse with money found in one hand of a lady, and a key in the other, supposed to be the lady of the house. The skeleton was found with most beautiful gold ornaments, necklace, earrings, and armlets.

When you view the streets, houses, and monuments of Pompeii, and look not only upon specimens of most exquisite art, but also upon the utensils of the kitchen, the materials for eating and drinking, and even the marks of cups and glasses upon marble tables in the drinking-shops, there remains upon the mind an impression of astonishment, for Pompeii was destroyed, or covered entirely, by the ashes of Mount Vesuvius in the year 79 after the birth of Christ. All the articles at Pompeii are not burnt ; but those at Herculaneum are burnt black like charcoal ; and the pictures brought to light, painted on the walls at Pompeii, are most beautifully preserved, and, what most astonishes me, of the most perfect style of art. Some of them deserve to be classed with the finest specimens of painting of the best periods of modern art.

I am looking out for original drawings by the old masters for Sir Thomas Lawrence ; but I am afraid that I shall not be at all successful, as the French have carried away everything that was at all worth taking, and since then so many English have bought and taken away pictures that the gleanings are scarce, and if anything good and genuine is found, it is exorbitantly dear. I drank all your healths on the 20th of October, knowing that you would all be together in the evening. Farewell.

Early in the following year Mr. Bewick's correspondence shows that he was again in Rome, where he was executing some commissions with which he had been favoured. The copies of the pictures in the Sistine Chapel which he had sent home met with the highest approbation of Sir Thomas Lawrence, who had them put up in his rooms.

In a letter to Bewick Sir Thomas says : ' I have sincere apologies to make to you for not sooner informing you of my receipt of the two pictures, which I had immediately placed on substantial frames. Unfortunately their large size makes it difficult for me to exhibit them in the rooms, which, with my own too numerous works, their superior dimensions convert into very small apartments. But let me now speak of the works themselves. I am not disappointed in their grandeur and noble simplicity of effect, but I will own to you that I am not equally satisfied with two or three of the details. In the "Sibyl" my impression is that something has been lost in the expression of the countenance, which my memory tells me has in the original a more softened abstraction of thought in the character. Then in the advancing leg the shadow comes on so far and harshly on the sight that the width, fulness, and substance of the limb, are injured by it.

'Is there so great a distance from the nose to the ear of the " Jeremiah," which by-the-bye is small, and not accurately placed, and have you sufficiently attended to the fine anatomical drawing of the upper hand, the first joint of the forefinger ? The knuckle appears rather a large swelling than the form itself, which in Michael Angelo is generally pronounced.

'These are my criticisms, and being anxious for the complete defence of this greatest artist, and its successful effect by your pencil, I have at present abstained from showing the pictures, but shall soon exhibit them to my friends. Of the sale of the " Jeremiah " you may be certain, as should other purchasers not be found, I shall gladly retain it at the price I sent you for the other.

* * * * * *

' I cannot well undertake the responsibility of employing you on another figure from the same noble work ; but should you, without building on my assistance, choose to dedicate your time to it, let me hope that your judgment will coincide with mine in selecting the "Sibyl" half rising and closing the book.'

In reply to this letter and the criticisms which it contains, Mr. Bewick writes :—' I am sorry that the size of the "Jeremiah" and the "Sibyl" prevents you from placing them in apartments where perhaps distance and light properly arranged might be favourable. The space in the chapel where they were painted is, as you know, immense, and the distance of the originals sixty feet from the spectator, with a light rather obscure, which may tend very much to soften any harshness of effect or expression that may have impressed you with a confined distance and concentrated light close upon the pictures.

' In answer to your very obliging criticisms on one or two details that you have been so kind as to make to me, I feel inclined rather to acknowledge the defects for my own than endeavour to make a feeble defence at the expense, if it was possible, of the original author. I confess to you that the expression of the " Sibyl" I found to be most difficult to hit; and I made the observation at the time that by approaching close to the head the individuality in a great measure lessened that abstraction that distance and obscurity gave. Whether this may be true with regard to my copy I will not pretend to say—no one made the remark when comparing it with the original in the chapel. I should have been too happy for a remark of this kind, for it is a head which I took great trouble to get well. The advancing leg, which you may depend upon being exactly copied, always appeared to me to have something of the objection you mention. The defect of the ear and the upper hand of " Jeremiah" I should be most glad to take as my own; they are both very much defaced in the fresco. The upper hand is not at all comparable to the one below, hanging, the veins surcharged, and every articulation beautifully and powerfully pronounced. Perhaps nothing could be finer than the expression of this hand, but the other is feeble, flat, and rather awkwardly drawn—as you say, lumpy. It must have lost much of its original force and character.'

Haydon, it may be remarked, though he admired the manner in which Bewick had accomplished the task which he had undertaken, did not approve of it. 'What absurdity,' he remarked, 'to pull things from dark recesses, sixty feet high—things which were obliged to be painted lighter, drawn fuller, and coloured harder than nature warrants, to look like life at the distance, and to bring them down to the level of the eye in a drawing-room, and adore them as the purest examples of form, colour, expression, and character. They were never meant to be seen at that distance or in that space.'

The following letter is addressed by Bewick to his sister :—

Rome, March 25th, 1829.

DEAREST BESS,—I have waited ever since I wrote to you from Naples, but in vain, neither my brother Robert nor yourself have sent to me an answer, although it is two months since I wrote to both. Since my arrival here I have been working very hard at the small picture for Lord Durham, which I hope to finish soon. The subject is 'Cornelia' and her family, from Roman history. A Roman lady exhibits her jewels to Cornelia, who in reply shows her her two boys; you remember the story. As Lord Durham is the father of a beautiful and interesting family, I thought it would please both himself and Lady Durham. He was satisfied, and I am now going on with the picture, which, I am sorry to say, is but small, but it is according to his orders. Sir Thomas Lawrence has written to me that he has put up the pictures in his room—that he is struck with their 'noble grandeur,' &c., &c., and that the scale being so large his rooms have become small apartments. Sir Thomas says, 'He will be glad to see Robert when he does him the honour to call upon him.' I hope that my brother has already called, as I wrote to him to do so. Sir Thomas tells me not to be uneasy about the sale of the other picture, as if no purchaser appears he will take it himself, and requests me, if I have time, to occupy myself upon another 'Sibyl,' which he names, and likewise desires me, if possible, to make him a facsimile copy of a large original drawing by Michael Angelo, which is in the Museum of Naples.

It is unfortunate that he had not told me before I left Naples, as I could have made a drawing very well when I was there. I am afraid that it will not be possible for me to deny Sir Thomas what he requests, though it will cost me a run over to Naples for a week or two. He has been so remarkably kind to me, as you know, that I think it might be imprudent not to do any little thing I can to please him. I am extremely anxious to hear from you, to know how you are, and still more anxious to be at Darlington, which I hope now will not be long. I work hard every day in this hope, and trust soon to see you all. I wonder and wonder you have not written, and more so at Robert, because his marriage was to take place about this time, and he may well guess how glad I shall be to hear it has taken place. How does Jane's affair come on? Is Thomas gone to London? Pray tell me all news.

On my coming to Rome I met a number

of English travellers and foreigners, who were leaving on account of the death of the Pope. All the theatres were closed, and every amusement was stopped, so that this Eternal City was, if possible, more dull than ever. The defunct sovereign was placed in state in St. Peter's, and a most splendid cenotaph erected to his honour, or his memory, in the centre of the Cathedral. The ceremonial was in the usual pompous style, and might strike an English stranger as a gaudy show for the living rather than sincere tribute of respect to the dead.

The Romans are now in lively suspense for the election of the new pontiff, which must take place shortly. The conclave of Cardinals is sitting, and the only amusement that the people enjoy is to go to Monte Cavallo, before the Royal Palace of the Quirinal, twice a day to see the smoke and inquire the news of the day. The seeing the smoke is this. You must know that twice a day the votes for the new Pope are collected from the Cardinals, and if a sufficient number do not vote for the Car-dinal proposed, the votes, which are written on paper, are burnt in a stove, from which there is a pipe to convey the smoke outside, in front of the palace. This, so long as it continues, is a sign that the Pope is not yet elected. When the smoke ceases, the votes are not burnt, and of course no smoke appears. The whole of the Cardinals are locked up for the time, without the slightest communication with any one. Their victuals are conveyed to them every day, as in a nunnery, by a wheel, without their seeing any one. There is a strong guard at the entrance of the palace, and no one enters it or comes out. It is exactly like a prison. Every one has his two apartments and one servant, and thus they live a tiresome and unwholesome life. The whole of the Christian world is waiting anxiously the result of their holy deliberations.

I still find the air of Rome very heavy, and often damp, producing a low tone of nerves, from which arise melancholy and dulness of spirits ; and I have no doubt that the air of Naples suits me much better than that of this city, which is so irregular that scarcely two days are at the same temperature, one hot and another cold or damp. Pray write immediately and tell me all news. How are mother and father? Mary?—Jane?—Is John Graham in Darlington, and what is he doing? My journey from Naples was, although a little cold, very pleasant. Pray give my kindest compliments to Mr. Wilson of Sunderland, Dr. Burn, and all friends, and believe me to be,

Yours affectionately, and ever truly,

W. BEWICK.

CHAPTER V.

IT was not without considerable injury to his health, long delicate, that Mr. Bewick had painted his copies of the 'Delphic Sibyl' on a scaffolding sixty feet high, erected by him in the Sistine Chapel, and afterwards of 'Jeremiah lamenting the destruction of Jerusalem;' but the warm approval of the President and of the artists to whom they were exhibited on their arrival in England was a rich reward to him, and he was in high spirits at receiving Sir Thomas's order for copies of the whole series of Prophets and Sibyls. He had executed four large copies in oil, and the whole of the studies in detail, when the sudden death of Sir Thomas Lawrence put a stop to his labours, and induced him to return to England. The Academy did not feel itself called upon to carry out the purpose of its great President, and the four careful and magnificent copies were sold at the sale of Sir Thomas Lawrence's effects, and are hidden away in some corner where they are useless, alike to the student and the connoisseur. A large collection of drawings, however, from which the paintings had been made remained in the artist's hands, and in his declining years it was his happiness to be able to add a gallery to his house in Leskerne, where he could show them with other original drawings and paintings of his own, as well as with some choice specimens of the old masters gathered in his travels. But surely such works are of national interest, and should be placed in some national museum or gallery as pendants to the Cartoons of Raffaelle.

The first record in Bewick's own handwriting of what befell him on his return to England is an account of a final meeting with Hazlitt and an interview with the painter Northcote.

On my return from Italy I met my old friend Hazlitt near Trafalgar Square. When he saw me he rushed up to me and caught me by both hands, exclaiming in amazement, 'My dear fellow, where have you come from? where have you been? I have lost sight of you for an age.' I replied, 'I have been in the sunny clime, and am just on my way to Northcote to show him my "Jeremiah."' 'Ah! I am so glad you are just come as my redeeming star,—my credit is at this time very low with him; you must know I am editing his Fables—I may say writing them—and he is just now very peevish and impatient at my not sending him some "copy." I shall be ready to-morrow. Now if you see him to-day and put him into a good humour, which you will do by showing him your "Jeremiah"— you must speak of me, tell him you have just seen me, and that I shall see him to-morrow with more "copy," and then you can tell me how his pulse beats,' &c. ·

We then shook hands and parted, he going his way, I to Northcote. An old servant, almost blind, who had lived with him for half-a-century, and who had been ordered to leave scores of times, but would not go, opened the door. I sent in my card, and was ushered into the miser's study. I found him alone in his studio, dressed in an old dingy green dressing-gown, and cap to match. He received me very graciously, and when I told him I had just returned from Italy he opened his eyes with amazement. I said I had brought my drawing of ' Jeremiah' to show him. ' Thank you, thank you, Mr. Bewick,' he said. I then unrolled my drawing ; and he, holding up his hands in amazement, said, ' Ah ! wonderful — strange ! How grand ! Ah, sir, Raphael and Michael Angelo were grand fellows —we are puny and meagre compared with them, and I fear ever shall be. The style of education in the arts is so effeminate, if I may so speak, in this country.' Then in a sententious manner he added, ' No, sir, they will never be able to comprehend the grandeur of Michael Angelo ; you may show " Jeremiah " upside down for the next century, and no one will see the differ- ence, so unaccustomed are they to see, and so little do they know of the grand lines and bold conceptions of Michael Angelo. Now, there is your friend, Mr. Hazlitt ; he is clever, and has a critical conception of art, but he cannot comprehend Michael Angelo. For instance, he tells me respecting the Sistine Chapel, that he was disappointed with the " Last Judgment," that the Prophets and Sibyls are grand figures, but that they are wanting in elevated expression.' 'But,' said I, 'had he been upon the cornice where I was he would have seen the expression better. I do not think that from a distance of sixty feet below he could distinguish their characteristics. He speaks of " Jeremiah" not being so fine in the expression of the features as in the action of the body, and drapery, hands, &c. Now I do not agree with him. The absorbed expression of grief or abandonment to lamentation in the face of " Jeremiah" is as fine and concentrated, as elevated and perfectly worked out, as finished as a miniature, as anything I know of Raphael; and I question if Raphael has ever given such grandeur of conception in any one figure. Then there is the face of the Delphic Sibyl, what can be more inspired, more elevated, poetical, or even beautiful ?' N. 'He mentions Zachariah, Daniel, &c.' B. 'But then there is Joel, Isaiah, the Cumæan

Sibyl, all equal in characteristic expression, intense, abstract, in unison with the action of the figure—with that grandeur of epic art which Sir Joshua says there is nothing to equal. Mr. Hazlitt has not been near enough to see the individual peculiarities or wonderful artistic excellence of their heads. By-the-bye this conversation reminds me that I have just seen our friend Hazlitt.' *N.* 'You have, have you? He is the strangest being I ever met with; what did he say?' *B.* 'He is ready with fresh " copy," and will see you to-morrow.' At this piece of information Northcote rubbed his hands, and smiling said, ' Well, Hazlitt is a clever, but original genius; I can make nothing of him, but hope he will come—very odd, very odd!' I then rolled up my ' Jeremiah,' bid Northcote good morning, and beset my steps to Mr. Hazlitt, who was anxious to learn my success. I told him the way was all made straight for him, and that Mr. Northcote would be glad to see him. He shook me warmly by the hand, and we parted. I left town for a time, and an occasional correspondence was kept up. But I never shook hands with him again.

On his return to England Mr. Bewick took a house in George Street, Hanover Square, for the purpose of exhibiting his works. They naturally excited much interest in artists, though unhappily for the country they were left on his. hands, and not secured for any school of art. The following detailed account of the drawings exhibited by Mr. Bewick, and of the manner in which they were taken, is copied from a contemporary notice in the *Art-Union:*—

'In the year 1826, Sir Thomas Lawrence commissioned Mr. Bewick, then in Rome, to make a series of copies from the most famous works of Michael Angelo—the Prophets and Sibyls that adorn the chapel of the Pontiff. It was the intention of the President to present these copies to the Royal Academy, in order that the future student might be enabled to consult the magnificent creations of a mighty mind, and derive from the continual study of them that incentive to emulation, and that instruction in his art, which these wonderful productions could not fail to afford him. Unfortunately for the artist and the country, the

President died before the labour was completed. Four only of the copies had been made; and these, unhappily, having been disposed of at the sale of his property, are hidden in some corner to which the student is debarred access. A large collection of drawings, however, from which the paintings were to have been made, is still in the possession of Mr. Bewick; and to these we desire to direct public attention, with the hope that we may be the means of consigning them to their original destination.

'When Sir Thomas selected Mr. Bewick for the performance of this arduous duty, he had, no doubt, entire conviction of his fitness for the task; he had the power to choose from the whole range of students; for probably there was not one who would not gladly have undertaken it, as conferring a high and honourable distinction, and as supplying the surest and most effectual mode of professional improvement. The wisdom of the choice is proved by the manner in which the work has been executed. The finished paintings we have not seen; but the drawings are of so admirable a

character, that we cannot doubt their preserving
the amazing power and beauty of the originals.

'The difficulty of procuring them was by
no means small. The influence of Sir Thomas
Lawrence overcame the first obstacle; and
permission was granted to Mr. Bewick to make
the copies. The height of the Sistine Chapel
is sixty feet; and the scaffolding was carried
up close to the ceiling. This scaffolding, it was
necessary frequently to remove and re-erect in
consequence of the ceremonials appointed to
take place therein. The time required was
necessarily very great; and a residence in
Rome during the summer months—so peril-
ous to health and life—is what few are disposed to encounter. There are, indeed, many
ways of accounting for the fact that of the
students resident in, or visiting Rome, none
have had the courage, energy, and industry
to grapple with difficulties which appeared
almost insurmountable, even after the labour
had been promised recompense, and permission to undertake it had been obtained. Notwithstanding the strong incentive to exer-

tion supplied by Sir Joshua Reynolds, a few sketches of the great works in the Sistine Chapel have been all that artists have brought away; and neither the French, the Germans, nor the Russians, who throng in crowds to the Eternal City to study the mighty master, have obtained a more advantageous mode of making the world acquainted with his greatness. It is therefore most unlikely that other copies than those of Mr. Bewick will be made; and in duty to him, as well as the students in Great Britain, we express an earnest hope that these may not be scattered, and so lost to the world. The whole of the interior of the Chapel Sixtus is divided into compartments, varied in size and form, all occupied with subjects relating to Holy Writ, or in that sublime circle, exhibiting the origin, the progress, and final dispensations of theocracy, or the empire of Religion, considered as the parent and queen of man, as taught by the sacred records. In this imagery of primeval simplicity, whose sole object is the relation of the race to its founder, there is only God with man. The veil of eternity is rent: time, space, and matter, teem in the creation of the elements and of earth. The awful synod of Prophets and Sibyls are the heralds of the Redeemer; and the host of Patriarchs the pedigree of the Son of Man. Such is the spirit of the Sistine Chapel.

'Among the copies are the five Sibyls—Delphica, Cumæa, Persica, Lybica, and Erythræa. The first is the most wonderful—a combination of beauty with power in the countenance, such as no other painter has ever executed, or, perhaps, ever conceived. The aged Persica pores over a book. Lybica is rising and closing a volume. Of the Prophets, Isaiah is listening to a sacred messenger; Jeremiah is mourning over the fearful nature of his own prophecies; Joel is perusing a scroll; Ezekiel, Zachariah, and Daniel, are the others. But any attempt to describe them would be absurd. The drawings are larger than life-size, and upon a scale of about one half of the originals. They may, we presume, be seen where we have seen them, at the house of Mr. Bewick, No. 27 George Street, Hanover Square.

'It is unnecessary for us to state that in

thus strongly lauding this series of copies by Mr. Bewick—and in treating them with some portion of that enthusiasm all artists have felt in examining, and afterwards remembering, the originals—we are influenced only by an earnest desire to assist in securing them, as the property of the country, for the benefit of British students in art.   We look upon them as certain sources of future greatness to many a young and yet uninformed mind, and trust there may be no danger of their being withheld from a national depository.   But as the Chancellor of the Exchequer may, from a score of causes, plead the inability of the nation to spare from its coffers the enormous sum of a few hundred pounds to bestow them on the country, we hope the members of the Royal Academy will, if the Chancellor do not, carry out the design of their late President, and expend some portion of their funds upon the most legitimate purpose to which they can be applied.

' We are naturally anxious to secure them for the metropolis, where they might be studied by and teach the greater number ; but if any difficulty should arise to prevent this—and if any do we shall feel no little sorrow and shame for the apathy of promoters and encouragers of British Art—we still hope they may not be so divided and scattered that, when a more auspicious time arrives, it will be impossible again to gather them together. Some provincial town will, perhaps, possess the treasure, and we may foresee a period when the student will make a pilgrimage to visit them with as much enthusiastic zeal as ever bore a devotee through toil to some sacred shrine.

' Sure we are that if our observations induce artists to look at these glorious works, the creations of the mightiest mind that has existed since human beings ceased to be directly inspired, they will consider us fully borne out in the earnest enthusiasm with which we speak of them.'

Mr. Bewick's health at this time was so delicate that he was unable to visit much at night, but his friends still cherish the recollection of the happy evenings spent in George Street, with him, his wife, and his bright and pretty sister.

But Darlington was his home, and thither he returned, finding large occupation for his ready pencil, for everybody in that part of the world who could afford it considered it his duty to have his portrait painted by ' Bewick,' or to have his walls adorned with some specimen of his handiwork ; so that before long the artist was enabled to retire from painting as a profession.

When the Commission was appointed, in 1843, to award prizes for designs of high art calculated for the fresco adornment of the Houses of Parliament, Bewick arose, like a war horse at the sound of the trumpet, and prepared a cartoon, entitled ' The Triumph of David,' which he announced thus in a letter to Sir C. Eastlake :—

DEAR SIR,—I have finished a drawing for the forthcoming competition, and as I have no place near Westminster Hall, where I could have a day to sketch it and retouch it privately, in case of accident by friction, or by conveyance from such a distance as this, I write to ask you if any such convenience will be accorded to artists from the country like myself. The very frail material of chalk on such a scale makes it rather an anxious consideration, when it is not fixed by any process of steaming, and I have not attempted to try the experiment with mine. I trust there will be sufficient forethought and provision for the treatment in hanging drawings on this large scale without frames, when the subject fills to the very edge of paper, as mine does; a thumb-mark or rule would be an injury.

I had almost given up the idea of sending a drawing, by reason of the delicate state of my health during the winter, and the promising information given in a former number of the *Art - Union* — 'that the walls will be so crowded,' but as a very contrary expectation is expressed in the *last* number of that publication (that the competition would be only a remove from a failure), I feel stimulated to send you what I can get ready; and although it is not done with the advantages of models, &c., that I might have had in London, I still entertain a humble hope that the 'judges' may not pass my design without discovering traces of some former acknowledged power in this particular department of chalk-drawing.

Sir Charles Eastlake replied courteously to this letter, as he did on all occasions, but as there is nothing in his letter beyond the details of business, it seems hardly worth while to print it.

The cartoon appears to have been rather too delicate in its treatment to excite much attention among the large number of drawings sent in for competition; but in the autumn it was exhibited at Darlington together with the artist's Sistine copies, and attracted much interest.

Henceforth he came forward but little into public life, his easy circumstances at home and the delicacy of his health alike persuading him of the charms of his fireside. The letters written in his declining years to his friends, Mr. W. Davison of Hartlepool and Mr. H. Cromek of Wakefield, show how completely he was devoted to his art, and how he loved to recall the circumstances of his early life, and especially all details connected with his ever-regretted master. While he was in Rome, and intimate with Gibson, the sculptor had made a cast of Bewick's head, which Mrs. Bewick subsequently desired to have executed in marble. With reference to this subject Gibson writes from Rome :—

Rome, March 1st, 1847.

DEAR BEWICK,—Many thanks for your kind letter and remembrance of me. I hope your health will improve. I continue to enjoy pretty good health, though never very strong—always careful, abstemious, and regular in my habits.

I devote all my soul and body to my art, and rise up with the sun. Since you left Rome I have produced many works in marble and original drawings. My life being so active, months and years gallop over my head with great rapidity. Old age and death will ere long put an end to my labours. My labours will live to be judged of by man, and my soul by God.

The cast of your bust has been preserved. If you wish to have it I can send it to you—executed in marble it will cost you twenty pounds ; for such a bust I charge seventy pounds. I think my agent in London, Mr. M'Cracken, Old Jewry, will charge you five pounds for case, packing, and carriage from Rome to London. So your bust, to which I should give myself some finishing touches, would cost you twenty-five pounds put down in London.

I remain, dear Bewick,

Yours very sincerely,

JOHN GIBSON.

The bust was put into marble, but did not reach Haughton-le-Skerne until the August of 1855, and the pleasant excitement produced by its arrival is described in a letter of the period.

Mr. Bewick was now in that happy position in which he could pursue his art, not as a means of living, but for the pleasure it afforded him. In his correspondence with the two intimate friends to whom the following letters were addressed, we see how deep was the artistic feeling by which he was animated, and how anxious he was to obtain to still higher excellence. Ever mindful of the difficulties which he had encountered in the early part of his career, he was at all times eager to encourage struggling artists, always urging them to perseverance as the road to success where there is a foundation of true talent.

As he had been unable to dispose of his large copies of the cartoons, he had rooms prepared for them connected with his own house; but symptoms of mildew soon showed themselves, and he found it necessary to use some necessary precautions in order to preserve them. At the same time, he still executed occasional commissions; his works were becoming known far and wide; and he was even solicited to allow his copies of Michael Angelo's cartoons to be exhibited in New York. These and similar matters are referred to in the following letter to his friends; and this portion of his correspondence is particularly interesting for the insight it gives us into his domestic life, showing his amiable character as a man, his obliging disposition as a friend, and his affectionate character as a husband and father. These letters are valuable also for the occasional reminiscences of artists with whom he had been associated at various times in the course of his life. His observations on the peculiar methods of the different artists whom he had seen at work are very interesting. How characteristic are the pictures which we find in one of these letters of the manner in which Turner, Wilkie, and Haydon, went to work, each bringing out in some manner peculiar to himself his wonderful effects!

Letters to W. Davison, Esq., Hartlepool.

Haughton Cottage, near Darlington,
Nov. 23rd, 1845.

My Dear Davison,—It is quite delightful to hear from you again. Mrs. Bewick and myself are much concerned for Mrs. Davison, that she still continues to be a sufferer ; certainly the air of the sea-coast must be too strong for her. I am quite sure that it is so for me, or we should have been down to the sea-side not unfrequently this summer, for the benefit of a change ; but my health, although at present pretty good, is so precarious and delicate that a *dry* and sheltered situation seems necessary, and the place where we are now is extremely so. Indeed, this place has been called by physicians ' the Montpelier of the North.' We live upon sand and gravel, and the moisture is absorbed rapidly. Collins, the landscape-painter, was the same, and he was ordered to remove to Hampstead to a dry sub-soil, and I believe he is living there still. The air here is mild, and the situation so sheltered that vegetables are ready in the season three weeks or a month earlier even than in Darlington, which is only a mile distant.

Miss Ada, I have no doubt, will be a ' sonsie' lassie. Let her draw *everything* except French specimens of chalk drawing, as they are very ' mannered.' He who would be a draughtsman must draw from the round, beginning with hands and feet and heads, or parts of these; but it requires great application. I drew for half a year, every day labouring and sighing to produce what I saw before me. But it is very different with a young lady who wishes only for an accomplishment. I should recommend her to draw trees, ships, rocks, clouds, waters, plants, or railing, as well as parts of the figure. I mean drawing from nature out-of-doors, for her health as well as practice, exercising the hand and eye. *Application*—application—application, is the thing, Miss Ada Davison; and therefore I would have it partly out-of-doors.

In this place I have not a single plaster cast, but probably at Newcastle some hands or feet or heads may be had. Mr. Quelch has everything of this kind at his house; he brought them from London; and I have no doubt but that he would willingly lend anything to you. A hand, and foot, and head, would be quite enough for some time, and they ought to be drawn in chalk the full size, in every possible view. I began to draw upon common cartridge paper, with black and white chalk, and had some difficulty in getting the outline and proportions. A few outlines merely will be very good to begin with— the full size; and never mind how rude, say some encouraging words to induce more trials. When I began I had never seen a port-crayon, and often had not the means to buy bread to rub out with; but nothing deterred me. Neither hunger nor declining health prevented me from beginning at five o'clock in the morning, and working till twelve o'clock at night, until I had mastered the difficulties; and this application told so much upon me, that my legs were swollen, and I had to keep them upon a chair while I worked, until I was told that confinement was killing me. But I had mastered the beginning, and looked onward, little dreaming of that future of which Hazlitt spoke to the boy at Dulwich College.

I am glad you keep painting, and, with all due deference to Miss Ada, I must say that your department—landscape—is the most pleasurable. I should like to see some of your recent works. Wilkie's 'Village Festival' must have been a very laborious undertaking, but I have no doubt that you have made a beautiful copy, although I confess to you this is not a picture that I like so well as many of his other works. The figures always strike me as being small for the size of the picture, and so not sufficiently prominent, and leaving a good deal of space to be filled by other material. It may be considered something between a landscape and a figure picture, and is neither the one nor the other, although the subject is one in which the figures ought to be the all-important part. The copy you made from would be Burlison's, no doubt; and a very good copy it seemed to me, and one that I should like to possess.   You were lucky to get hold of the sketch of Constable's, and in a frame it will be delightful.

I have not been from home for a length of time.   I am obliged to keep as quiet as possible, and I assure you to live here is to be as quiet and retired as any tired person need wish to be.   The house I live in was built by myself for the purpose of letting, but I came here because my health required retirement.   We have not got all complete in the inside, as my painting affairs throw certain parts into confusion.   I make the best room into a studio (not a very good one), and the room adjoining contains paints, canvas, and a heterogeneous mass of pictures and frames, &c. &c.   Our living room is to your taste, I dare say ; the whole of the walls are covered with old pictures on a crimson paper ; the furniture is of carved oak. My Vandyck is over the fireplace, in a beautiful light. I paint an occasional portrait or fancy head.   I was employed lately to paint a portrait of one of the Carmelite nuns, with a very picturesque and interesting costume—that, literally, of the ancient Spanish peasant, which they wear to this day without the slightest modification.   It is the portrait of a lady who paints and draws. She has travelled often in Italy, and all over the world, and, although now a nun, is an extremely interesting person. Mrs. Davison may imagine me—the palette on my thumb, in the nursery, surrounded by nuns, veiled, with musical voices, and some young, interesting, and beautiful, with this picturesque costume, and sandalled feet. Mrs. Bewick desires her kindest regards to Mrs. and Miss Davison and yourself, in which I beg to join, and am, my dear Davison,

Yours truly,

W. BEWICK.

Haughton Cottage, Jan. 15th, 1850.

MY DEAR DAVISON,—With all due decorum I begin my long-delayed note to you by wishing a happy new year to you, not forgetting Miss Ada ; who I hope, and do not doubt, will add to every other cause of happiness in store for you both, and all three.

My friend Miss Quelch has told Mrs. Bewick that you intended to write to me, so I take the will for the deed, and have no doubt that you are prevented by the usual causes, procrastination, or too much ' of that same' writing in the ledger, daily accounts, &c. To me, I confess, in my younger days, this was ' the hatred of my soul,' and, indeed, now, after all the romance of life is over, and I am settled down in a staid country retirement, with nothing to do, I still make a stumblingblock of this 'keeping accounts,' and do it as little as possible. I regard this as a weakness, and always think it a defect in my organisation, or lack of the faculty of calculation. I am glad to let my wife be the money-keeper, the payer of bills, and the buyer of everything, except bricks and wood. No doubt, then, you will wonder how I get through my time. I do as well as I can; and tell Mrs. Davison I endeavour to laugh as much, and as often, as I can get an opportunity for exhibiting the risible expression of my now old-looking visage,—old with so many years of dire experience and buffeting with difficulties (in art), and the seriousness, if not the peevishness, of mankind. I amuse myself by looking out into the little world around me, and diving into character, real or pretended, and finding out innumerable little curiosities, all highly edifying in their way; and these I sometimes put on paper.

'Well,' you will say, 'this is about anything rather than art.' Really, Sir, I never talk about the arts at all, simply because here there is no one to talk to on that particular subject. It comes upon me as quite a new thing, a novelty, and I can hardly get hold of the usual terms and expressions belonging to the mystery, —such as, the 'subtleties,' 'manipulations,' and other German novelties in the code of art-language. I am quite at a loss how to commence with you on this our old score. I hear you constantly paint and draw; and I want to know if you still have the enjoyment of pleasing yourself with your greys, and browns, and half-tints?—your 'bit' of positive in a sea of 'breadth?' I see you, on a certain day, very busy; with Mrs. Davison full of admiration at everything you do, which is the delight of life! We shall be together again some of these days, I hope (I mean you and I, and our two wives).

Mrs. Bewick joins me in earnest regards to

both of you, and to Miss Ada ; and in the hope
of having good news from you,

I am, my dear Davison, yours very truly,

WILLIAM BEWICK.

P.S.—I inclose you a very beautiful pro-
spectus of a work proposed to be published
by that very ingenious and extremely clever
artist and friend of mine (perhaps of yours
also), Mr. Archer ; the intimate friend of Balmer,
and the author of the short memoir of him in
the *Art-Union*, at the time of his death.
Mr. Archer and Mr. Lance married sisters.
The author of the work on London is an extremely clever draughtsman and engraver, and
writes in a very nice, understandable style.
He is member of and lecturer at the Archæological Societies, and therefore well educated
and fit to carry out the beautiful work he is
now about. He has Prince Albert, and a host
of noblemen and *dilettanti* subscribers.

CHAPTER VI.

CONTINUATION OF CORRESPONDENCE WITH MR. DAVISON — A FRIEND OF KEATS THE POET — ADVICE TO HIS FRIEND — MR. SEVERN — PYNE THE ARTIST — PORTRAIT OF MARY BEN-TON — EXHIBITION OF HIS CARTOONS DESIRED AT NEW YORK — TURNER — REMINISCENCES OF GREAT ARTISTS — LETTERS TO MRS. DAVISON.

Haughton-le-Skerne, near Darlington,
Nov. 17th, 1850.

MY DEAR DAVISON,—I have your two nice and chatty letters. The first came when I was from home, painting an extraordinarily aged person. What do you think of one hundred and nineteen years?—a face all wrinkles and puckers! I painted two pictures from this person; one is a front face, and the other a profile.

I am now building a house in which I shall have a good gallery for my cartoons from Michael Angelo, that are at present rolled up, and have not seen the light for ten years.

Your imaginary bliss as a picture-dealer I can well understand, and fancy you scrubbing and rubbing up some antique Van Spruggen or Signor Linkermfeedle, and after you have taken away with 'essence of salt,' or 'spike lavender,' whatever there might have been of good on the canvas, delighted to see how 'fresh' it is, how new-looking and clear of dirt, as they say, and that you had indeed got to its original state, 'pure as it was when just painted!' and so forth. You then spend days filling up cracks and holes, matching the colour and varnishing, and crown the accumulated sin by blandly asserting the name of the original artist, say Claude, or Waterloo, or, perhaps, Vandeveldt: is this endurable? Oh! I have seen these dealers spoiling, scrubbing, smoking, and swaggering, spending perhaps five or six days in skinning a picture, and most valuable and national works spoiled by these pretenders. All artists have a just horror for these chapmen; they certainly do come in contact with gentlemen connoisseurs, and often rule them; but their pleasure in art is only in proportion to the gain they make by it, and it is astonishing what influence some of these fellows have over gentlemen of real feeling for art merely by their swagger and appearance.

But, to turn to something else, I am truly glad to learn that you are determined to spare nothing in the perfecting of Miss Davison's education. Speaking of education puts me in mind of an old friend who married, and is come into the possession of a large family, and who has written to me describing his children, and how they are advancing themselves. He is a poor artist, but rich in affection and talents, industrious, and a gentleman. I only need say that Mr. Severn was the friend of Keats the poet, and tended him until his death at Rome. His tenderness and affection for the poet was as strong as the love of woman; and as I knew Keats, poor fellow, I now love my friend Severn, and rejoice to see how he has pushed his family forward with nothing but his pencil to help him. He is as honourable and dear a fellow as ever breathed, with a noble and generous spirit, and the feeling of a true gentleman.

My gallery for the cartoons will be 30 feet long by 18 feet wide, and 15 or 16 feet high;

and my painting-room 20 feet by 15 feet. All to be ready to move into it by May-day next, as I have let my present abode from that time. Mrs. Bewick desires me to convey through you her kind regards to Mrs. and Miss Davison, in which I beg to join heart and hand, and am, my dear Davison,

Yours very truly,

W. Bewick.

Haughton-le-Skerne, Dec. 7th, 1850.

My dear Davison,—I should like to see your Rembrandts very much, but had rather they were original things. I cannot but long that you should be doing, what in your own peculiar line you do so well, those delightful bits of sea-side scenes. Why not combine some extraordinary effects in nature, of colour, or light and shadow, taking for your material the objects and forms you know so well, and can draw with such correctness and propriety? You would certainly do something fine in this way, some effects of sky, broad and true to nature. Cattermole did some fine things with Rembrandtist effects and colour; but then he does not paint in oil, and his things are in water-colour, a material not quite so manageable as oil. Now, Turner's are extraordinary works, but then the effects are imaginary, and one cannot reconcile them in any way to our ideas of truth and nature; and hence the difficulty, or rather the impossibility, of this being satisfactory, or truly pleasurable, to the eye, or even to the fancy. I speak only to Turner's latter works, for his early productions are very superior in all the requisites of pictorial harmony, truth, and execution.

My dear *Willie!* (as Mrs. Davison says) do be constant (don't be ashamed at the word) to your *sea*-scapes. Give us every pictorial variety your imagination is capable of. Be most extraordinary, most eccentric, in your productions; but then *do*—do!—what you *can* so easily, and harmonise it to nature, or the appearance or possibility of nature; do this with constancy, and I will warrant you will surprise and delight everybody you care about pleasing.

You ask me about Severn. Mr. Severn is well known in the arts; he was resident in Rome when I was. He paints pictures historical and poetical, and has a fine imaginative fancy, and does some things charmingly. He has been greatly patronised in high quarters. He painted such subjects as ' The Vintage' to admiration, and the King of the Belgians bought one of these admirable works at a great price. He is also a poet and musician, composing and playing on the piano his own music. Dear, dear Davison! here I am; can do nothing, as Hazlitt used to say of himself—' Damn it, nothing, Sir;' and when he missed a ball at rackets, he shouted in despair, ' Sheer incapacity, by G——.'

Ever yours most truly,

W. BEWICK.

Michael Angelo Gallery! ! !
Haughton-le-Skerne, near Darlington,
June, 1851.

MY DEAR DAVISON,—Happiest of mortals, you have seen everything the metropolis of the world contains in 1851! And now for once I do envy you. I do covet your opportunity, your leisure, and your discriminating selection of all the choicest products of nature or art, and at every symposium at which you feasted.

I cannot follow you in your remarks on the works of artists. You speak highly of Pyne. He is a very superior artist, and, at the same time, a remarkably clever man, and as to theory, will outrun you (theorist out-and-out) in nostrums, and propositions, and experiments, and ifs, and buts, and whys, and wherefores, and all the jingle of right angle, triangle, A B C, &c. &c. It appears that you were at Sunderland just a day too soon, for the day after the Doctor received the profile portrait of Mary Benton, the old woman of whom I spoke in a former letter. The other picture which I painted of this fine old lady has been engraved in the *Illustrated London News*, and there is an account of her obtained from the gentleman who purchased the portrait. I will send you (for lack of news) a note from the proprietor of the picture—Mr. Fox, of Westbourne Terrace, Hyde Park—into whose collection it has found its way. Indeed, he wrote to me to inquire if I would part with the picture. I named my London price for it, and when he received it he was good enough to send me a cheque upon Coutts for double the amount. Several artists have written to congratulate me upon this successful production, particularly the hands, expression, &c. You will be good enough to return the notes to me, and of course you must consider them confidential. My gallery progresses, and is nearly finished. If it were dry enough, my cartoons would be up in a twinkling, and then, 'my dear fellow!' you will be no longer excused. I have some good rooms in my new house, although they are all wet, except a little breakfast-room and bed-room, which are dry, and in which we keep rattling fires every day, so making an increase in the coal-trade.

Mrs. Bewick desires me to convey to Mrs. and Miss Davison her kindest regards, as well as to yourself, in which I beg to join, and am, my dear Davison,

Yours very truly,

W. BEWICK.

Haughton-le-Skerne, near Darlington,
Jan. 2nd, 1852.

My dear Davison,—Here is 1852. What do we promise ourselves in the shape of work? Are you looking forward to exercising your brush at all? I am in great anxiety about my cartoons, as they are beginning to mildew from the damp, although I have a large fire in the flue night and day. I fear they will have to be taken down, and from the straining frames. How grand they look! I have ten stretched, and five in frames. The Americans want to have them in their forthcoming Exhibition at New York, but the guarantee is not sufficient for me; and, besides, I would like it better that they remained in this country somewhere secured, as most probably no other copies will ever be made, by reason of the great expense and difficulty, and I am told the frescoes are much decayed since mine were done. Now, Sir Davison! be in good humour with me, make my genteelest bow to the ladies, and do tell me how Mrs. Davison is, as Mrs. Bewick will be anxious to know; and I send this off by the post, in the hope that it will reach you before all the merry-making and Christmas cheer are ended.

Yours, very truly,
My dear Davison,
W. BEWICK.

Haughton House, near Darlington,
Feb. 3rd, 1853.

MY DEAR DAVISON,—Having written a few days ago to Mrs. Davison when in a very sullen and moody humour, and feeling myself rather lively and spirited to-day, I take it into my head to talk to you in the serious and prosaic way most suitable to our usual subject, the Arts. I am sprightly because I am just left alone, after being cheered up by two bright ladies shining in their satins — Quakeresses, with as fine bred horses and trappings to their carriage as any nobleman in this fair England. The coachman has a modest living. How these fair Quakeresses have laughed! What happy faces, beaming with goodness, telling of good cheer and happy homes! My wife is gone out, albeit it snows, and I am free for a gossip with you.

Your two last notes lie before me. I should like, indeed, to see your experiments *à la Turner*. I must beg to inform you that I have myself seen my friend Turner paint, and and that too upon some of his finest works. You say no one was ever let into his secret by seeing him paint, but seeing him paint would not let you or me into his secret. Indeed, he did not know that he had a secret. To know how he painted when he was thirty or forty would be the desideratum of those who play follow-my-leader. Although so very close in money affairs, he was a cordial old chap. I was never introduced to him, but he came boldly up to me and held out his (extraordinary) hand, and being, as I am, a judge of shakes, his shake told me his character, and we thereupon gave a double shake. He was very pleasant, and you would have been mighty fond of him, but you could have seen no rainbow or prismatic colours in him or in his costume. His complexion was of a very healthy hue, as if mellowed by the sun and fine weather, like ripe corn. Indeed, there is a friend of mine at Sunderland, the very man, in figure, face, and complexion, and about the age; so that, if ever you want to see how Turner looked, our Doctor can contrive you a meeting, and he is just as likely to surprise and astonish you with his extraordinary effects in his way as the real Turner. Indeed, the painter was as natural and simple as any real landscape, and did not look as if he represented 200,000*l*.

But, seriously, I have seen Turner paint, Wilkie paint, and of course Haydon (although I was the only painter, or pupil, or student allowed to be present while he was at work), and Landseer, with some others of not equal eminence in the executive or effective departments of the art; and I cannot say that any *scumbled* at the rate you speak of, although Turner had a very curious and almost unaccountable process of bringing up the ultimate perfection of his tones and effects. I suppose you would like vastly to hear me describe their methods— secrets if you will—but, my dear Sir, what an inquiry it would be — to what fearful discussion would it lead — the analysing the palettes of each of these eminent painters, after they have

been painting a few hours. Nobody could suppose that Wilkie could produce execution so
near perfection from such a furbished up palette, the scrapings, the savings, and the skin,
with just a bit of the surface rubbed clean to
wet his pencil on and mix his tints. His palette
was a save-all, with bits of tints of colour
remaining for days and weeks.

Then, as to Haydon, his palette — but why
bother you in this way, who enjoy the imagination, the unreal, the mystery of men's ways in
their studio? If you knew exactly how, why, and
wherefore, it would prevent the exercising your
invention and imaginative faculties, stop the experiments that you so delight in, and delight
everybody else with. I say again I should like
very much to see some of those Turners of yours,
either the Italian ones or that 'sea-storm' that
is now left in your head, and was so sublimely
exhibited before your eyes a few days ago in
fearful reality. I have never seen Burnett's
work; but Turner's early works are upon a
different principle to his last. Which do you
like best? We wish we were nearer you, by
'earthquakes' or any other process. Mrs. Be-

wick joins me in kind regards to Mrs., Miss, Davison, and yourself, and

I am, my dear Davison,
Yours very sincerely,
W. BEWICK.

Not the least pleasing peculiarity in the correspondence of Bewick is its variety, passing with perfect ease from grave to gay, from discussions on art to the ordinary details of domestic life. After the more serious letters which he had written to Mr. Davison, the following letters to that gentleman's wife afford us delightful specimens of his lighter and more sportive mood :—

Haughton House, near Darlington,
July 21st, 1853.

MY DEAR MRS. DAVISON,—I do bless that blarney-stone with all my heart, no matter by what name it goes. I had it very racy and sweet when I was in old Ireland in my youth, in the mild South, where the hot sun melts the icy hearts of both men and women. In the north I own to its rarity. I am chilled by the rigidity and the sternness of so cold a phlegm as reigns in these Northern regions ; and when something that smacks of heart-warmth comes to our deadened finger-ends, there is a tingle all over one's nervous sensibility, quite unusual, and one cannot help asking what it means,—how?—where are we?—is it real?—does it come from a southern or northern latitude ; and we remain in a maze of pleasant sensations ; and I for one do not care a straw, why, or whence, or how you call it, civility, amenity, or other fine names in the catalogue,—no, I meant to say category of pleasurable sensations.

But mine, Mrs. Davison, is a curious fatality. I love the South, the Southern people, the refinements of a Southern hemi-sphere, arts, literature, science, the natural frankness and generosity accompanying high attainments and the possession of great genius bestowed upon the few. And look at me! I am thrown into a place here where, literally speaking, there is not one individual being that possesses the slightest inclination or taste for any of the humanising accomplishments. Here is a cold humid atmosphere—cold people, who

take a poet for an exciseman, a painter for a
fellow not to be trusted further than ready
money will take him, and who, astonished to
find that an author who has amused them at a
feast is only an author, exclaim, ' We thought he
had been a gentleman!' And a gentleman he
was, ma'am, as well bred as any of them, though
he had stooped to literature, and now enjoys a
world-wide fame, known to these Northern folk
by his exuberant wit and original genius; and
we boast of him as the author of *Vanity Fair*,
the Thackeray, and my friend. Mrs. Bewick
desires her love to you all, and so does, my dear
Mrs. Davison,

Yours truly,

W. BEWICK.

Haughton House, near Darlington,
August 24th, 1853.

My dear Mrs. Davison,—We have, it
seems, reciprocated thoughts, for Mrs. Bewick
and myself have often wondered how Mr.
Davison was going on, and I have procrasti-
nated, ma'am, from day to day, hugging the
delightful satisfaction of having shirked a duty,

avoided a pleasure, until your note this morning 'brings me up to the scratch ;'—scratchy enough my hand is, for I never could write an 'office' hand, although I have whilom tried. Hazlitt used to say, 'He liked to see how painters formed their tottering letters,' and I have heard a fine landscape-painter swear a tremendous oath at these words, and offer to write with any man living for one hundred pounds ; and he showed me his handwriting, which was certainly beautiful. Alas ! both these great spirits are in the dust. Is my dear William mad,—to walk seven miles, and remain in bed next day ? Is it possible that an old business-man like my friend William should do such a mad freak ? Had I done it, it would have been nothing to surprise anybody, a harum-scarum fellow like me, that gets on to the moon and off again, rides on the thistle-down, blowing bubbles to the winds of heaven, and nobody thinks it strange ; they only wink, and point, and say, 'Ah ! he—he's west-north-west,' and leave me to my dreams and vagaries.

Well, Mrs. D., have you read that extraordinary book by Mrs. Crow, *The Night Side of Nature?* If you have not, get it ; it is quite in your way; it will take you to the seventh heaven, and more. I am at present going through it. I have not taken any of the cherry-bark, because I have none ; but I have been going on pretty well without any drugs whatever ; and now it is fine weather, I get out as much as my frame will bear, and go to bed after dinner, which refreshes me. I avoid all invitations out, and deny myself the pleasure of fine dinners and pleasant company, even in this village. Though a lady desired to drive me in her carriage three miles off to a delightful dinner, I had the heart to refuse the risk. What does my friend William say to this self-denial ?—*he* could not do it. Everybody wants to drive me off to try change of air, but I think of the comforts of home, and cannot, as yet, make up my mind.

I must tell you of the arrival of a marble bust of me from Rome. It came last week, and was found dropped outside my gate early one morning by the servant. The woman tried to carry me, but could not. You may rely upon it, I was in a flurry when told in bed where my other head was lying, being sure the nose would be broken off, or that some mutilation would disfigure it; and when it was brought into the house, I heard,—nay, I felt that something or other was knocking about in the inside of the case. I exclaimed 'It is the nose! depend upon it;' and we were all impatient to open it and see. It was delightful to see how it was packed, so secure and safe; and when it was at last got fairly out, Mrs. Bewick exclaimed, 'How beautiful!' and kissed its cold lips. The bust is by the great sculptor Gibson, my friend. It was modelled twenty-five years ago, and cut in marble in 1853—mind, not at all by my desire. Gibson, in the first place, asked me to sit to him. The model was seen in Rome by some friends, and a drawing of it brought over for Mrs. Bewick by a lady, and they have persuaded her to get it done in marble. Everybody exclaims, How beautiful it is! I must say as a work of art it is quite equal to the antique. It is life-size. Our kind regards to William and Ada, and I am,

My dear Mrs. Davison,

Yours truly,

W. BEWICK.

Haughton, near Darlington,
Sept. 9th, 1853.

DEAR MRS. DAVISON,—As I am desirous not to lose Gibson's note, I write for fear that you should have forgotten that it was my wish that it should be returned. Indeed, my having occasion to show it to a friend of Gibson's who paid me a visit yesterday, put me in mind that it was at Hartlepool, and I thought it better to write to you in case it had escaped your memory.

There is a strange and unexpected revelation quoted from Tom Taylor's Autobiography of Haydon inserted in the *Durham Advertiser* of this day. When I read the quotation, it brought back the dim remembrance of those early days. Of course, I got through it with palpitating heart, for I had great difficulty to manage my feelings. Little did I think it would ever be recorded in the language of the moment. When we consider the extraordinary circumstances under which Haydon painted the figure of Lazarus, it often occurs to me what wonderful powers of mind were possessed by this man; for be it known to you that he has recorded his being arrested at that time ; and in the middle of his work, he was again arrested two separate times. I was mounted upon a box, upon a chair, upon a table ; and when he came back a third time and mounted the steps, he said to me in accents not to be forgotten, 'Bewick, if I am called out again, it will be impossible for me to go on ; that is the third time this morning that I have been arrested.' He painted the head, hands, and drapery all in that day ! and it has never been touched since. Sir Walter Scott told me, whilst looking at the picture, that it was a perfect realisation of what he himself imagined when reading the account in the Bible. I hope Mr. Davison continues to improve and to be prudent. I am going on pretty well at present. Mrs. Bewick joins with me in our kind regards to Ada, William, and yourself, and

I am, my dear Mrs. Davison,

Yours very truly,
W. BEWICK.

CHAPTER VII.

Haughton-le-Skerne, near Darlington,
Oct. 12th, 1853.

MY DEAR DAVISON,—I am very much obliged to you for sending me the nice, freely written letter from the Lakes. I remember the time when I was at Sir John Leicester's gallery to view the fine collection of modern works. It is, indeed, a long, long time ago, and I remember I was there in company with Mr. Leigh Hunt, Keats and Haydon, the Landseers, and others.

Mr. Haydon had asked permission to take this party; and Sir John gave orders that when he and his party came he should be informed. He and Lady Leicester and their friends came in to see those remarkable men, and we all were introduced (a very unusual thing on such occasions). Lady Leicester was beautiful, and there was a full-length portrait of her by Sir Thomas Lawrence, equally beautiful. Looking at me she asked Mr. Haydon if all his pupils had black hair (the Landseers have all flaxen polls); and when I read Mr. F.'s remark about my 'black hair,' it brought the circumstance to my mind. Leigh Hunt had a profusion of black hair at that time, and he was pale, and altogether a remarkable-looking man, with a searching, dark, and beaming eye, and everybody seemed struck with his uncommon and intellectual appearance. Keats and Haydon were not so tall, but both remarkable in their appearance. With our united love to you, William, and Ada,

I am, dear Davison,

Yours very truly,

W. BEWICK.

Haughton-le-Skerne,
Oct. 21st, 1853.

MY DEAR DAVISON,—Your note written on the 18th duly came to me this morning. This brings me to the 'chromatic scale' again, and I wish very much you would fulfil your promise of supplying me with your recently discovered improvements, together with a plan of them. That the grounds of the old painters are known as to colour is pretty correct; but what 'grounds' have you for supposing that they laid those grounds on a principle of contrast? It seems very like saying, I shall prove my argument by the power of contradiction. The Dutch masters had a white ground. Then, supposing that Rembrandt painted in a head or other subject *at once*, or Rubens—both of whom, it is known, often did so—how could they have a chromatic or 'accidental' ground for such pictures, painting in red under blue, purple under yellow, and so on? The fact that the Venetians painted upon a brilliant system of glazing cannot be a part of this chromatic principle, although I have seen Titian copied by laying in the *whole* in grey; but there was a very different reason for this, seeing that the under-colour in the original was *cooler* than the upper transparent glazing.

Here is the first volume of Haydon's Autobiography brought in to me, so I shall have a feast, I guess. Only fancy twenty-seven folio volumes for his journal! His correspondence, it appears, is not published in the life, but very probably will come afterwards. Of all lives, ' autobiography ' is the most interesting. Benvenuto Cellini's is a romance that no fancy or imagination could have invented. It is interesting, because he writes of his feelings, his peculiarities, and his habits. He takes you to the time in which he lived — to the home, the place, his acquaintances, enemies and friends, his occupations, his successes, his difficulties, anxieties, sufferings, pleasures, loves, and disappointments. And although this may be egotism, when years are past and another generation has come, it has grown into the interest of history, and is a valuable illustration of the state of society at that particular period.

And now, my dear Davison, I have had my chat with you, and will turn to my old master and see him again as he lived. Mrs. Bewick unites with me in kind regards to you and all that to you do belong.

And I am, my dear William,

Yours very truly,

W. BEWICK.

The following letter is of great interest, as containing Bewick's judgment on the master who had been so friendly to him in the early part of his career. These remarks were occasioned by the appearance of Haydon's Autobiography :—

Haughton-le-Skerne, near Darlington,
Nov. 20th, 1853.

MY DEAR MRS. DAVISON,—I suppose you will have read Haydon's memoir by this time. Everybody is reading it, and everybody is reviewing it. I have just finished the third volume, and I suppose the second edition is required, which will be corrected and improved ; so if you have not yet read it, wait for the second edition. The third volume gives me some acid falsities which I think I ought to correct, either in the papers or some other way. I should not like to reflect upon the memory of one who seems to have had everybody upon him, who, like most other men, was not quite perfection, but had many fine qualities, and very great genius and intellectual power. If these had only been kept quite devoted to the great task for which he was fitted, his noble efforts might have astonished the world and honoured his country. We may indulge in the speculation that the painter of the finest work of high art in this country, 'The Judgment of Solomon,' must, under favourable circumstances, have achieved things which would have done honour to the country and to our School of Art. But after the painting of 'Lazarus,' when a terrible pecuniary embarrassment beset him, and his canvas could only obtain divided attentions, while his mind was 'ill at ease,' and anxieties frittered away noble genius, what wonder though life became a burden intolerable? As it was, under all the unfavourable circumstances, he earned, by his industry and talent, at the rate of 500*l.* per annum, or more; yet he could not keep the bailiffs out of the house! Some years he cleared from a thousand to two thousand. Mrs. Bewick and myself hope you are all well, and we unite in our loves to you, and I am,

My dear Mrs. Davison,
Yours truly,
W. BEWICK.

Haughton, Dec. 6th, 1853.

MY DEAR DAVISON,—I shall set you down as 'the silent man,' or 'the narrow-necked bottle' of Shakespeare. You go to Paris, and I hear nothing of it from you until the pith and marrow of your impression is retailed in gossip to the nobodies of every day, and utterly frittered away. You pass up to London, and not a word you have to tell me of anything that either pleases or displeases you. It appears you rave about the Turners; you have gloated upon them; and you have set up poor old ruddy-faced Turner as 'the god of your idolatry.' Of course I want to know all about your impressions before they evaporate, and leave only perhaps faint the steam of your effervescence anent this old conundrum; and as a contribution to the hodge-podge you keep boiling and bubbling in the cook-shop of your brain-pan. I send you a curious revelation about pictures in Queen Anne Street. If you have not seen it before, it will interest you as to the materials Turner put into some of the examples of his genius, and his grudging parsimony with regard to finery in his mansion. In an appendix to Haydon's Life, vol. iii., there is a copy of Sir Joshua's memorandum of his colours and pigments; the wax and balsams he brushed on his canvases, with Beechey's and Haydon's notes upon the same. To you, who are scientifically and chemically hodge-podgy, and up to the gamut of chromatic tinctures, the airy evanescences of light, or the Rembrandtish darkness of scene, of the colours that stand, and those that *turn* to airy nothing, of all the vehicles that are good, who know all about table-turning, this knowledge of Turner's use of materials will be marvellously interesting.

My life has been a life of frankness, but I sometimes like to be as dry and mysterious as any clockmaker or barber-politician. I try to mystify and wrap up simples in a labyrinth, or to tie them in a true-lover's knot, that can only be cut by the short ' twig' of a woman's eye. I had a bold tenant once, a hero who told some one that he did not like a smiling landlord (meaning me). Ever since that I have tried to look serious, grave, or sour, as business men seem to do, even if they are only selling a ha'porth of needles or a twopenny doll, a child's cradle or little Tommy's rattle.

But to return to Sir Joshua. What a melancholy thing it is to think that he should have pestered his mind with such abominable theories and humbugs of practice as are recorded in his memoranda ! And what a fickleness he exhibits in so many times changing and experimenting, and at every change he writes down that he is ' *stabilito in muno*,' &c. This repeatedly occurs, and is as often changed again by new and unheard-of experiments.

My wife desires her kind regards to you, Mrs. Davison, and all, in which I beg most cordially to join, and I am,

My dear Mrs. Davison,

Yours sincerely,

W. BEWICK.

Haughton, Dec. 17th, 1853.

MY DEAR DAVISON,—I have, then, done what I wished,—made you speak out in four sheets of note-paper. Anything is better than bottling all your blue ink in self-possession and passive silence. I am equally an admirer of Greek architecture, Turner, and Sir Joshua, and cannot turn over to Mr. Ruskin all at once. The critics say that Haydon was insane (never was there a greater mistake), and now they say Ruskin is over the moon. I have not read his *Stones of Venice*, nor his remarks about Turner, except by snatches and odd bits. Setting aside fine writing, I do not see why one may not admire Greek architecture and Gothic at the same time, without running to the extremes of determined hatred and rapturous attachment. Each possesses its peculiar merits, fitness, and beauty; comparison and preference of one or other serves no object. They will still exist to the admiration of all posterity. It is something like the dispute about the superiority of Shakespeare and Milton, Michael Angelo and Raphael. I warrant you there is something superlatively good in all. Wherefore should we not feel the beautiful harmony and purity, the just proportions and classic taste of Greek architecture? Are we to be tied down to accept impressions of one man's mind, when taste is the guiding influence? Surely I may be impressed with the solemnity — sublimity, if you will — of a venerable Gothic structure, without being thereby disqualified from perceiving the beauty of another equally harmonious, but of a distinct character of architecture? And, without pretending to any knowledge of the character of Mr. Ruskin's mind, there does surely seem something very peculiar in that he sees nothing good in architecture but in Gothic structures, nothing so perfect in art or so wonderful as Turner's pictures! Surely, Mr. Davison, there are certain qualities of colour surpassing every other painter in the landscapes of Titian, in those of Giorgioni rich and deep harmony, and in those of Salvator Rosa a power of handling, a vigour and truth, and, what is more, a distinctive character in his forms, in his touches, and in his foliage, that Turner, with all his excellencies, never attempted.

I doubt that I am becoming serious, and that will not do. So now you see me smile, and I am reflective, as one is when treading on delicate and tender ground. Mrs. Bewick desires to unite with me in kind regards to Mrs. Davison and yourself; and I am, dear Davison,

Yours, very sincerely,
W. BEWICK.

Haughton-le-Skerne, near Darlington,
July 16th, 1854.

MY DEAR DAVISON,—I am, and so are all our folks, sorry that you could not get up the steam sufficiently to be here at our party, particularly as my cartoons looked better than ever I saw them before. Night-light is the thing for them; it throws a glow and tone over them that an eye accustomed to the richness of oil-painting feels wanting in fresco. There is all the force and power peculiar to fresco, and the tone of an artificial light that enriches its dryness. I could have wished to give you longer notice of my intention of lighting them up, but I only thought of it the day before, and the chandeliers only arrived just in time from Darlington. It was quite an experiment. It was pretty nearly a rout; and when the folks paired off into the gallery, surprise and wonder seemed to be the effect of the extraordinary beings that started from the walls as if into life,—a gigantic race, with extraordinary expressions and grand solemnity, that seemed, indeed, to awe the spectators. Imagine the contrast: coming out of the drawing-room costumed in modern elegance, with social smiles, and stepping at once among the Prophets and Sibyls of patriarchal times, the embodiments of supernatural intelligence!

Everybody I meet now asks to see these wonderful things. Their effect is magical, it appears, for I have never shown them here in their present completeness before.

Fortunately for myself and for my visitors, I keep up pretty well, but cannot go very far from home; for if I step over the mark of a mile or so, I am obliged to go to bed on my return; and I cannot go out to parties of any kind.

With our kind regards to all of you and Miss Quelch, I am, my dear Davison,

Yours, very truly,

W. BEWICK.

Haughton House, near Darlington,
Jan. 1st, 1857.

MY DEAR DAVISON,—I write to wish you and yours a happy new year, and many returns of the same. I hope you have had a merry Christmas, and that your health, and that of Mrs. Davison, is such as to enable you both to enjoy the good things of this season of the year with all the zest and jollity of your youthful days.

What a fuss there is about our old friend Turner! How he has at last astonished the world of property! What would you not give for a scrap of Turner? Your little finger, I dare say. What would you have given for a shake of that mighty hand? or to have had your eyesight blest with a peep at the giant doing his wondrous work, a sly peep past the curtain to see him handle the brush, to see him poking away at his little shabby palette of dirty colours?

What a wondrous artist Genius is! What a coiner,—what a 'philosopher's stone!' What transmutations it can effect, and how it can make the lieges stare, ope their 'glazed eyes,' and strike their illiterate senses with strange sensations, and pluck admiration from ignorance, envy, or jealousy!

Be good enough to tell Mrs. Davison, with my love to her (if you are not jealous), that I am going on slowly with my recovery, and hope to come round again to something like myself, although lopped of the spring of youth, and my black locks changed to venerable grey. I hope to be well enough to go to Manchester to see 'the Treasures' of Art there. You, of course, will go. Can we hope to meet there? If I can stir up enough of courage to pack up a rubbing in of Turner's, some fine day I will send it to you. It is about two feet long, old and dirty;—a bridge of one arch, high up between two rocks, thrown into shade, with a spurt of water jumping over them. If anything is Turner's, this dash of water is. Mrs. Bewick desires to unite with me in our best regards to you and to Mrs. and Miss Davison, and I am, my dear Davison,

Yours truly,

W. BEWICK.

Haughton House, near Darlington,
July 11th, 1857.

MY DEAR DAVISON,—We have just returned from Manchester! I ran all risks, and set off on Monday last, returning last night, so that we had three clear hard-working days. The fatigue has been too much for me, and we returned two days sooner than we intended. My stars! Willie, but if you have not been there yet, what a joy you have to come to! Do not speak of Turner, *there* you have him in all his glory, in oil, in water, in marvellous revelry! Poor, old, farmer-looking fellow—how I love him for his genius!—how I cry 'Bravo' at every wonder of his pencil! Constable is not sufficiently repre-sented. Wilkie's early pictures are capital, his late ones are going to pieces like old ships, cracking so that the cracks cannot be filled up. Here is his 'Hookabiadar,' which cost Mr.

Jacob Bell 150 guineas,—it is quite a marvel how paint could so split up into small square bits, three quarters of an inch square, with wide gaps between. The hand looks as if he had some kind of scale armour on, and people take it for that, or for some peculiarity of the glove. The puff of smoke floating from his mouth, in the background, is quite gone,—it does not exist; and the way it was put in was a fine piece of skill and thought.

Well, sir, there are such Rembrandts, such Vandycks, Titians, Raphaels, in numbers, and in painting quite admirable; and as you gaze upon such marvels, you cry 'Wonderful! wonderful!' as each seems to surpass the other in depth, or breadth, or brilliance, or sleight of hand, or glazing, or power, or transparency, or negative combinations of hues, or vivid and striking identity of character, living, speaking, looking out at you, expecting you to say, 'How do you do?' to them. In these Rembrandt seems glorious. Vandyck, too, is wonderful in flesh, and beauty, and drapery; and so is our Reynolds. Here is his 'Nelly O'Brien,' equal to anybody, beautiful and highly finished, quite an example of lady painting; nothing can be finer, more pure, or powerful, or transparent, or beautiful. What a charm it is! There are some brilliant Titians, and landscape-painters should look at his depth, richness, and brilliance of colour. How he makes the sun shine! Cuyp, and Ruysdael, and Claude are fine. Indeed, this exhibition is a most wonderful one, and the general effect is almost overpowering. Art here is transcendent in every shape; the paintings are numerous, rich, rare, and of superlative excellence; and though your sense of admiration is roused to the utmost, the study of each picture becomes a laborious task. The noise, the hurry, the bustle, and the crowd, with the music of the organ booming in my ear, afterwards drove away sleep; while the buzz and tumult continued still present to me. On the Thursdays all the fashion of Manchester attend, and everything is genteel and delightfully quiet; the music is superior, and you have ladies there with costumes costing 150l. Now, Davison, you have all the Exhibition, except the English Water Colours; and let me tell you that they surpass the whole world, being wonderfully beautiful, chaste, and elegant. The English school of Art is favourably represented, and stands up well.

Mrs. Bewick's kind regards to Mrs. Davison and Ada, and I am, dear Davison,

Yours truly,

W. BEWICK.

P.S.—There is a donkey painted by me for Haydon—it is the property of Lord de Tabley, and is called Haydon!

Haughton House, near Darlington,
Feb. 21st, 1859.

MY DEAR DAVISON,—We are so glad to see your handwriting again! Have you heard of the exhibition of French pictures at Newcastle? Dr. Burn has sent me a catalogue, but he does not say if they are fine or the contrary. There are many landscapes, and some fine sea-views. One is 'Fishermen hauling a Boat on Shore.' This is a capital subject for you; do try it; you have all the subject with you at Hartlepool, and have not to go to look for it at the 'Dogger Bank' or 'Yarmouth Roads.' I should like very much to see Mr. Burlison's pictures, as I have no doubt they will be full of genius and originality. His *Florence*, is it bright and sunny ? I have a delightful memory of Florence and its people, its squares, its statues, its galleries of paintings, and its churches full of interesting art. There seemed nothing there but sun and love ! enriched by vineyards and pleasure—with laughter to satiety. I lost myself in Florence, having no map, knowing nothing of the language, and seeking my dinner without knowing the name of the street or of the hotel, or where there was an eating-house, or what to say for 'dinner,' or for the word 'hunger.' Just imagine yourself alone in this predicament, after wandering about in search of churches and pictures all day, not able to find your hotel, nor any friend to speak a word for you, and then, my dear sweet William, you will confess how glorious you are at the town wall, when the nicest of dinners awaits your appetite.

Our love to you all at home, and I am, my dear Davison, yours very truly,

W. BEWICK.

Haughton, Dec. 10th, 1860.

MY DEAR DAVISON,—I am so glad that you are making yourself happy by pleasing yourself with your work. There is no department of painting so much calculated to give pleasure as landscape (or ' sea-scape') painting. You create your sky,—your effects of light and shadow,—your tone of colour, be it spring, summer, autumn, or winter,—your eye will direct the proper key,—and you work away, lopping or changing,or adding, or bringing out, or hiding in obscurity unfavourable objects; and thus you produce to your educated fancy the breadth and truth of nature. You stand off and view your handiwork with the satisfaction of a superior being,—a creator as far as effects go,—as far as artistic manipulation will carry you; and, as daylight fades, you wish for an hour more of light to complete your work.

Your two pictures mentioned in your last letter will by this time be quite complete, and I shall be glad to learn if you have finished them to your entire satisfaction. Our friend the Doctor mentions your questions about Wilson's beautiful green, whether it has changed to its present purity, or was originally of this particular hue or tint? There can be no doubt that it remains as it was first painted; but if you try to mix any blue and yellow together, you will fail to produce the particular green seen in Wilson's pictures, especially his mid-distance. Now, when I was a young lad at home, and stole to my room by five o'clock on holiday mornings to wrap myself up in seclusion for the day, warm in enthusiasm, and labouring as for some great reward, — with colours, canvasses, and brushes in the most primitive style,—no master,—no adviser, —I was only too glad to seize hold of any little book or pamphlet that might by chance come into my hands; and there did fall into my possession a pamphlet published about the time of Wilson, and mentioning the particular colour to be used for different parts of pictures. I remember very well being delighted with one particular green for different parts of a landscape, which I used, and no mixture that I could invent would produce the delicacy, lightness, and purity of this peculiar green. Many years afterwards I had the opportunity of seeing the landscapes of

Wilson, and then, to be sure, I recognised my old favourite 'green.' You will be surprised to learn that in this early youth I was bold enough to make a large copy of Wilson's 'Niobe' from a print—the colour, of course, all my own. I remember the figures, &c., were highly finished. I took it to London on my first visit, and I had some very great compliments paid to my picture, although it was but a copy. You may imagine my surprise, when I saw the original picture, to find it upon quite a different key to mine, and all the colours of draperies, sky, rocks, and trees quite different. As I studied the peculiarities of colour and breadth of effect from nature, I put in composition my own ideas of colour, and the contrast with the original was very curious indeed.

I have been often told that I ought to have turned my attention to landscape, as that department seemed my peculiar *forte*. However that may be, nothing could give me greater enjoyment than painting a landscape ; but my attention and time have been concentrated on work more difficult and more laborious, and, if you like, higher in character. I dare say, what

you say of Mr. Burlison's ' Florence' may be correct. I remember Florence, as I saw it and its
neighbourhood from a villa a mile distant, built
in the midst of vineyards, with a terrace in front
looking down upon the city. It was a charming
place. On the terrace wall were orange-trees in
full bearing, and below nothing but the vine,
the olive, the almond, &c., in every direction
up to the walls of the city. When I stood
upon the terrace for the first time, the city
seemed to lie basking in the broad sunlight.
It looked as if uninhabited. There was no
smoke, nor any of the usual appearances of a
town in England, where the canopy of smoke
bred by our coal fires keeps us moody and melancholy. The brightness of the town seemed
half lost in airy, vapoury heat. All was still,
for everybody in it was taking his *siesta*. I felt
anxious to make a sketch, but I had been invited to dinner, and to listen to the reading of a
manuscript novel that a friend was going to
forward to England. So we had much to talk
of, and when dinner was over came visitors, two
gentlemen and a lady—an English gentleman
and his wife, and an Italian Prince. It so hap-

pened that the lady was lively and full of enthusiasm. She had sat with her sister very
often to Harlow ; and, ordering the Prince from
the couch, she sat by me to tell me of the extraordinary character of Harlow, whom her
father quite idolized. He would come down
into the country where they lived and call them
all out of bed at two or three o'clock in the
morning. Some fine idea had come into his
head, and he must have one or both of the sisters up to sit to him. This lady was the most
vivacious and quick speaker I ever heard.
There was not a moment's pause, and it was delightful to hear her, so sensible were her observations, so well told her anecdotes. This party
remained all the evening, so that I spent the
night at the villa, sleeping in a grand state-bed,
all gold carving and damask. I was enchanted
with the view from my window in the morning
—the sun dispersing the dew—the city bathed
in the most delicate effects of morning colour.
As I sauntered through some of the apartments,
where there were pictures and statues in abundance, I came to the billiard-room—an extensive hall, with niches all round, filled with

marble busts of the Cæsars, &c. ; and it seemed to me more like enchantment than reality. I have got a fine, massy new frame for my 'Entombment,' and one for the Velasquez. The effect is mighty fine.

Mrs. Bewick begs to unite with me in our love to Mrs. Davison, Ada, and yourself; and I am, my dear Davison,

Yours truly,

W. BEWICK.

Haughton House, near Darlington,
Jan. 1st, 1861.

MY DEAR DAVISON,—Mrs. Bewick cordially unites with me in wishing you and Mrs. Davison and Ada a happy new year, and many returns of the season. I am glad you know all about the peculiar green that Wilson was in the habit of using, and that is one of the many charms we find in his works.

If you think that I hit off the 'yellow green' in my copy of the print of 'Niobe,' you are quite mistaken. I had at that time never seen a Wilson picture, nor indeed any other picture of any note; I used the green merely because it was a colour I had. I do not think that Wilson got his purity or his aërial effects by their glazing of this colour. As to his greens having changed by using macgilp, if it were so, his blue skies and other pure colours would have changed in like manner. I remember well an exhibition in Bond Street of Glover's own pictures, which were sold by auction, and they were exhibited without frames; alas! I was horrified, they looked so crude, so much green of the gross blue and yellow mixture, and at that time I had a mellowed tone in my eye that ill agreed with Glover's 'painting on the spot.' The wall was full of these gamboge and blue effects; but there were no Wilsons there, as you mention. I am glad you were amused with my account of my visit to the elegant Florentine villa. Mrs. Bewick desires her love to Mrs. Davison; and I am, my dear Davison,

Yours truly,
W. BEWICK.

Haughton House, near Darlington,
Sept. 4th, 1861.

MY DEAR DAVISON,—I write to say that we have arrived all safe, and that I am still alive. We came here on Friday last. As I felt sufficiently recovered from my late severe illness at my brother's at Dagenham, we determined to come home *viâ* London, our object being to see the exhibitions. We were too late for the Royal Academy, and also for Holman Hunt's picture; but we did feast upon the rarities at the National Gallery, the British Institution, and the Kensington Museum. My eye! Davison, but our friend Turner is great at the last place; and, indeed, at the National he compares well. He stands his ground between two of the finest Claudes. Are you not proud that he was an Englishman, and not a Scot or an Irishman? So much noise is made by these latter, that one is glad to find modest merit eclipses all their pretensions, and an Englishman step over their heads by sheer force of genius.

When Turner was painting these glorious works, Sir Walter Scott said to me at Abbotsford, that, 'if we did not mind, the Scotchman would be beating us in the race.' This was in 1824, when Wilkie had painted his best works,—he was at Abbotsford the same time with me. Is it not a triumph to see such wonderful combinations of poetical conception, breadth of treatment, and colour that rivals the brilliancy of the sun? His contrasts also are so masterly and effective. How one revels in the Turner Gallery! what a feast of colour! how the eye is filled with gorgeous effects! what delight he must have felt in pouring out such imaginative creations of his ethereal soul! One is at a loss for language to express one's admiration,—it is so unbounded,—one's feelings, when viewing such exalted and varied emanations of a genius so original and incomparable.

Why, Davison, why don't you go mad when in the Turner Gallery? how do you contain yourself? One should be always alone with Turner, unless one has a companion capable of feeling the magic wonders of his pencil, and thus you can enhance your ecstasy by sympathy in the comprehension of his unrivalled powers. You turn to Landseer, and find wonders of execution, the perfection of manipulation, to which Turner had no pretensions, neither hand nor mind was made for this most beautiful department of the art; it is purely artistic, the mechanism of the brush, which we as artists always estimate. We do not look for it in Turner. Landseer is sensitive —delicate—with a fine hand for manipulation, up to all the *finesse* of the art; has brushes of all peculiarities for all difficulties; turns his picture into all manner of situation and light; looks at it from between his legs—and all with the strictly critical view of discovering hidden defects—falsities of drawing or imperfections. See to what perfection he carries his perception of surface—hair, silk, wool, rock, grass, foliage, distance, fog, mist, smoke—how he paints the glazed or watery eye! Turner could never paint any of these details. No! But can you tell what has become of the latest of his pictures, painted to illustrate a manuscript poem—'The Fallacies of Hope,' I think?

Don't you envy a man who has seen Turner paint these fine things, or who has shaken the right hand that did all those extraordinary works!

I have been blest with both these honours!
'Think of that, Master Brook!' Sir Edwin has
a fine hand, a most correct eye, a refined perception of character, and can do almost anything
but dance upon the slack wire. He is a fine bil-
liard-player, plays at chess, sings when with his
intimate friends, and has considerable humour—
all of which Turner could not do. He looked
liked a farmer, and there was nothing about
him to denote the possession of great genius.
He was ruddy, and stiff in the joints; awkward
and ill-dressed, although he had mixed in the
best circles. He liked the retirement of his own
studio, into which he admitted no one, except
one or two particularly favoured friends.

I wish Mrs. Davison could have seen our meeting with my *old*, old friend, Tom Landseer, the
elder brother, who came to the hotel at King's
Cross to see us. We had been up to the Villa
during the day, and intended to start for home
the next morning. Landseer was not at home,
but Mrs. Landseer was overcome when we entered the house, after an absence of twenty
years. She hugged and kissed Mrs. Bewick,
and squeezed our hands, and showed us every-

thing the house contained, in her delight, and said Tom would be in such a way when he returned to find that we had been, and would be sure to come down to see us; and so they both did, and stopped with us till midnight. Well, my kind old friend seized my wife, and then me, the tears streaming down his cheeks with emotion. We talked so fast, and so much in the short time, that, being weak from recent illness, I became exhausted. We had all former times to talk over, and familiar and distinguished friends we so often met at Landseer's, so many of whom had passed from us. The scene became deeply interesting to all of us, and my sensitive friend was often moved to tears as he tried to persuade us to return once more among old friends. While I sit writing to you I am coughing very badly, for I caught a cold at the Kensington Museum. Long galleries, with open doors at the ends, and the sun burning upon the skylights.

My wife desires to unite with me in our love to you, Mrs. Davison, and Ada, and I am,

My dear sweet William, yours truly,

W. BEWICK.

Haughton House, near Darlington,
Nov. 16th, 1862.

MY DEAR DAVISON,—I should like very much to see your collection of photographs from Raphael, and Michael Angelo, and Rembrandt. It is true I have not seen any of these fine things, except a very fine one from Raphael at my friend Landseer's, which is framed and glazed, and is hanging up in his studio by the side of a fine cast of the 'Apollo,' mounted upon something which raises it three or four feet from the floor. I had to look up at it, and it appeared very fine. The photograph is one of a Madonna and child, from a dark drawing in chalk, mighty fine! I was introduced at Landseer's to an American artist, who is in possession of an original picture by Raphael—5000 guineas—very fine indeed.

I have had an idea that Gibson's 'Venus' would disappoint me in regard to the tinting, but I was glad to be told by a person who has seen it that the colour is a warm flesh colour, for I was afraid it might be pinkish. I wrote to Gibson to mention what I had observed in some portions of the Elgin Marbles, where the wet or weather had not come, and it appeared to me that they had been painted with some kind of body-colour, perhaps with a vehicle of wax. Now, it is known that the Greek sculptors had painters to colour their statues, and there was one in particular who was famous for his success in imitating flesh. Some of the Greek marble is of a heavy grey colour, and this may have induced the sculptor to paint it, to improve the effect; but I suppose that all the varieties of tint would be given with the skill of a good painter.

At Rome, when rambling among the ruins, I picked up a fragment—a most exquisite foot of a youth—in this kind of marble. It was in the grounds of Cæsar's Golden Palace! I gave this beautiful piece of art to a kind friend of mine in London. I think I will enclose Gibson's last note to me. You will see what sort of man he is. He has the simplicity of a child. So had Thorwaldsen, who surpassed Canova, who seems to have been influenced by French taste, and whose general works I cannot say I like. Thorwaldsen's works are simple, natural, and very fine; and this reminds me of an ovation

I witnessed in Rome. Three German regiments passed through Rome from Naples, and the the commanders ordered all three bands to meet before Thorwaldsen's house to give him a serenade. Imagine three German bands united, playing their finest music, all the officers in the windows above, the streets crammed with the population of Rome, the simple, grand fellow, the sculptor, appearing amongst the officers, smiling with delight. This is, indeed, to be an artist! Can you and Mrs. Davison fancy this fine old fellow, with his massive white head, playing at children's games, such as 'musical magic,' 'hunt the ring,' &c. &c., among a squad of youths of both sexes, as I have really seen him do in the ancient city of Rome?

I am, yours truly,

W. BEWICK.

Haughton House, near Darlington,
July 19th, 1863.

MY DEAR WILLIAM,—When I awoke out of my sleep yesterday morning I could not help thinking to myself how exceedingly kind of you to come this way home and call at Haughton upon us, and give us the pleasure of your company, if even for so short a time as you proposed to yourself; albeit that my wife and I had determined to lock you up for the whole of the day, and send you off the next morning. But see how the finest plans of human thought are disappointed or frustrated! I had no sooner opened my eyes than Mrs. Bewick handed me your half-sheet of a note, blowing into nothing all our fine-spun plans, and leaving me and my two pictures, set for your examination and criticism, to silence and disappointment, till your highness be pleased to come and see us. The pine-apple pines upon its plate, the prize-strawberries sent from Richmond Gardens must be enjoyed by others, because, forsooth, 't' railway doesn't *fit*,' and the object of our expectation cannot come. So my wife, myself, my pine-apple, and my pictures, remain like fish out of water—as sad, as gloomy, as sorrowful as the picture of the three Marys that hangs by my side. We — the two who can — express our sorrow with 'open mouths;' and we express a conviction that no reparation can be made, or consolation imparted, but by your coming over and bringing with you the magnetic charm that attracted you so swiftly back to Hartlepool— meaning your 'better half,' *i. e.* Mrs. Davison, who, Mrs. Bewick says, must come for a few days for change of air, &c., and must feel that she may do as she likes in every way with us, and be at home as fully and as completely as in her own house.

You must have had a high treat at Tatton Park. It is true, when you see the finest things of the great masters, when you examine their dexterities of mind and hand, you are tempted to ask if there are no hands in our boasted school that can go so far as these old fellows.

I was lately at Raby Castle, and was surprised to find such a fine collection of works of art, paintings and sculpture. It is many years since I was in this famed old stronghold— famed in history and romance—and at that time there was literally nothing of art; but now there is a full collection, all of old masters, except one or two pictures—one by Turner, a good size, a view of Raby, with the pack of hounds in full cry in front of the castle. This picture reminds me of the painter to the King of Naples, who was paid by the square yard, and to suit his majesty, who liked a good deal for his money, painted huge skies—half his large pictures were skies.

Mrs. Bewick joins me in our best regards to you and Mrs. Davison; and I am, my dear Davison,

Yours, very truly,
WILLIAM BEWICK.

Haughton House, near Darlington,
Jan. 22nd, 1864.

MY DEAR DAVY,—I am quite aware of the results of body colour in water-colour drawing, as I used it extensively in my cartoons from M. Angelo, and I hope to see your success in it. I have seen drawings by Rembrandt when he had put white with his colours in the sky. Allan* showed me a picture in the Royal Academy exhibition, 'The Broken Fiddle,' entirely painted with body colour (water and

* Sir William Allan.

then varnished). It was placed on the right line, and was a beautiful picture. We are still proposing to give our evening, and hope for your company alone, if Mrs. Davison cannot accompany you. My bad cold has delayed our fixing the event, but we hope to be able to do so soon. Bonnington was *first-rate*. I admire his feeling and freshness, and breadth; he was very masterly. With our united kind regards to you and Mrs. Davison, I am, my dear Davison,

Yours ever truly,

W. BEWICK.

Haughton House, near Darlington,
April 18th, 1864.

MY DEAR DAVISON,—Now that you have sent back those fine drawings, and that your mind is at ease and your time more at liberty, I think I may venture to trouble you with a few lines, to ask how you and Mrs. Davison are after the fatigues of going through such a treat as Mr. Cromek has afforded you. Did you get to Byron Hall to the sale? I understand some things sold well, and others not so well. I am sorry that I was unable to go, as I hoped to have had a treat in the pictures, books and furniture, all which, I am told, were of first-rate quality. Bewick's birds sold for ten guineas; fine impressions are rare, or rather early impressions; my copy I bought from the hand of Thomas Bewick, and the impressions are fine.

Mrs. Cromek seems highly delighted with my introduction to the Misses Bewick. They have sent him a desirable autograph of their father, and they remember well the father of Mr. Cromek passing a night with their family at Newcastle. They also have sent him four letters from his father to Mr. Bewick, so you may be sure that the suffering invalid is pleased with those ladies.

What a lamentable thing it is for a man of such genius and power in the Art to be afflicted with racking pains and suffering, so that life seems a drag, and he is unable to realise the ambition for distinction to which his natural ability, hard study, and acquirements entitle him! His interior of St. Peter's is a marvellous piece of art and labour; how it is all made out and worked, and what delicacy and breadth is preserved! how flat the marble floor! The drawing of the interior of the cathedral at Sienna struck me as quite wonderful; so does the chapel at Warwick; but there are so many excellent things, that one is quite puzzled to select. With our united regards to you and Mrs. Davison, and to Ada if she is with you, I am, dear Davison,

Yours truly,
W. BEWICK.

Haughton House, near Darlington,
May 22nd, 1864.

MY DEAR DAVISON,—When the sun shines I am idle. Our friend Mr. Cromek is now in London, in the heat and turmoil, sweating in exhibitions or suffocated in omnibuses, fatigued by walking, and restored by Turkish baths! He seems disgusted with pre-Raphaelitism, and to get into the National Gallery out of the Royal Academy is quite a relief to his eyesight, and to his pictorial sympathies and tastes. He is a very amusing writer, and his tastes and judgment are refined and critical.

I hear that Cattermole and J. Lewis are now into oil. I think it a pity, if true; but Lewis painted in oil before he went abroad, so that he may be said to have returned to it again. I suppose they both wish to go into the Royal Academy, the members of which, it appears, will be increased to fifty. Mr. Herbert's fresco is making a great noise. I hear it is very fine, but in what way has not been explained to me. I suppose the scenic part of it is from photographs, and it is a real scene of the place where Moses is said to have received the tables of the law. The crowded host in the background, I am told, is very fine.

The season is very enjoyable. The perfume of the laburnums and lilacs coming into our bedroom, reminds me of sailing in the Mediterranean, opposite the Spanish coast, when I was walking the deck of the good Columbian Packet. The breeze brought a strange, bewildering aroma. I snuffed and snuffed, then asked the old carpenter if he smelt a delicious perfume. ' Oh, yes, sir; it is the smell of the vintage in Spain, which is wafted to us by this fine breeze.' Ah! what a time of enjoyment youth is, and what blessings there are in store for us if we only have the taste or perception to find them out, and the gratitude to acknowledge the gifts of Heaven! As I sit writing this short note, I am surrounded by such infinite variety of tint and colour and form of foliage, that I have abundant material for enjoyment in the wonders contained in the small space before my own house. You have the fine effects of the ever-varying sea, always interesting, always sublime. I am a great admirer of a noble tree, its arms and foliage, blown by the wind, giving to the scene variety of form, colour, and graceful movement; so also of a field of ripe corn moved by the breeze.

I am much obliged to you for the list of prices, &c., of the Spearman sale. The portrait of Bewick is very finely painted, and very like him.* Bewick was a hearty, fine creature. When I first visited him, after having been in London, he invited me to his house. The conversation about my aspirations, my enthu-

* Thomas Bewick, the celebrated wood-engraver, and now in the possession of the Rev. Edward Chase, M.A., Rector of Haughton-le-Skerne. By Ramsay.

siasm, &c., impressed him, as he had had feelings akin to mine when a youth; and he seized
my hands, the tears filling his eyes, and
encouraged me by squeezing them, and saying
with the finest feelings, 'God bless you! I
wish you all the success your industry and
genius deserve.' Was not this very fine of
the old hero?

Mrs. Bewick unites with me in our best
regards to you and Mrs. Davison, and to Ada
when you write.

Ever yours truly,
W. BEWICK.

Haughton House, near Darlington,
Oct. 23rd, 1864.

MY DEAR DAVISON,—It is now so long since
I have received a scratch of your pen, that I
have forgotten the end of your last conversation; so we must begin *de novo*, and try new
subjects, if possible, to hit upon them. First
of all, what is new to me is that my wife and
self have been to Leeds for three weeks. We
had pleasant lodgings on the side of a moor—

Woodhouse Moor—and we were quite in the country, although in the midst of Leeds. What a fine place for a breath of air!—always wind, sometimes storms. There the gay people of Leeds turn out at all times of day; and the women who have good ankles are rather glad to have crinolines to show their understandings.

We took a fine sunny day for Kirkstall Abbey, and were charmed with it. As a fine ruin, I think it is the most picturesque in composition of any I have ever seen. What beautiful pictures might be got of it! The east neighbourhood would be avoided, as the modern mills and manufactories jar with the sentiment of indolent monastic life that impresses you when absorbed in the admiration of the splendid architectural ruin before you. The intelligent old man that has charge of the place showed us two or three beginnings of drawings by artists who have to return to finish them. We missed the alder-tree that grew near the altar, from which 'Mary the Maid of the Inn' so fatally took a sprig, when the moon broke through a cloud, and she saw two men carrying a dead body. You know the story. The hat of one of them rolling to her feet, she took it up, and, carrying it home to the 'Star and Garter,' where she was waiting-maid, found in it, to her horror, the name of the man she was affianced to. Southey, in his famous ballad, makes her go mad. There is before you still the famed ruin and the said 'Star and Garter' on the same spot where poor Mary was fated to listen to the traveller's request to bring the sprig of alder at midnight. You fancy you see her — bright, beautiful, spirited, and firm of character — determined not to be daunted by so lonely and irksome an errand. The alder is gone, but we plucked a sprig of something else, to remind us of 'Mary the Maid of the Inn.' Curiously enough, the late Edward Pease, of Darlington, used to come every year to the 'Star and Garter' at Kirkstall to meet a Leeds gentleman, and these twain fixed there and then the price of wool for the season. The son of this wool-merchant told me himself this curious circumstance.

The ruin is in a valley. There are fine old trees growing in part of it. The river Aire, only a stone's-throw from it, ripples past the grassy banks, with boats and fishers, and every object to charm one who loves scenery. Then the river is backed on the north by wooded banks as far as the eye can reach.

We shall be glad to have a good account of you and Mrs. Davison; and Mrs. Bewick unites with me in our love to you, Mrs. D., and Ada. And I am, my dear Davison,

Yours truly,
W. BEWICK.

CHAPTER VIII.

Haughton House, near Darlington,
Feb. 9th, 1864.

MY DEAR SIR,—I am extremely sorry to hear that you are an invalid. I sympathise the more with you as I have been myself an invalid for the last twenty years, and have been at death's door two or three times. I own with gratitude to have been greatly benefited by homœopathy : indeed I may say that I am now comparatively well, although still very delicate and easily fatigued; but I can and do enjoy everything connected with my beloved art.

We had Mr. Davison here on Friday evening. He brought a portfolio of drawings by himself and others, as well as a collection of photographs from the drawings by Raphael in the Louvre. My house is full of works of art, fine pictures, and a gallery, with a portfolio of original drawings by the old masters, Correggio, Rembrandt, &c. You may be sure that we enjoyed each other's society vastly. We had a large company of ladies and gentlemen, some possessing general taste for art, but none with the soul to feel it like our friend. He was delighted with some experiments of a chromatic character shown by Dr. Malcolm. This is one of Davison's hobbies.

I paint a little occasionally, and I am greatly obliged to you for the characteristic sketch of the poet Cunningham. You will see what Miss Bewick says of it, and of a larger drawing of the same gentleman. She sends for your acceptance the only autograph (of her father) she has; and I forward her note, that you may have her own autograph. It is Jane, the elder of the two daughters of Thomas Bewick: she has lately published her father's life. The younger sister is called Isabella. I have photographs of both of them. You speak of the voraciousness of collectors: it is true. I had no rest from them until I was denuded of almost every autograph I possessed of celebrated people with whom I have come in contact. I did manage to keep one, which happens to be framed and glazed, being a letter to myself from Sir Walter Scott: it is a long letter, and you will see that I could not part with it. I was twice at Abbotsford, and saw the great magician in his domestic circle. His conversation was delightful, very much in the Waverley style. The persons I met there were all distinguished for rank or genius. Besides this one autograph, I have others attached to drawings of celebrities whom I have met in society. The drawings are by myself in chalk, of the size of life, and are intellectually characteristic; and I made no attempt to idealise.

I am greatly obliged to you for your kind wish to send me your valuable book of original drawings; and if you can risk them I should like very much to see them, if you can put in some of your own doing. Dr. Malcolm speaks of them so highly that I feel a great desire to see some. Your idea of writing ' your recollections' is a good one, and I have often thought of jotting down anecdotes and memorials of persons that have passed away and have become part of the history, if I may so say, of our times. Indeed I have done something of the kind, but it remains incomplete and sketchy. I am, my dear sir,

Yours very truly,

W. BEWICK.

Haughton House, near Darlington,
Feb. 12th, 1864.

MY DEAR SIR,—I am greatly obliged to you for the interesting book. The binding at once revived my Italian reminiscences, and Haydon's name too, with other associations of the past, filled me with melancholy interest. When I was in Edinburgh in 1824 a friend called upon me with a book that he said I ought to possess. It had been bought at the sale of Mr. Haydon's things, and brought to Edinburgh. This was 'Reynolds' Lectures,' in three volumes, with notes and sketches by the well-known hand. The work had been given to me by Haydon as a keepsake, and after I had had it some time he said to me, 'Bewick, I think you must give me back the Reynolds that I gave you.' So I took it back to him, and it was curious enough that I should be fated to get it by purchase after all, and in the round-about fashion I did. I still have the work, and treasure it as containing re-marks and sketches by Haydon in his younger days.

He was an extraordinary man, a great en-thusiast in art, and evinced wonderful power, as in his 'Solomon' and 'Christ's Entry into Jeru-salem;' but after that period there was a falling off. He did not believe that man ought to be influenced by events, yet it is curious that his career was completely influenced and coloured by external circumstances; and if one believed in fatalism, one might say that he was driven by fate to the dire destiny which over-came him. And yet the circumstances of his early life appeared to promise the happiest results.

He married for love, his wife was beautiful, and yet his marriage seemed to be the cause of his ruin, for it was more than he could do to make 'both ends meet,' and petty worries and daily cares broke his strength of mind and crushed his genius.

I sincerely sympathise with you in your anxiety and vexation regarding the aspersions thrown out in the Life of Blake. Surely serious untruths, when published to the world, ought to be contradicted; the public ought to be set right if you are in a position to do so without much trouble to yourself. I have not seen the Life of Blake. Who was or is Nollekens Smith? There was Smith, of the Print-room in the British Museum—it is not he? Is Gilchrist a Scotchman? I think I have seen the Life of Blake severely criticised. But Blake, although poetically constituted, was sadly wanting in artistic acquirement, and his books to me are unsatisfactory. I have fallen upon a note from my late friend Captain Basil Hall, the son of Sir James Hall, who wrote his Travels to Chile, &c. If you have not an autograph of his, perhaps you might like to add one to your collection, and if I meet with anything else in this way I will take care to send it to you.   Believe me, my dear Sir,

Yours very truly,

W. BEWICK.

T. H. Cromek, Esq.

P.S.—The copy of *Reynolds' Lectures* contains notes by my late friend W. Hazlitt, who had borrowed it to write his essay on Reynolds in *The Edinburgh Review.*

Haughton House, near Darlington,
Feb. 18th, 1864.

MY DEAR SIR,—I hasten to tell you that I have ascertained that Nollekens Smith is the person I supposed, late of the Print-room, British Museum.   I remember him well.   He was a notorious gossip, and I knew ladies who used to go to the Print-room to be amused by his endless and amusing tattle.   He was a great retailer of anecdote and scandal, dealt largely in inuendo, and had a keen relish for any story of doubtful propriety.   He had great expectations from Nollekens; and when the sculptor died looked to inherit considerable part of his wealth, but, like many others who live upon expectation, he was sadly disappointed. And he then wrote his *Life of Nollekens*.

I tell you what I know of the character of Smith, that you may not be annoyed at anything related by him. Nobody who knows him cares for or believes anything from Nollekens Smith. If you get his *Life of Nollekens* just for your amusement, you will, I dare say, see for yourself the character of the man. It shows the spite and venom of a disappointed man. I am, my dear Sir,   Yours very truly,

WILLIAM BEWICK.

Extract from a Letter to T. H. Cromek, Esq. dated 29th Feb., 1864.

You know, of course, Gibson and Severn? Did you know poor Wyatt?—and then there were Uwins and Havell? Both the latter were sensitive and nervous. Havell never could be satisfied with his food! How he grumbled! I used to laugh at him. But I took pity upon him, he seemed so miserable, and invited him to dine privately with me at my lodgings. What a change came over him !—and as he praised the dishes set before him he seemed comparatively a happy man. He used to compare the Fratoria of Rome with his style of living in India.

Ever yours truly,

W. BEWICK.

Extract from letter to T. H. Cromek, Esq., dated March 7th, 1864.

The Roman artists were a curious ungenial set, take them altogether. There was a great division between the Scotch and English, I remember—but I seemed to stand very well with both. I took no part with either, but valued each man for himself, and always returned civilities or attentions. Gibson used to say, ' *That* Eastlake, sir, is a curious kind of chap, you never know what to make of him.' He did seem to keep himself aloof, and was cold to many of the young fellows. But he was the first to take me to church, where he was one of the most regular attendants. He had been disciplined to this at a public school.

He was a hard student, and talked to me of 'the business of life.' Beginning life, too, with an independence, he has been a prudent and a most fortunate man, and now is happy with a handsome and talented wife. Everybody liked Wyatt, I have him before me with his guitar and his peculiar voice. It was very nice to see the two sculptors on opposite sides of the street so friendly, and Gibson sending visitors over to Wyatt's studio, speaking a good word of his talents and works. I am glad that Severn has become Consul at Rome, as he always liked to live there, and he will fulfil his duties well, and give great satisfaction, I know, to visitors. You will know he has lost his wife. I have not seen any of the young Severns. One of the daughters drew or painted small portraits very nicely.

 . . . .

Ever yours truly,
W. Bewick.

VOL. II.

Haughton House, near Darlington,
March 26th, 1864.

MY DEAR SIR,—I have this day sent off the case with the smaller portfolio in it, and also my drawing of George Thompson, with the sketch done in Rome for a picture which has never been painted; for, as I said before, I lost the sketch for some years, and when it turned up it was offered to me, as a Wilkie, for a picture I then possessed. I have written what you desired upon both sketch and drawing. I am not able at this moment to state when George Thompson died; but I think it is stated in some of the recent publications connected with Burns.

As the Thompson is a chalk-drawing, you will be obliged to put it under glass to preserve it. There has been no copy taken from it. The spot on the forehead is quite correct.

I shall be most happy to give you an intro-duction to my intelligent friend Bonomi. How his brother, the architect, would be delighted with your fine drawings of the temples and buildings of Italy and Greece.

I send you the autograph of James Hogg,

the Ettrick Shepherd, friend of Sir W. Scott. It is the original MS. of one of his songs—he gave it to me when I visited him at his farm.

Ever yours truly,

W. BEWICK.

T. H. Cromek, Esq.

Extract from letter to T. H. Cromek, Esq., dated March 31st, 1864.

The picture in the Pantheon is the 'Lazarus' of Haydon. You are right about my sitting for the 'Lazarus,' which was all painted in one day, the painter being arrested three times during the painting of it. What a day! I sat for other heads. In the picture of 'Christ riding into Jerusalem,' now in the Academy of New York, I sat for several heads. One is very like what I was at the time; it is that of a person speaking loud to another, to give an idea of the noise and crowd. That other is John Keats, the young poet. Hazlitt, Wordsworth, and others, are introduced into the same part of the picture. Of course, they were all heads that suited the painter for character, and he painted them from life, giving the expression he wished.

.   .   .   .

Ever yours truly,
W. BEWICK.

Haughton House, near Darlington,
April 2nd, 1864.

MY DEAR SIR,

I have a finished chalk-drawing of W. S. Landor done in Florence, with his autograph at bottom. Wilkie saw it in Rome, and said in his quaint way, ' Like ! it it more than like — it is the man and his character.'

When in Rome I called upon a friend one morning (a Mr. Brown, a literary man, friend of Severn's), and a gentleman sitting at a desk, whom I had never seen before, joined our conversation about trees, their beauty, character, &c. I was very much astonished at the powerful language he used, and the knowledge he possessed of the subject. He went into the planting, the growth, the proper soil and situation of every kind of tree, and its particular capabilities and uses. His whole bearing struck me as being that of no common man, and afterwards I took care to inquire who he was, and Mr. Brown told me he was one of the most remarkable and talented man of the age, and was the author of *Imaginary Conversations of Great Men,* &c. Walter Savage Landor. I afterwards made my drawing of him, and he very good-naturedly gave me as many sittings as I required. He said, when speaking of tree-planting, that he had planted some large plantations upon an estate where he had built a mansion, and going abroad, had left his land in the tenancy of a fellow who destroyed all his trees and ploughed up the land. When he came back and saw the bare condition of his estate, where he expected his well-grown plantation, he was so disgusted that he pulled down the house, sent the tenant across the water (meaning he had transported him), quitted England, and went to Florence, and there I had an opportunity of meeting him.

The hands of Haydon are fine specimens of chalk-drawing, and are engraved by Thomas

Landseer in soft ground. It is to this Thomas to whom I propose to give you an introduction. He is a fine, good-hearted fellow, and, like his father, very deaf, but ought to have been a painter, as he is vigorous and spirited, and draws well. Many drawings of animals on wood are by his hand. I hope the next letter from you will give me a better account of you.

Ever yours truly,
W. BEWICK.

Haughton House, near Darlington,
April 16th, 1864.

MY DEAR SIR, — It is curious that you should have gone to anatomical studies first, like myself, who dissected at Sir Charles Bell's theatre of anatomy for three seasons with the Landseers. We dissected every part of the muscles of the body, and made drawings in red, black, and white chalk, the size of nature. These drawings were thought by the professor the finest ever made from dissection.

Your dear mother must have been a person of great energy of mind, and you have been fortunate in having her to encourage your advancement, and accompany you in your progress; and what a satisfaction it must have been to you to listen to her praises of your successful labours!

We surely take everything, or nearly so, of good or great from our mothers. We have just been reading *Family Troubles*, by Miss Hardcastle; and when I perused your account of your early life, it seemed so like a part of this book of cross purposes, that I laughed at the touches of nature you had described.

There has been a sale of book treasures, some drawings and paintings, and a portrait of Thomas Bewick, painted by Ramsay. I am sorry that I could not attend the sale. I have unfortunately got the skin rubbed off my left foot, so that I am obliged to wear a slipper just as if I had gout.

The portrait of T. Bewick that I possess was painted by Bell, in the style of Rembrandt, with the hat on, the light falling on one cheek and the side of the nose; and this, with the white neckcloth and frill, is the only light in the picture. It is artistical, but not a domestic picture by any means, and no one would like a family likeness to be so treated. But it is well painted, and I am often asked if it is a Rembrandt.

Mrs. Bewick will write ten thanks for the two photographs of the Misses Cromek. I have only to admire them. Mrs. Bewick unites with me in kind regards to you and the young ladies,

And I am, my dear Sir,

WILLIAM BEWICK.

Haughton House, near Darlington,
April 28th, 1864.

MY DEAR SIR,— So you have seen the memoir of me by Longstaff. I do not remember what there is in it. There are two other memoirs in two histories of the County Palatine of Durham. One of them has a line engraving from a painting exhibited in the Royal Academy. It was done on my return from Italy by a friend, now no more.* They are, perhaps, none of them exactly like. The drawing by Landseer was good, nearly life-size, but the engraving wants something. Mrs.

* Macarthur.

Bewick has found an impression from the painting, which she begs your acceptance of. It is well engraved, by (I think) Brown.

So your amiable daughters are amused by the particulars given in Longstaff. Well, my dear Sir, there is a great deal left out that would have been probably more amusing to young ladies in the way of romance; for, in the life of a young fellow like myself, there were often occasions for strange vicissitudes, both connected with art and other matters. The 'ups and downs of life'— all the vagaries of a chequered existence — hopes, ambitions, successes, and disappointments—hard work and anxieties—the 'fight' to get through the bogs and quicksands in the road of life — reality would be as romantic as a well-plotted romance, if we had only the skill to set it down.

We have been busy for the last few days with our tercentenary of Shakespeare. We gave a lecture with music, recitations, &c. The first lecturer in the North was invited by me to come, and being an old friend, he consented, and recited beautifully. He was our guest. He lectured here on Saturday and stayed over

Sunday. His name is Grant. He is a friend of Mulready, Tom Taylor, &c.; is a poet, and author of the historical romance of *Rufus, or the Red King.* He is also an artist, teacher of drawing, professor of elocution, and connected with the press.

I was present at a stylish Quaker wedding the other day. The chapel was crammed full, and outside in the street the crowds were kept back by policemen. Tell your daughters there were eight bridesmaids, all in the fullest fashion of the day; in white, with blue flowers or feathers to their bonnets.

The bride was elegantly dressed; she could not have been more so at Hanover Square. The ceremony was most solemn and serious. There was an address by an elder — (I sat with him on the same form at school) — dreary pauses — silence! The bridegroom, a handsome fellow, rose from his seat, took the bride by one hand, and said in a distinct voice that he 'took friend Maria Jane for his wife,' &c. &c. The same words were repeated by the young lady, the proper distinction of course being made; then a long pause of silence, and a tedious, gloomy prayer by another elder, followed again by a pause ; and finally the agreement on parchment was read aloud, and signed by the contracting parties, and any other friends. The affair lasted two hours.

The portrait of Thomas Bewick that I mentioned to you was for sale at a gentleman's house near Durham, and has been bought by the rector of this parish. It is a fine portrait, size of life, painted by James Ramsay for a friend of Mr. Bewick, of the name of Scruton, of Durham. Had I been able to go to the sale, the picture would no doubt have been mine. With our united best regards to you and your daughters, I am, my dear Sir,

Yours, very truly,
W. BEWICK.

P.S.—I have a vivid recollection of Miss Mitford and her father, but I have no drawing of her. Haydon made a beautiful drawing of her. She had fine eyes, a very happy face, and beautiful expression. I thought her very pretty, full of spirit and genius. She was fond of her father, who spoke with a Northumbrian accent, and had a boisterous, hearty laugh. He ran through two fortunes. After he had spent the first, he was walking in London with his daughter, and they stopped at the shop-window of an agent for the state lottery. She thought she should like to try her luck. It was on her birthday. So the father bought her a ticket, and she chose the number. The ticket turned out a prize of 10,000*l.* Could you think it possible that the father could or would run through all this? But so it was. He spent all she had, and was then dependent upon her genius and labours for bread and butter.

To see her genial goodness and affection for her father, after all the mishaps he had occasioned her, made one's heart ache, and kindled an almost enthusiastic admiration of her filial love and devotion.

I have no drawing of Turner. The last time I saw him was at the Royal Academy dinner. I was talking with Shee, and he came up smiling, and held out his right hand — the hand that has astonished all lovers of the brush !   I have seen him paint (in oil).   What a slobbery palette! what brushes!—what poverty of colours !

Haughton House, near Darlington,
May 5th, 1864.

MY DEAR SIR,—Your photograph has come home from the frame-maker, and is hung under one of Mr. Tom Landseer, and opposite one of Thackeray.

We are exceedingly glad that you are so much better, and sincerely hope you will be well enough to start for London on Monday ; but don't hurry yourself.   Should you not feel quite up to the mark on Monday morning, better wait a day or two longer at home than hurry away to strange lodgings.   Do the Misses Cromek go with you ?   You will hardly be comfortable without them.

It is very curious that there should be two portraits of Thomas Bewick in the market at the same time.   I should have liked to see the one you speak of.   Miss Bewick will tell me if there was a portrait painted of her father by Raeburn.   I never heard of his having done one. But I saw a very fine one by Nicholson at Edinburgh, and I have an impression that Lord Ravensworth bought it after Nicholson's death.

I wish you would describe the picture at Wakefield—size, dress, and if there is any inscription upon it at back or front, or date. A slight sketch in a letter will enable me to judge if it is intended for Bewick.

In the first Royal Academy Exhibition I saw there was a portrait of Bewick. It was No. 1 in the catalogue, and painted, I think, by Ramsay. He was dressed in a brown coat.

The Misses Bewick have a small, highly-finished picture by Good, of Bewick. It is a very interesting portrait, with his peculiar light and shade,— the lights crossing, — that is, a bright light on one side of the face, and another light, inferior, on the other side.

You quite surprise me with regard to the Water Colour Society. I should have thought members had priority of place.

I have had to-day a visit from the mother of the Quaker bride I mentioned in my last letter. She brought another lady from the south, a great admirer of art, &c. But it rained, and the fine horses in the carriage could not be kept in the rain long enough for them to see all I had to show them. They are both fine women, and dressed in the height of fashion. Quakerism is creeping out fast, both with men and women.

When I first drew from the Elgin Marbles at the British Museum, there came to me from Darlington a Quaker gentleman, without buttons to his coat—which was of the old cut and colour—hat of broad brim, and shoes with silver buckles. He was mild, smiling, and innocent-looking. His name was Nathan Robson; and I attended him over the establishment without my hat. I was then in appearance what you see in Landseer's drawing of me. The contrast between us was remarkable enough. This was the last appearance of the William Penn style of Quakers; and I have no doubt the Misses Cromek would have been amused to see youth and age so strangely represented. I only remember that people stared very much at us both. I had my port-crayon in my hand, having just left my drawing of the large group of the 'Fates,' or the full-sized drawing that I made for Goethe, the German poet.

The anticipated visit to Mr. Beresford Hope must be delightful to you, and I sincerely hope you will be able to enjoy the treat.—With our united kind regards, I am,

Ever yours truly,
W. BEWICK.

Haughton House, near Darlington,
Aug. 22nd, 1864.

MY DEAR SIR,—Both Mrs. Bewick and myself are extremely sorry to learn of your sad sufferings, and very much disappointed that medical skill does not relieve you.

Davison has been from home, but he has no cause of complaint against me, as I wrote to him last, although it is some time ago, and I wait in expectation of some kind of reply. At the same time, our intimacy is of such long standing, and we have so many tastes in common, that if I had anything to interest him I would not wait for his reply, but write immediately; and indeed I will now do so to remind him that

I am still alive. He is a nice fellow, and clever, and Mrs. Davison is also a great favourite with us.

We were invited to meet the celebrated Professor Pepper, of 'Ghost' notoriety, and of the Polytechnic Institution. I found him a very pleasant, joyous, and gentlemanly person, and his lady very handsome and ladylike. As I live in the midst of Quakers, he told us that he lectured at Stoke Newington to a Quaker's establishment of young ladies, and after the lecture they came to him with a set of difficult scientific questions, which he answered in the best way he could on the spur of the moment. After all was over the young ladies came forward, and each shook him by the hand, saying, No. 1, 'Fare-thee-well;' No. 2, 'Fare-thee-well;' No. 3, 'Fare-thee-well;' and so on through the whole of the establishment. I observed that the last young lady might have varied her good wishes by adding, 'And if for ever, fare-thee-well.'

My friend, with whom the Professor is staying, lives some eight miles from here, and the day being fine we enjoyed the drive very much, and arrived at home at 10 P.M. The dinner was a champagne one, and the grapes at dessert were excellent; I never tasted finer, and they were grown in the vinery behind the house. These was a kind of grape of a flesh-colour, which I do not remember to have tasted or seen before, and which was delicious. Our host is a sufferer like yourself, and was scarcely able to walk with me to see his garden, flowers, &c. We were boys together. He has a taste for art, and his dining-room is decorated with his own paintings—copies. He is now failing in health, but we had some pleasant recollections of early days. His accomplished daughter wrote to me that, as her papa was so unwell, she was sure a chat with me would do him good. He did rally, seemed in good spirits, and we had a merry day, with a good deal of laughter, in which the learned Professor joined most heartily, oblivious of his 'Ghost.'

And now, my dear Sir, I have written all sorts of nonsense with the view of amusing you, but fear that in your torments my gossip may be tiresome, if not annoying, to you. As soon as my photograph is ready I will forward it to you. From what I have seen of it, it looks ten years older than I really am, and *this* no one likes.

I wish I could get a cast of the bust by Gibson—profile—which is a fine work of art.

With our united kind regards to you and your dear daughter,

I am, my dear Sir,

Yours very truly,

WILLIAM BEWICK.

Haughton House, near Darlington,
Sept. 20th, 1864.

MY DEAR SIR,—I hasten to return you the interesting photographs of your two old and valued friends. They are both intellectual, and both appear characteristic of truly English gentlemen, of the good old school. As you observe, I should not have recognised them, for time has changed both; but it has improved them, as their leading trait is goodness, which in young men is not generally so predominant as to be remarkable. I should like to see what manner of man Mr. Ralph has turned out, as he was a handsome boy, but a mischievous, harum-scarum fellow.

I do not remember to have met the author of *Hajji Baba.* As you are a water-colour hero, I will tell you of a singular character that was to be seen at Mrs. Chenie's—a young German water-colour artist. He was rather tall, thin, and worn, a shred of a man, as ugly as sin, with a voice like a trombone, and a noble genius. It was curious to see so precious a shrine in so rude and coarse a temple, and it was delightful to observe Mrs. Chenie—refined, elegant, and fresh —paying her gracious attentions to this uncut diamond. Her sweet and musical voice, and her delightful smile, irradiating her features, made her such a striking contrast to her guest that I have never forgotten either the lady or the extraordinary water-colour painter, or his works, but his name I really quite forget. Then there was an amiable Italian, with his guitar and sky-blue ribbon, and pimpled, crimson face. These were shining lights in the elegant crowd at Mrs. Chenie's delightful evenings in Rome. I think I met Mrs. Chenie at dinner at Lady Westmoreland's. There was my Lord Seymour and other gentlemen, and Eastlake—no ladies. I was unfortunate in being called to take the bottom of the table to carve roast beef, but everybody was too refined to partake of it. I have not half described the German water-colour painter. His works were landscapes, grand and noble in character.

Is it Mrs. E. Chenie that draws so beautifully? How enviable it is to be so gifted, and to possess so many resources of happiness!

With our united kind regards to you and your daughters, I am, my dear Sir,

Yours truly,

WILLIAM BEWICK.

Haughton House, near Darlington,
Nov. 5th, 1864.

MY DEAR SIR,—I hope by this time you will have returned and be quietly settled at home, and that you have had no renewal of your troubles. The weather has been for some time wet and cold and stormy, and I thought that you would hardly be able to leave Richmond, as you intended.

Speaking of Lord Byron and his daughter, Ada Lovelace, Dr. Malcolm showed me some of her letters, and said he had a few left. I thought of you, and begged him, if they contained nothing of a private nature, to spare one for you. Last night he brought me one of her notes to him, and as it mentions Miss Martineau's cow and mesmerism, it is interesting. I should have liked it better if her name had been in full, but we must be thankful for what we can get. Should you not possess her autograph, I trust you will prize her note as that of a lady of great intellectual gifts, and, as it appears, of singular spirit and independence of mind and grasp of thought. I have read some other letters of hers, in which her originality, I may say singularity of expression and humorous jollity, reminds one of her noble father and his extraordinary genius. Surely, my dear Sir, we live in a wonderful age. The age of Elizabeth was splendid for a galaxy of brilliant men of genius, and perhaps the present century may rank in after-times with any age for remarkable talent in certain lines, especially for inventive genius.

With our united best regards to you and your amiable daughters, I am, my dear Sir,

Yours truly,

WILLIAM BEWICK.

T. H. Cromek, Esq.

Haughton House, near Darlington,
Nov. 28th, 1864.

MY DEAR SIR,—I asked for the paragraph about young Stothard for you, and by consent I send it, to place with your other scraps about the family.

Mrs. Bewick is very much obliged to you for the copy of the beautiful lines on the death of Mr. Charles Stothard. It is melancholy to think of the sad end of the sons of so gifted a man as the father. Old Mr. Stothard was librarian when I was a student drawing at the Royal Academy, and well do I remember the first time I saw him in the library. He had a large volume before him, and he looked over his spectacles at me with a steadfast gaze for a long time. As I was bashful, this quite disconcerted me, and I blushed up to the ears; but his expression was so kind, and his smile so paternal, that I was soon reassured. I have often wondered, however, why he gazed so long, and what could be passing in his mind. I felt a great desire to speak to him, and to know something of him. I felt sure he would teach me something. I was then eager for knowledge, and anxious to improve. Nothing would have been lost upon me, if he had only given me a little encouragement. Perhaps he was equally modest, as I had no letter of introduction to him. I came more in contact with that strange but learned character, Fuseli, the 'keeper,' whose extraordinary language astonished and rather alarmed a raw country lad, as I was at that time—so sensitive that I blushed at my own name. Imagine my horror when a white-headed old gentleman spoke to me in language bordering upon obscenity, or swore like a trooper. It was curious in so little a man, with his odd figure and foreign accent. His peculiarities and his sayings were so odd, that more curious anec-dotes were reported of him than of any other person of the time.

I am glad you continue to improve, and that you have finished your drawing of Rome to your satisfaction. I shall be glad to know what is your next subject. Mrs. Bewick unites with me in kind regards, and I am, my dear Sir,

Yours truly,

W. BEWICK.

T. H. Cromek, Esq.

Bowburn, near Ferry Hill, at J. G. Quelch, Esq.
March 25th, 1865.

MY DEAR SIR,—We arrived here yesterday, and I am glad to say Mrs. Bewick has borne the journey very well, though somewhat fatigued.

We had the better day for the journey, as there is now a storm of snow and wind that would have prevented our risking the chance of getting cold. As it is, I have a bad cold in my head, and last night I indulged in a good stout glass of hot brandy and water before going to bed.

It appears that Thomas Bewick, from great liability to cold in the head, kept his hat on whenever he could, and Miss Bewick tells me they made him a velvet cap, which he wore when at home. The portrait I have of him, painted by William Bell, has his hat on.

Whilst I was looking at a full-length photograph exhibited in a street at Newcastle, two workmen were looking at it at the same time. I asked one of them who it was intended for? They both looked at me contemptuously, not to know the great Newcastle Bewick; and one of them answered loudly, 'Bewick.' I said, 'Is it Thomas Bewick, the celebrated engraver?' The man called out, 'Aye,' in the Newcastle dialect. You should have seen how simple and innocent I looked, as if I had never heard the name of Bewick in my life before. I told the Misses Bewick this, and they enjoyed the joke vastly. Miss Bewick gave me Thomas Bewick's walking-stick; it is a blackthorn, full of knobs, with a silver hoop, upon which he engraved his name and the date; above that is a horn of some animal forming the gib. It is just as he used it the last time, with all the dirt upon the ferule, and Miss Bewick says he never had any other stick. In the full-length picture he has it in his right hand. Of course I bought the photograph.

I am sitting in a room at my sister's, with a large original Cuyp. In the picture cattle are in the bright glow of warm sun-light, whilst outside the house is a large stretch of landscape covered with snow, the air stormy, cold, and windy.

I should like to possess a photograph of your drawing of the library, even if it is not satisfactory to you. With our kind regards, I am, my dear Sir,

Yours very truly,
W. BEWICK.

Haughton House, near Darlington,
March 8th, 1866.

MY DEAR SIR,—In the midst of this fearful snow-storm one naturally asks every day, 'I wonder how Mr. Cromek is?' And I write to ask the question, trusting that he bears up wonderfully against it, and comforts himself by nursing a good coal fire, rubbing his hands together, and cheering himself and those young ladies of his who nurse him and are so fond of him. Formerly, in the time of Mortimer and Morland, they would have shut the window-shutters and got in some bosom friend, and with the gin-bottle and pipe turned day into night, and forgotten the storm in hot gin and water, or steeped their forgetfulness in the fumes of the weed, singing that good old moral song, 'Tobacco is an Indian weed,' &c.

But, my dear friend, neither you nor I can take to the gin-bottle for consolation. We hug our maladies, and try with the doctors to be resuscitated and made well again, and look upon this beautiful earth with the admiration that God has endowed us with the power to feel. You see what a stir has been made by the death of our old friend Gibson. Imagine, as you can, the man Gibson being aware of a file of soldiers firing into his grave, over the Emperor's graceful presentation lying on his coffin!

I will enclose some papers to the credit of the sculptor, which your young ladies can put into their scrap-books. They are written by one who knew Gibson personally, and is a great admirer of his genius and worth.

I have not heard lately of our friend Davison, but hope he is going on well; nor have I heard from Miss Bewick.

Poor Harvey! Have you seen what the *Illustrated News* says about him? The writer appears to be totally ignorant of Harvey's 'Associates.' I could put him right, but do not think it worth while. The writer, no doubt, thought it better that his memory should be embalmed in the society of *Sir* This and *Sir* That, rather than speak the truth, and make him associate with plain *Thomas*, or *Charles*, or *William*, who were the real friends and companions of this clever and prolific man of genius.

Mrs. Bewick joins me in wishes, and hopes that you are going on well, and that your daughters are all quite well.

And I am, my dear Sir,

Yours truly,

WILLIAM BEWICK.

CHAPTER IX.

WE now draw towards the close of a life which was full of vicissitudes. From the period when he left Darlington, almost a fugitive, Bewick had experienced many varieties of fortune, and had at last raised himself to a respectable position as an artist. The man who had acquired the friendship of Scott, Hazlitt, Wordsworth, and others of the more remarkable men of his day, as well as that of many members of his own profession belonging to different parties or coteries, must have possessed talents of a superior order—must have been endowed with virtues which recommended him as a friend.

After his return to the North, Bewick, as we have seen from the preceding correspondence, still continued to practise his profession. Although in his early youth he had expressed something like aversion to portrait-painting, he found it necessary, after his return to Darlington, to give way to the wishes of his numerous friends and patrons who were anxious to have their likeness taken by his hand. Darlington and the surrounding country includes a district inhabited by numerous wealthy Quakers, country gentlemen, and retired men of business, and there was scarcely one of these who did not desire to have his portrait taken by one who, they considered, had, by his career, done honour to the North of England. The consequence was that he was kept in constant employment; and the works of this nature by his ready pencil may be counted by the hundred. It must not be supposed, however, that he confined himself entirely to portrait-painting. As long as his health lasted he took pleasure in the production of historical and fancy pictures; and in the mansions of many gentlemen of the county of Durham, and the neighbouring counties, may be seen paintings which do honour to his taste and genius.

No artist can be expected to pass through life without experiencing to some extent the jealousy of rival artists or of carping critics. The claims of Mr. Bewick to any high rank as a painter have more than once been assailed; but without venturing to assert his right to one of the highest niches in the Temple of Fame, we are justified in asserting that the artist who received so many testimonies of approval, not only from the public, but also from brothers of the brush, must have possessed more than ordinary talent. It was no light gratification to an artist to receive the approbation of so thorough a judge of art as the poet Goethe, who, through the German Consul, commissioned Bewick to execute for him a large cartoon of some of the figures in the Elgin Marbles, that the German men of taste might obtain some idea of these sculptures. The poet was highly pleased with the work, and stated that his sovereign, to whom he had presented it, had ordered it to be placed in the Royal Academy of Arts, and would be pleased to know when the artist should visit his kingdom, that attention might be paid to him. In company with his friends the Landseers, he made full-sized copies from Raphael's Cartoons, which were publicly exhibited with great success. A head painted by Bewick at Darlington was mistaken, both by Wilkie and Calcott, for a Murillo. He also made copies of Rembrandt which few could distinguish from the original. 'The Kyloe Heifer,' which he painted for Mr. Hilton Middleton, of Archdeacon Newton ('High-priced Hilton'), was engraved by Turner, A.R.A. His picture of 'Jacob meeting Rachel,' which was exhibited in London and Darlington, was specially admired by many men of taste and genius, particularly by Haydon ; and the figure of Rachel presented one of those evanescent expressions belonging to un-ripened innocence so difficult to portray, and which bore out Keats' opinion that 'Bewick would do some of the tenderest things in art.'

After continuing to exercise his profession for some time in the North, Bewick, who had amassed a sufficient fortune for his modest wants, determined to retire from its active pursuits. The interest which he ever afterwards took in art proceeded solely from the pure and lofty pleasure with which it inspired him. In his house at Haughton-le-Skerne, he had a gallery of paintings which was deemed worthy of a visit by all artists and amateurs whose footsteps led them in that direction. It was at all times a pleasure to him to exhibit his treasures; and his eye still flashed with true artistic fire when he descanted on their beauties of conception and execution. His correspondence, as we have seen in his letters to Messrs. Davison and Cromek, bore very much upon artistic subjects; and with the friends whom he collected round his fireside it was his delight equally to expatiate upon the subject which so completely occupied his mind, to recall his reminiscences of the past, and to amuse and delight all who listened to him by his anecdotes of his old friends Wilkie, Haydon, and Hazlitt.

Bewick also continued in his last, as in his earliest days, to cultivate the predilection for literature and literary men which had all along been so marked a feature in his character. He was naturally proud of the intimacy which he had enjoyed with Keats, Hazlitt, and Wordsworth, not to speak of the attentions which Sir Walter Scott and James Hogg had lavished upon him; and these reminiscences were not without their influence in giving a certain literary bent to his mind. The interest with which he remembered the distinguished literary men of an era that was fast passing away led him to hail the advent of new essayists, poets, and novelists. The works of Dickens and Thackeray afforded him great delight, and the comic spirit and poetic pictures of the one filled him with no less admiration than the deep knowledge of human life and the heart of man displayed by the other.

Though Bewick, on the whole, paid comparatively little attention to political matters, he was in his heart a true Conservative. The character of his mind—his love of ancient art—led him to be a *laudator temporis acti*. A friend of the artist's writes, 'During the years 1846-7, I had several opportunities of seeing and conversing with Mr. Bewick. I was then but a youth, in my " teens," somewhat ardent and enthusiastic, and having a firm belief in the " rights of man " as set forth in the People's Charter. Mr. Bewick was a Conservative, and in the kindliest manner combated my arguments in a way that produced a powerful impression on my mind. I had been attending meetings where the wildest schemes had been discussed, and plans for a revolutionary movement proposed, which fortunately were never attempted to be realised. Under these influences I became imbued with red-hot Republican ideas, and firmly believed that all monarchs ought to be sent about their business as speedily as possible. Mr. Bewick, however, from time to time, kindly reasoned with me, and explained how property had rights as well as people,— that if all were on an equality to-day, there would be a change to-morrow,—that reforms, to be lasting, must be, like the oak, of slow growth—and that the wild theories of the Chartists were utterly impracticable in the then state of society. Although my notions of " liberty, fraternity, and equality," were great favourites with me, the kind words and logical reasoning of Mr. Bewick tended greatly to lessen my enthusiasm for them.'

Such was Bewick's life and character, as represented chiefly in his own reminiscences. His latter years were almost entirely uneventful, no incident of importance interrupting the placid tenor of his way. Though he reached the period which is commonly considered the allotted span of man's life, he was generally free from suffering, and on the whole enjoyed good health; but it is probable that the remarkable assiduity he had displayed when a student of art, working from an early hour in the morning till late at night, may have entailed some consequences which would prove to him that the laws of Nature are never violated with impunity.

Mr. Bewick died at Haughton House, on the 8th of June, 1866, leaving a widow, but no issue. He was buried in a charming spot in the well-wooded ground which had been recently restored to the churchyard of Haughton ; and the esteem in which he was held by those who knew him best was testified by the regret and sorrow of many who took part in that last ceremony.

THE END.

INDEX OF PEOPLE

INDEX OF PLACES